# Positioning the Missionary

*Brett Christophers*

---

# Positioning the Missionary: John Booth Good and the Confluence of Cultures in Nineteenth-Century British Columbia

**UBC**Press / Vancouver

Printed in Canada on acid-free paper ∞

ISBN 0-7748-0654-0

---

**Canadian Cataloguing in Publication Data**
Christophers, Brett, 1971-
    Positioning the missionary

    Includes bibliographical references and index.
    ISBN 0-7748-0654-0

    1. Good, J.B. (John Booth), 1833-1916.   2. Church of England –
Missions – British Columbia.   3. Ntlakyapamuk Indians – Missions
– British Columbia.   4. Colonies.   5. British Columbia – History –
19th century.*   I. Title.

BV2815.B7C57   1998   266´.3711    C98-910251-3

---

This book has been published with a grant from the Social Sciences Federation
of Canada, using funds provided by the Social Sciences and Humanities Research
Council of Canada.

UBC Press also gratefully acknowledges the ongoing support to its publishing
program from the Canada Council for the Arts, the British Columbia Arts Council, and the Department of Canadian Heritage of the Government of Canada.

Set in Stone by Brenda and Neil West, BN Typographics West
Printed and bound in Canada by Friesens
Copy editor: Randy Schmidt
Cartographer: Eric Leinberger

UBC Press
University of British Columbia
6344 Memorial Road
Vancouver, BC V6T 1Z2
(604) 822-5959
Fax: 1-800-668-0821
E-mail: orders@ubcpress.ubc.ca
http://www.ubcpress.ubc.ca

*He was running to prove that all that separated him from them was ground that could be covered. He gave no consideration to what might happen when he arrived.*

— David Malouf, *Remembering Babylon*

# Contents

# Figures

# Acknowledgments

I acknowledge with gratitude the support of a University Graduate Fellowship for the duration of my studies at the University of British Columbia.

Many people have contributed to the completion of this book. Much of my initial research was carried out at the Vancouver School of Theology, where Anglican archivist Doreen Stephens introduced me to the records of the Columbia Mission. At UBC Press, Jean Wilson believed in the project in its early stages and gave me great encouragement to progress, while Randy Schmidt has been an attentive and diligent editor. I also thank cartographer Eric Leinberger.

I owe a tremendous debt to Cole Harris, who supervised the thesis around which this book took shape. One of my earliest memories of British Columbia is of a field trip Cole led to the Fraser Canyon in the fall of 1993, when he spoke about the region's past with a passion and humanity that inspired me to focus my work on precisely the issues he raised. Over the next few years he became a close friend and a tireless critic, scouring successive drafts of both the thesis and the book with a thoroughness for which I was initially unprepared, later receptive, and ultimately enormously grateful.

Several other people read and helped to improve the text. I especially thank Dan Clayton, a constant provider of generous and constructive advice. Two close readings of my thesis – by John Barker and Derek Gregory – helped me to realize just how much work had to be done to turn it into a book. Averil Cameron and David Ley were invaluable commentators on Chapter 2, as was Kamala Todd on Chapter 6. And both of my reviewers offered material suggestions at an important stage in the book's development. Any remaining shortcomings are of course entirely my own responsibility.

My decision to prolong my stay in Canada to write this book was made considerably easier by the friendships I made in Vancouver. In addition to those I have already mentioned, my thanks go to Trina Bester, Terry

Cardle, David Demeritt, Martin Evans, Andrew Hall, Andrew Hamilton, Nicky Hicks, Phil Kelly, Loretta Lees, Wendy Mendes-Crabb, Daren Smith, Judy Tutchener, Ben Watkins, and Bruce Willems-Braun for making my time in BC so full and so happy.

I have most of all to thank Averill Groeneveld-Meijer, my constant companion during the production of this book. It is yours as much as it is mine.

Lastly, my family, to whom I owe more than I can express or ever hope to repay. Thanks so much to you all. This book is dedicated to the memory of Donald Christophers, my grandfather.

# Introduction

In the summer of 1860 William B. Crickmer, an Anglican missionary based in Yale, British Columbia, made his way up the canyon that extends north from Yale to the town of Lytton, where the Thompson River joins the Fraser. Sponsored by the Colonial and Continental Church Society, Crickmer had arrived in the Pacific Northwest in 1858, when the huge territory west of the Rocky Mountains and north of the 49th parallel became the colony of British Columbia. The Fraser had seen a flurry of activity during the colony's first two years as thousands of men, mostly from California, converged on the river in search of gold. While not the first people of European stock to see British Columbia, their numbers were unprecedented; a new era in relations with Natives had dawned. Crickmer likened the confluence of the Fraser and Thompson Rivers to the clash of two cultures, and in the dominance of the Fraser he claimed to find the tragedy of empire: 'Below the cemetery is the junction of the two rivers, the Fraser and the Thompson: the former, large and discolored; the latter, clear as crystal, – an emblem of the two races of Whites and Indians, now, in God's providence, united. And truly the type stops not here; but, if the truth must be told, the larger, more fierce, rolling and filthy stream of the sinful White, after flowing for a short space apart, gradually pollutes, absorbs, and destroys the unsophisticated children of nature.'[1]

In the Fraser Canyon the Native encounter with Europeans began in 1808 when Simon Fraser passed through the territory of the Nlha7kápmx (Thompson) people, who lived, and still live, in riverine communities from Spuzzum north almost to Lillooet, east along the Thompson to Ashcroft, and in the Nicola Valley (see Figure 2). Crickmer's vivid geographical metaphor was only a rough gloss on contact and conflict, yet his fatal impact thesis was not entirely misplaced. Before and after Fraser, European diseases, principally smallpox and measles, were in the canyon, killing many. Then came miners energized by the discovery of gold, with

*Figure 1*    The confluence of the Thompson and Fraser Rivers

itchy fingers and modern guns. Hostilities escalated. And on the heels of miners came settlers, whose objective was to occupy land and for whom the Native presence was a direct impediment.

This book is concerned with how missionaries interpreted and intervened in these developments. Its chief protagonist is John Booth Good, who for sixteen years served as Anglican missionary to the Nlha7kápmx, mostly in Lytton, the heart of Nlha7kápmx territory. Here, as Crickmer intimated, was a microcosm of colonialism at large – Europeans and Natives had collided in a cramped canyon space and, together with immigrant Chinese, had crafted a pluralistic society in which ill will reigned. Good knew this locality well and knew that Crickmer's reading was not quite right. White power certainly impinged on Native life, especially in that good land had been taken by settlers, but the Nlha7kápmx had not capitulated; they resisted colonialism in Good's day, and still resist it now, though its name has changed, its forms have proved mutable, and its exercise is increasingly veiled. When Good arrived at Lytton in 1867, he found cultures in tension: rivers had met and their flows had combined, but one stream had not subsumed the other.

As an emissary of the Society for the Propagation of the Gospel (SPG), Good was expected to minister to colonists and to evangelize Natives, but the latter duty was closer to his heart. This book considers his mission to the Nlha7kápmx from the late 1860s until the beginning of the 1880s. It is neither a biography nor an insular study of one mission in colonial British Columbia.[2] It is, first and foremost, a study of Good and his charges, but to understand his endeavours and the Nlha7kápmx response to him, I have had to situate his mission at several scales. One is the local ethnographic literature, primarily the work of an Orcadian, James Teit, who lived among the Nlha7kápmx for four decades and spoke their language fluently. Teit's publications and fieldnotes offer a tantalizing glimpse of Nlha7kápmx life, both before contact with Europeans and in the last decade of the nineteenth century, when he researched and wrote his major study. Among other things, his writing provides explicit and implicit evidence as to Good's influence with the Nlha7kápmx. He spoke to several elders with personal experience of the first Anglican mission to their people, some of whom recalled it with indifference, others with bitter resentment.

Of course, we need to be very careful with Teit's salvage ethnography, and not only because his perspective was partial. One reason why the first wave of European anthropologists often clashed with missionaries is that the latter reshaped the 'authentic' cultures that ethnography sought to capture. Indeed, Teit's mentor, Franz Boas, claimed, on visiting Lytton in 1888, that the Nlha7kápmx had been Christianized to such an extent that their former ways could not be retrieved. Thus, although Teit spent many years studying the Nlha7kápmx, there is inevitably a degree of historical slippage in his account; he wrote at the turn of the century and it was his Nlha7kápmx contemporaries he knew best. As far as my own use of Teit is concerned, there are two implications. First, it is important to acknowledge that Teit's image of the precolonial Nlha7kápmx probably fails to fully erase the impact of colonialism. Second, and equally important, where I rely on Teit's comments about the Nlha7kápmx response to Christianity, I generally assume that what was true of one generation was broadly true of its precursor.

Another frame of reference for Good's work is the Anglican mission, particularly as it materialized in British Columbia. When he arrived in Victoria in 1861, Good joined an Anglican clergy presided over by George Hills, who came to the field in 1859 as the first bishop of the Columbia Diocese. By this time Roman Catholic missionaries had been active for two decades, and crude forms of Christianity, introduced during Spanish explorations and by Native or Métis employees in the fur trade, had circulated earlier still. The first Anglican on the scene was the Reverend Robert J. Staines, chaplain at Fort Victoria from 1849 until his death in 1855, when he was replaced by the Reverend Edward Cridge. When Vancouver Island and British Columbia became a single colonial diocese in 1859 (they remained distinct colonies until 1866), and an endowment, the Columbia Mission Fund, was established to maintain it, the Anglican mission began in earnest. To situate Good's experience I probe the views of his peers, Bishop Hills in particular.

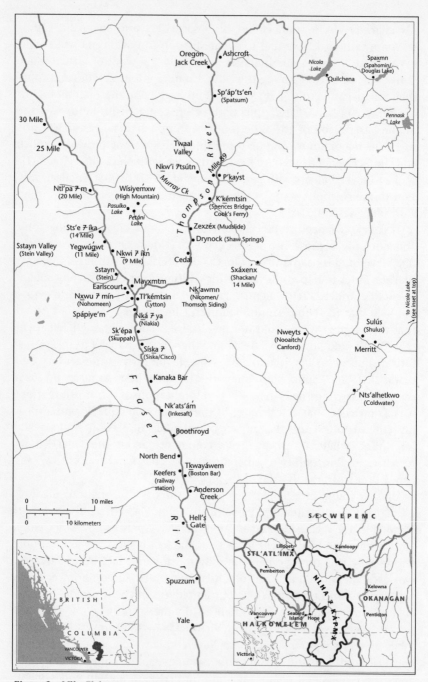

*Figure 2*   Nlha7kápmx territory

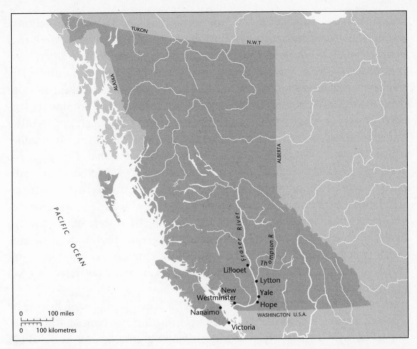

*Figure 3* British Columbia c. 1860. The shaded area indicates the extent of the Columbia Diocese.

It is important to emphasize that the Anglican Church in British Columbia was no monolith. Its diversity is apparent in the two debilitating schisms it suffered during Good's time in Lytton. The first pitted Hills against Cridge, Dean of Christ Church Cathedral in Victoria; the second pitted William Ridley, bishop of the Caledonia Diocese that emerged from the subdivision of the Columbia Diocese in 1879, against William Duncan, the Church Missionary Society (CMS) catechist whose mission to the north coast Tsimshian has been well documented. Although each schism involved personal friction, theological disagreement also surfaced on both occasions. Cridge, like Duncan, was an evangelical Anglican sponsored by the CMS, a Low Church organization that downplayed ritual, the sacraments, and the authority of bishops. Hills and Ridley, by contrast, were High Churchmen who promoted a *via media* religion in the tradition of the ancient and undivided Catholic Church. This theological breach was at the forefront of Cridge's quarrel with Hills, and contributed to Duncan's eventual break with his parent church.

But CMS missionaries were a small minority among Anglican clergy in colonial British Columbia. Most of Good's colleagues represented the High Church SPG, and many, like Good himself, were schooled at St. Augustine's College in Canterbury, England, which had close links to the

SPG and shared its theology. In the sense that Good's was the majority position, his ideas reflect the local Anglican consensus (to the extent that there was one) more closely than Duncan's, whose mission has often been considered the prototypical Anglican operation in British Columbia.[3] The Anglicans regarded Good's Nlha7kápmx mission as their finest next to Duncan's, yet by comparison it has received little critical comment. This book focuses on Good, but, significantly, when it does reach out to other Anglican missionaries to provide perspective, Good's thinking often tallies where Duncan's would not. This is not to suggest that Good always observed Anglican dogma as posited by the SPG (effectively the missionary arm of the Church of England) and his bishop. Nor should we assume that SPG and CMS missionaries never saw eye to eye; despite differences in doctrine and methods of worship, they were all Anglicans. Heathenism and Roman Catholicism were far greater foes. Indeed, in mission theology High Church and evangelical Anglicans could often find common ground, and on more than one occasion I shall refer to CMS positions that paralleled Good's.

If church structures and doctrines offer a lens through which to view Good's mission, so also do the nineteenth-century colonial discourses unpacked by recent literary scholarship. In both England and British Columbia, Good was exposed to powerful models of cultural and racial difference, which permeated his vision of empire without quite dominating it. Although Good's imagery of 'heathenism' was indebted to this racialism – he often branded unconverted Natives 'savages' – his sense of what constituted otherness was not. To Good's mind religion rather than race separated his charges from himself. Thus, while the critical literature on colonial discourse does help us understand how Good thought about and addressed Natives, it must be approached carefully, for the texts analyzed by colonial discourse theorists frequently contradict Good's most central convictions. Rather than accepting postcolonial theory at face value, we must read Good back into it and, where necessary, unsettle its assumptions.

Good did not align himself with the popular colonial conventions of his age because he did not need to. The nineteenth century saw a proliferation of discourses that served to justify and consolidate colonial occupation, but grounds for empire had deep roots in ancient Christian thought, which nourished missionaries such as Good with imperial concepts that merely *seem* secular and modern. When Good described the 'heathen' as the Other of a Christian self, his parameters appear to be those of nineteenth-century imperialism, yet they are not. They derive, rather, from debates in the Early Church on questions of purity and paganism, and of universality and election. In effect they turn on the question of sameness and difference – the very issue that animated nineteenth-century imperialists. Was difference innate or acquired? Could differences be reconciled in sameness? Was it *right* to impose a single identity on all? Such concerns troubled the church from its earliest days and were only given a new twist when, starting in the late fifteenth century, Europe exceeded its borders and contemplated the peoples it encountered beyond.

Thus, throughout this book we return again and again to what Anthony Pagden has labelled the 'imaginative dependence of the new upon the old.' The colonialism charted in these pages is a strange hybrid: firmly secured in early Christian theology, it is also wrapped in a modern mantle of capitalist imperialism and reformed faith. Pagden's argument is that recent European ideologies of empire are all tainted by history. He says that 'for all their apparent, and much discussed, novelty the theoretical roots of the modern European overseas empires reached back into the empires of the Ancient World. It was, above all, Rome which provided the ideologues of the colonial systems of Spain, Britain and France with the language and political models they required.'⁴ Pagden's comments are aimed at those scholars (and there are many) who claim to find in modern imperialism an original configuration of Western thought. He maintains that if the Roman Empire never achieved the scope of nineteenth-century expansion, it prefigured its philosophical logic. These observations pertain to postmedieval European imperialism in general, but are especially salient to discourses of mission, most obviously because Christianity for many years legitimized the *Imperium Romanum*.

Like many other missionaries (Anglican and otherwise), Good's inspiration came straight from the early Christian thought that Pagden identifies in all European theories of empire. Good's appeal to antiquity was undoubtedly a function of his training. The SPG and St. Augustine's were High Church, and this theological tradition, manifested in the mid-nineteenth century by the Oxford Movement, placed heavy emphasis on patristic study. Whereas continental Protestants saw the Early Church through the eyes of the Reformation, High Church Anglicans (Tractarians) looked more directly to the Scriptures and the Church Fathers. St. Paul and St. Augustine were especially important and, as we shall see in Chapter 2, both could be mobilized towards a theology of empire that scarcely required, and in many respects resisted, a theory of race.

And so this book offers an eclectic cast of characters. Paul and Augustine figure prominently, but so do men named Sashiatan and Spintlum, Nlha7kápmx chiefs with no obvious connection to the two fountainheads of Western Christianity, but coupled to them by an Anglican missionary for whom the Early Church, not England, was the real cradle of empire. Still, Good's mission was closely tied to developments in contemporary Britain. Until the latter days of the eighteenth century, European missions were largely Roman Catholic; it was only in the nineteenth century that the Anglicans began to make much of an impression on the mission field. That British imperialism had hitherto lacked a humanitarian impulse is reflected in the failure of an evangelical petition to Parliament in 1793 to permit mission work in India. The success of another petition in 1813 is a measure of changing attitudes. As the movement to abolish slavery gained momentum and economists started to question the hard value of colonies, the concept of empire as a civilizing mission gained currency. The British government now looked favourably on mission work. In a series of lectures given between 1839 and 1841, Herman Merivale, permanent undersecretary at the Colonial Office, argued that 'history has no example to offer us of any successful attempt, however slight, to introduce civilization among savage tribes in colonies, or in their vicinity, except through the agency of religious missionaries.'[5]

Such was the prevailing political atmosphere when Good left England for British Columbia. As recently as 1858 Edward B. Lytton, secretary of state for the colonies and the man after whom the Fraser Canyon town was named, had reassured the archbishop of Canterbury that the government fully supported colonial church work. Moreover, moves were afoot to ensure better treatment of colonial subjects. For some years the Aborigines Protection Society had advocated the 'civilization' of indigenous peoples in British North America, arguing that the Hudson's Bay Company should have its charter repealed for neglecting its duty to protect Native welfare. Many in Parliament were of a similar mind, and when gold fever struck the Fraser River in 1858 they spied an opportunity to revoke the company's trading licence. It was clear to the government that to defend Britain's foothold in the Pacific Northwest against American encroachment, a colony would have to be established. It was also clear that the first governor of British Columbia should be James Douglas – Chief Factor of the Columbia District and, since 1851, governor of Vancouver Island – and that as a condition of his appointment Douglas should sever all ties to the company (which would relinquish its trading monopoly). A reputation for benevolence endeared Douglas to a British government that saw in empire a mission of moral improvement. As governor of British Columbia, Douglas was indeed concerned with 'civilizing' the colony's Natives, and support for missionaries, Anglicans in particular, was integral to this humanitarian platform.

As we shall see at various stages in this book, Good's was an ambiguous position within the matrix of British colonialism. In one sense at least, his and other Anglican missions served as what Gauri Viswanathan calls masks of conquest, which detach cultural imperialism from material oppression and thus cloak the ugly reality of colonialism.[6] Good often accused the colonial government of mistreating Natives and was especially critical of its land policy, but by distancing his mission from this malpractice he implied that Christian colonialism somehow stood apart. It was, however, part of the colonial project. The rise of the Anglican mission coincided with a dramatic shift in power relations between Europeans and Natives, as a fur trade economy from which both sides accrued benefits was replaced by a colonial regime geared to settlers. Though Good and other missionaries questioned the dynamics of this transition, their work must be interpreted in the context of the dispossession, marginalization, and cultural decay of Native societies.

Such considerations form one of this book's two main lines of inquiry – namely, the place of Good's mission in a broader analysis of Nlha7kápmx social and cultural change under foreign rule. But *how*, exactly, can we think of Good's mission as colonizing? This is no simple matter. Anglican church work was colonial to the extent that it operated under the aegis of British and then Canadian dominion. But in what specific sense were evangelism and moral instruction the strategies of a colonizing power? This book argues that the answer to this question is critical to any real understanding of Good's mission, for colonialism is a particular form of power that words such as coercive or authoritarian inadequately describe. It seems almost natural to describe mission work as a Christian form of colonialism, but what does colonial actually mean? Chapter 2 offers an answer of sorts, and later chapters follow through on its conclusions.

In the light of my understanding of colonial power, I confront a whole gamut of questions familiar to students of the imperial Christian mission. I ask why it was that the Nlha7kápmx first solicited Good in 1867, what it was about his mission that absorbed them through the 1870s, and why they deserted him towards the end of the decade. I examine Native gender relations and the patriarchal family unit that Good, like other missionaries, was keen to introduce. More generally, I identify Good's influence on Nlha7kápmx social structures, subsistence patterns, and cultural trappings as his most tangible legacy; evangelism was only one component of mission work, and there is reason to believe that many of those who converted did so but nominally. To the degree that they spoke English, farmed reserve land, and lived in permanent villages, the Nlha7kápmx of the 1880s were much closer to the assimilated Natives envisaged by Douglas than many white commentators gave them credit for, and Good's mission was instrumental on each count. Many Nlha7kápmx resisted and resented these changes, and continue do so, but the consequences of European intervention have been enormous, and Christianity has played a pivotal role.

A few words are necessary on my use of Native names. As we shall see in Chapter 5, Good held that to convert the Nlha7kápmx properly, each charge had to be individually known; to address the flock as a uniform body was poor form. Thus, Good recorded the names of all members of his mission and upon baptism gave each a Christian name by which, henceforth, he would recognize them. Because certain Natives assumed positions of unusual importance, with regard to both church affairs and relations with the secular authorities, I need to refer to them by name. For the sake of consistency, I use the one given by Good. In some cases an alternative is available, either from Teit or from recent oral histories.[7] But Teit rarely used individual names in his ethnographic work – his was a study of Nlha7kápmx *culture* – and only the most famous Nlha7kápmx of Good's day appear in today's mythologies. As a result, few of the people mentioned by Good can be identified by other means. Where another name is available it is included in parentheses on first mention.

The research for this book was carried out principally in British Columbian archives and libraries, and its main source is published volumes of missionary letters and reports. When Anglican missionaries wrote to their English sponsors with details of progress and observations on colonial life, they understood that their correspondence became public property, for it was these missives that missionary societies published to kindle interest in mission work and secure funds for its continuance. In Good's case published versions of official communication appeared both in SPG journals, primarily *The Mission Field*, and in the annual reports of the Columbia Mission. Yet the letters contained in these volumes have been heavily censored. As one example, Simon Carey points out that the printed extracts of Bishop Hills's journal 'have been edited by missionary society secretaries with such loyalty and tact that the human and courageous figure of the original tends, in the published version, to emerge as a sanctimonious prig.'[8] Carey's concern is that this censorship shrouds the real Hills from today's reader, but there are far more important considerations. Editors actually cut out contentious material, such as conflicts among missionary churches, disputes between missionaries and colonial officials, and so on.

To review missionary periodicals, then, is to encounter deeply sanitized narratives of empire. It is therefore fortunate that the original missionary reports have survived. What was censored and why are intriguing questions in and of themselves, for this politics of representation bears directly on our rewriting of colonialism; a sketchy discussion of these issues is offered elsewhere.[9] This book cites published and unpublished missionary correspondence – Good and other SPG agents were required to submit both quarterly and annual reports – but for obvious reasons published material is preferred except in instances where valuable information is missing. It goes without saying that it would be impossible to come to grips with Good's mission if we only had the censored texts at hand. Indeed, it is a testament to the circulation of colonial power and knowledge that Good's reports are housed in Oxford, England, at Rhodes House Library, and that to untangle the twisted braids of empire we must return to its very core.

# Abbreviations

| | |
|---|---|
| Add. MSS | Additional manuscripts, BCA |
| ADC | Archives of the Diocese of Columbia, Victoria, BC |
| BCA | British Columbia Archives, Victoria, BC |
| BL | Bancroft Library, Berkeley, CA |
| CC | British Columbia, colonial correspondence (correspondence inward to the colonial government), BCA |
| CCA | Canterbury Cathedral Archives, Canterbury, UK |
| CLR Series | Columbia Diocese. Copies of letters received, USPG |
| CLS Series | Columbia Diocese. Copies of letters sent, USPG |
| E Series | Missionary reports, USPG |
| RG10 | Canada, Department of Indian Affairs, Black Series, Western Canada, Record Group 10, University of British Columbia Library, Vancouver, BC |
| RQE | Report for the quarter ending ... (USPG E Series) |
| VST | Archives of the Ecclesiastical Province of British Columbia, Vancouver School of Theology, Vancouver, BC |
| USPG | Archives of the United Society for the Propagation of the Gospel, Rhodes House Library, Oxford, UK |

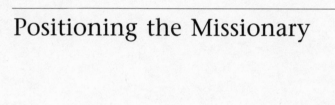

# Positioning the Missionary

# 1
# Beginnings

Having spent three years in Nova Scotia from 1857 to 1860, and five years in Nanaimo on Vancouver Island from 1861, the Reverend John B. Good moved to mainland British Columbia in May 1866 when Bishop Hills posted him to Yale, at the foot of the Fraser Canyon.[1] In March 1867 Good received three groups of Nlha7kápmx from their territory to the north. The first callers were delegates of the Lytton band. The leader of this advance party, Sashiatan, had approached the Lytton magistrate, Captain Henry M. Ball, to write a letter to Good on his behalf,[2] which he now presented to the Anglican missionary. It read as follows: 'I must now tell you what the Indian "Sashiatan," who gives you this, wishes me to

*Figure 4* Lytton c. 1867

write about. He is a chief and has great influence with Indians in this part of the country. He has taken a great fancy to you, and is determined that all the Indians shall be followers of yours ... He is a good and valuable Indian, and through him you may obtain an influence over, perhaps, a thousand Indians.' This was a revelation. After the two following groups had come and gone in quick succession, Good concluded that Nlha7kápmx interest was genuine. While Yale had some potential as a centre of mission work, Lytton appeared to promise a fuller harvest. It was 'a matter of grave and pressing moment,' Good decided, 'to have a Mission, opened as soon as possible, at Lytton.'[3]

Good's intention was to move immediately, and he indicated to the Nlha7kápmx that he would soon be with them. But his bishop dictated otherwise: for the time being, Good was obliged to stay at his post. Having gathered at Lytton in anticipation of his arrival, the Nlha7kápmx interpreted Good's delay as vacillation, and dispatched a telegram advising him that he 'had better make haste and come.'[4] Good read these words as a warning and was troubled by his inability to act. This impasse was, however, short lived. Towards the end of April Hills announced that a new SPG missionary, the Reverend David Holmes, was expected in Victoria any day and would head straight to Lytton upon arrival. With this news in hand, Good, whose station would remain Yale, set off to tell the Nlha7kápmx that Holmes, not he, would be their missionary. But so impressed was Good by the people he met at Lytton that on returning to Yale he petitioned Hills for a change of plan: if Holmes replaced him in the lower canyon, he could himself take up the invitation from Lytton. The bishop was persuaded; by the middle of June Good had moved.

As the genesis of Good's storied mission, the Nlha7kápmx call for help occupied a special place in Anglican writing on the Columbia Diocese. As Good saw it, the defining feature of this episode was the fact that the Nlha7kápmx had solicited him rather than vice versa, and he found a precedent with Saul of Tarsus, St. Paul, the greatest of all Christian missionaries. Acts 16:9 tells of the vision that appeared to Paul in Troas: 'There stood a man of Macedonia, and prayed him, saying, Come over into Macedonia, and help us.' The Apostle's divination bequeathed a touchstone to later generations of missionaries, Good among them. When he first informed the SPG of the Nlha7kápmx invitation, Good framed it as a Pauline call. The Native desire for Anglicanism was 'sudden, extraordinary & simultaneous,' and the 'burden of their united prayer' was manifest: 'viz. "Come over & help us."'[5]

Good situated this Native agency within God's will. As he reflected on being invited 'to come amongst [the Nlha7kápmx] and be their father, teacher, and guide,' he determined that 'God was thereby calling me to

spend and be spent in their service.'[6] This notion of providential intervention dominated Anglican accounts of the birth of Good's mission. It
was propagated, among others, by Bishop Hills and the Reverend Robert
L. Brown (Anglican missionary at Lillooet in the early 1860s),[7] and broadly
conformed to the rhetoric of the day. All European empires were ratio-
nalized, at some level, by the premise of godly favour. Providence was a
common, even prosaic, imperial axiom,[8] one especially germane to missionary discourse. The Anglicans frequently identified providence in the
expansion of their earthly dominion. God led missionaries to fields they
might otherwise neglect, and the heathen to Truth in the form of the
colonial church.[9] Good was a product of his age; it was in keeping with
prevailing wisdom that he deemed the Nlha7kápmx call 'a providential
opening.'[10]

The providence narrative assumed that God, not mortal volition, maps
out history. This much is evident in Good's discussion of his own role
in the events of 1867. On at least one occasion he justified moving to
Lytton on the grounds that to do otherwise was to resist God's will (as
articulated by the Nlha7kápmx).[11] Some members of the colonial bureau-
cracy accused Good of meddling in Nlha7kápmx affairs, but a summons
by God placed him above such critiques. In any case, by invoking providence Good minimized his own agency and also that of his charges. The
latter was far the more significant erasure. 'Did it not seem clear,' Good
wrote, 'that the hand of God was in all this and manifestly calling this
people through me to the knowledge of his Truth?'[12] The Nlha7kápmx
were not rational individuals, forced by circumstances to take charge of
their future; they were, according to Good, the unwitting beneficiaries of
God's foresight and care. Their agency was equal to that of a puppet on
a string.

Against these Anglican texts that efface Native politics, I ask why the
Nlha7kápmx turned to Good, something that appeals to providence tend
to preclude. Salman Rushdie argues that historicism is writ large in such
religious scripts. In thrall to God's will, humans cannot influence the fate
He determines. 'To make it plain,' writes Rushdie, 'we could say that religion places human beings beneath history.'[13] When religion is colonial,
as in Good's case, history is European and non-Europeans are subordinated to it. I do not mean to suggest that the story of providence was a
'flawed' reading of what happened (which is to confuse theology and
secular history); my claim, rather, is that providence folds Nlha7kápmx
history into Christian history, which is Western.[14]

Providence was a dominant but not exclusive presence in Anglican
narratives of mission. Tied to the belief that God led the heathen to the
gospel was a conviction that unevangelized regions lay somehow in wait
of Christianity. When Eugene Stock wrote his history of the CMS at the

end of the nineteenth century, he contemplated the state of the world a century earlier when the society was founded. Places that had not at that time encountered Christianity were identified as prospective mission fields, such that one word captured 'the condition of God's earth – *waiting*.'[15] This idea of anticipation implied that the Christianization of non-European space was not only possible but incumbent; to colonize heathen lands was to realize their latent potential and to set an inevitable history in motion. As several scholars have shown, a similar mental map underwrote secular colonialism: uncolonized space was considered empty waste (and thus open to settlement) until infused with the European modernity that its vacuity beckoned.[16] Though not quite equivalent, both of these imagined geographies turned on the *prospect* of European consumption.

The images favoured by Anglican missionaries were fields and doors. Heathen territory could be thought of as a field ready to be harvested, or as an open door offering access to untapped bounty. These were precisely the tropes that Good used to evoke Native want of Christianity and the Anglican obligation to provide it. On numerous occasions he told his sponsors of 'doors standing wide open' and of 'fields white unto harvest.'[17] Such powerful images implied that the people who inhabited these spaces (which were virginal, not empty) were in some sense unfulfilled; their time was yet to come, and the Anglican mission was its advent. Thus, when a mature Good recalled the Nlha7kápmx telegram he received at Yale, his memory was of God having 'flung wide an entrance for the propagation of the Gospel.'[18] This reading dismissed Nlha7kápmx agency and, in the sense that they awaited a Christian future, implied that the Natives' past was immaterial.

### Solicitudes and Dreams

Good had anticipated the cry of the heathen for many years, so there was a strong sense of vindication when his services were requested in 1867. Born in 1833, Good grew up in the small town of Wrawby in Lincolnshire, England, and from a tender age the 'Red Indians' of North America were the objects of his 'solicitudes and dreams.'[19] This preoccupation became an obsession. The focal point of Good's education was not an elementary school but the parish church, where the Reverend John R. West introduced him to the work of his father and namesake, CMS missionary John West, Hudson's Bay Company chaplain in the Red River colony in the early 1820s.[20] The younger West took the boy under his wing and familiarized him with his father's experience; Good was fascinated. It was his regard for the missionary West, an important figure in his own right, that persuaded Good 'to go out to evangelize the natives of the same race in the regions beyond.'[21] This 'beyond' was not necessarily prophetic; in 1824, West had urged fellow Anglicans to extend their mission field west of the Rocky Mountains,[22] and Good possibly knew of this.

If the elder West inspired Good indirectly, his son's influence was more tangible. When Good applied to St. Augustine's Missionary College in Canterbury in 1854, the vicar's commendation – 'good utilities, much energy, a strong body' – was invaluable.[23] After a successful training in Canterbury, Good left in 1857 for the mission field, going first to Nova Scotia where he spent three largely happy years before returning to England in 1860 to marry Sarah Ann Watson. Then, together they made the voyage to British Columbia, acknowledged from the outset as Good's 'proper field.'[24] Sponsored by the SPG, Good was something of a black sheep. Whereas his personal preference was for evangelizing Natives, the SPG was established 'to provide pastoral care for ... emigrants and for soldiers, officials and merchants in colonial outposts.'[25] Nevertheless, Good's sponsors allowed him his preference: other SPG missionaries catered primarily to European peers, but Good's focus was on the heathen. A letter from SPG secretary Ernest Hawkins to Bishop Hills clarified Good's brief. 'Will you kindly bear in mind,' Hawkins emphasized, 'that he is sent by the Society with the definite object of labouring as a Missionary among the *native tribes of Vancouver*.'[26]

George Hills had been chosen as the first bishop of the Columbia Diocese in 1859, when his close friend Angela Burdett-Coutts, the young philanthropist, pledged £15,000 to fund Anglican church work in Vancouver Island and British Columbia. By this time the colonial episcopacy was a seasoned strategy of Anglican missionary endeavour, the Church of England having overcome bitter eighteenth-century opposition in the American colonies, where Dissenters insisted that bishops would jeopardize religious freedom. In 1787 two American bishops and Bishop Charles Inglis of Nova Scotia – the first Anglican colonial episcopate – were consecrated at Lambeth. By the end of the nineteenth century over 100 more colonial bishoprics had been constituted, among them the Columbia Diocese. The role of the colonial bishop was argued over at length, with something of a sea change in church policy occurring around 1840, from which point Charles Blomfield, bishop of London, advocated using bishops as colonial pioneers. His thinking gradually dislodged the prevailing wisdom that the episcopacy should only be introduced to colonies in which missionaries were already active. Blomfield said that bishops should *lead* the missionary campaign, a view shared by Samuel Wilberforce, bishop of Oxford and zealous patron of the Anglican mission, who regarded Hills as a trailblazer in precisely this sense – a man 'who says to his brother clergymen, not, "Gentlemen, *go* out to Columbia," but, "Gentlemen, *come* out to Columbia."'[27]

Theoretically, as bishop of Columbia Hills controlled all Anglican clergy in the diocese, though in practice his control varied, especially between CMS and SPG missionaries. While the CMS paid its agents directly, the SPG sent Hills a block grant each year, which was distributed among the society's missionaries as he saw fit. Understandably, these clergy retained closer links to the bishop than a CMS man such as Duncan, who was suspicious of episcopacy in any case. It was a basic SPG tenet that funding for missionary churches should increasingly come from within the colonial diocese, and that independence was the ultimate goal. In this spirit the SPG gradually whittled away its contributions towards the upkeep of missionaries. In the case of British Columbia, SPG resolve to liberate its personnel was redoubled by the fact that funds were also available from the Columbia Mission Society, which raised money from private donors in England. The upshot was that Hills received £2,000 from the SPG in 1868, but only £1,200 in 1872 and £350 in 1880; funding was withdrawn altogether in 1882.[28]

In the early colonial episcopates the SPG generally determined the placement of its missionaries, but by the 1840s the scales had tipped and the bishops, some of whom had resented the society's power, were now firmly in charge of their clergy. When Good arrived in Victoria in April 1861, Hills allocated his stipend and decided where he would be stationed. His first posting was Nanaimo, a coal-mining town on Vancouver Island. Donald Simpson has written of Good's 'marked success' there,[29] but his principal British Columbia mission was later, among the Nlha7kápmx. When Alexander Garrett, another SPG missionary, spent a brief period in Nanaimo shortly after Good left, he found that one of Good's most celebrated converts had also been baptized by the Methodists and the Roman Catholics![30] Garrett took this as evidence of perfidy, but it could also be read as a comment on Good's mission. He never dominated church affairs in Nanaimo as he did in Lytton – the Catholics were strong, as were the Methodists under Ebenezer Robson, who was in Nanaimo before Good and protested his intervention.[31] In Lytton Good soon had the mission field to himself.[32]

To a man of Good's cast, the Nlha7kápmx summons of 1867 was irresistible; he would have taken the bait under almost any circumstances. As it was he was already unsettled. Having moved from Nanaimo in the summer of 1866, Good found Yale little to his liking. During the heady days of the Fraser gold rush Yale had boomed, but now that miners had gone north to the Cariboo and beyond, the town had waned. As the head of navigation on the Fraser from 1862, Yale was a town to pass through, not live in.[33] As such it was a difficult site for pastoral work. In the short time that Good spent in Yale, he concluded that it was virtually impossible, largely because so few people actually lived there. His congregation was small and unstable.[34] SPG missionary Alexander Pringle, who briefly served in Yale in the early months of 1860, had made much the same criticism as Good,[35] and conditions had worsened by 1866. That many of the men who were resident lived 'irregularly' with Native women only compounded Good's frustration.[36]

Furthermore, French Roman Catholic missionaries dominated this mission field. Father Charles J. Grandidier had built a church in Yale in 1860, and when he left the following year for the Cariboo gold fields,[37] other representatives of the Oblates of Mary Immaculate continued his work. Despite Bishop Hills's judgment that the Stó:lō were unimpressed with Catholicism,[38] and the fact that the Oblates never established a permanent mission in the lower canyon, it is clear that their influence over Natives was considerable, and that the Anglicans could do little to shake it. Pringle did not even try.[39] His successor, William Crickmer, took up the challenge, painting 'English Church' on St. John the Divine to mark the turf as Anglican, but made little real impression.[40] Reverend Reeve, who followed Crickmer, was resigned to the Oblate sway over Natives and, having worked as a missionary in China, resolved to evangelize Yale's immigrant Chinese population – only to find that the dialect he knew was not theirs.[41] Good, who followed Reeve, was determined to convert the Stó:lō, but he could not loosen the Catholic grip.[42] Given this predicament, the call from Lytton came at just the right time.

**Truth and Error**

Why did the Nlha7kápmx want an Anglican missionary? This is an important and baffling question, without, unfortunately, a simple answer. Archival sources are exclusively European, and James Teit, ethnographer of the Nlha7kápmx some forty years later, offered no specific insight. Good's summons to Lytton was a Nlha7kápmx initiative, and ultimately we cannot know the exact rationale. Some critics would argue that speculation about motive violates Native histories and knowledges, and that such epistemological violence sustains cultural domination. These are serious concerns. I write as a European and the records I use are those of the colonial project. Yet I think it important to consider Nlha7kápmx purpose, for the other option – limiting reconstruction of Good's call to his objectives and those of other whites – strikes me as more dangerous. If we rewrite colonialism purely through critical readings of European power, we risk reproducing a central fallacy of empire: the notion that Europe produced history and Natives submitted to it. British Columbia has been forged in interaction, and its cast bears many hands, Native and immigrant.

We must appreciate, of course, that powerful prejudices filtered white comment on Natives. All colonial knowledges are situated in one way or another, and must be read as tainted evidence. To this degree, Anglican reflections are of little help in explaining the Nlha7kápmx appeal to Good. Convinced that providence led the heathen to the church, the Anglicans could admit but one explanation for Good's summons: God recognized that the Nlha7kápmx needed proper spiritual direction. If God was the dominant force, how, in practical terms, did these Natives come to choose Good as their saviour? His own answer was that fleeting encounters with Bishop Hills had apprised them of Anglican teaching. Passing through Boston Bar in the spring of 1867, Hills met Nlha7kápmx whom he identified as old friends from previous tours of the mainland, the first in 1860. As he wound his way through the canyon on these annual visits to the interior, Hills acquainted Natives with Anglican belief.[43] Good held that this intermittent evangelism had paved the way for his call: 'The seed then sown broadcast by the wayside took root downwards, and has now also begun visibly to show itself on the surface of things.'[44] The Nlha7kápmx had taken to Hills and, steered by a higher power, now sought (in Good) direct access to the bishop's religion. The Anglicans emphasized that Nlha7kápmx motives were pure – it was faith alone that they desired, for this was God's decree.[45]

This was a persuasive but overdetermined interpretation of Native intent; Good's explanation was theological. Why, in his eyes, would the heathen seek out Christianity, if not for spiritual help? Good's understanding of sin and salvation was deeply entrenched, and told him that the Nlha7kápmx needed the gospel, that *his* church was best equipped to provide it, and that the bishop's groundwork had enabled them to identify the faith that God intended. Some commentators were not so sure. From his seat in New Westminster, Frederick Seymour, governor of British Columbia, eyed Good's progress through a political, not a theological, lens. His interest was in peace and order among the colony's Natives, and he identified Good as a troublemaker. The Nlha7kápmx, he argued, had long been charges of Roman Catholic missionaries – a fact that Good seldom acknowledged – so why was Good intruding? Just months after Good moved to Lytton, Seymour inquired of Peter O'Reilly, magistrate at Yale, whether he considered it 'expedient' that Good should 'disturb the minds of the Indians already converted to Christianity by the agency of the Catholic priests.' Seymour's worry was not with the details of Native faith so much as with the harmony of his colony; he suspected that even Hills would not countenance Good's tactics, which appeared combative.[46]

Seymour would repeat this query the following summer. 'What is going on at Lytton?' he now wondered. It seemed to him that 'Good is doing a great deal of mischief with the Indians.'[47] To Seymour's mind, the Anglican mission at Lytton was born of inappropriate missionary behaviour, not of Nlha7kápmx spiritual want. If Good's analysis was guided by his theology, what political considerations swayed the governor? From the first days of the colony, British Columbia's government publicly endorsed the division of church and state. In the late eighteenth and early nineteenth centuries, colonial bishops often conflicted with secular colonial authorities over the status of the Anglican Church. In England, state and church existed in symbiosis, but where the Anglicans tried to secure the privileges of an established church overseas, they broke with Colonial Office and metropolitan church consensus that the state-church couplet should not carry over to empire.[48] Disputes were especially common in the 1810s and 1820s when, for a variety of reasons, missionary societies that previously scorned state aid began to petition government for financial support and guarantees of security.[49]

Settler opinion in early colonial British Columbia was firmly opposed to Erastian principles, as it had been in the eighteenth-century American colonies, and in Upper Canada in the early nineteenth century. Yet the suspicion remained that both the Anglican Church under Bishop Hills and the colonial government under James Douglas were ill at ease with the religious voluntarism they were expected to nurture. Douglas publicly defended freedom of religion but enjoyed a close rapport with Hills,[50] and, in the estimation of other missionary churches, was bent towards the Church of England. This argument assumed substance when it emerged that a parcel of land in Victoria had been set aside exclusively for the Anglicans. This property, known as the Church Reserve, was ultimately graced by Christ Church Cathedral. When the disposition of this land became clear, the Congregationalists and Roman Catholics objected; here was evidence, they said, of an embryonic state church. Catholic Bishop Modeste Demers, who favoured the American model of church-state separation, was shocked that Douglas appeared to have sided with Hills, and while the governor denied that he was partisan, the charge clearly had basis in fact.[51]

This brings us to British Columbia after Douglas, and to Seymour. If Douglas was an Anglican patron, subsequent governors were perhaps less partial. Vincent McNally identifies seeds of church-state independence in the supposed secularity of British Columbia's public education system from 1865, though it was not until the School Bill of 1872 that fully secular instruction became the law.[52] There is compelling evidence that the new system was in fact neither nonreligious nor nonsectarian (it was Anglican),[53] but the vigour and persistence of Anglican protest shows that the government was at least modestly serious about secular schooling; in British Columbia, as elsewhere in the empire, Anglican missionaries condemned such policy – however weakly enforced – as an invitation to moral abandon. As one critic said with reference to secular education in general, and the discipline of geography in particular, 'there is no moral law conveyed in the latitude and longitude of Hongkong.'[54]

With the gradual demerger of church and state came, in theory, more even-handed treatment of missionary churches, although an element of bias undoubtedly remained. Methodist and Roman Catholic missionaries were not being fanciful when they complained that their Anglican rivals enjoyed not only the ear of government but the tangible fruits of this favour in the shape of superior access to medicines and supplies.[55] But Seymour was not an overt champion of the Anglican cause in the manner of Douglas. His somewhat more impartial stance is evident in the degree of anger he provoked in Good, who argued that Governor Seymour and his successor, Anthony Musgrave, effectively bolstered the Roman Catholic Church. 'How the Government of the day could so blindly and readily play into the hands of a power that had never sworn allegiance to its authority,' Good later mused, 'surpasses belief.'[56]

If Seymour had not challenged Good's move to Lytton, he could have been suspected of abetting the Anglicans. As it was, he worried that Good had violated an existing mission. This was not the first time that Good had been accused of such underhand tactics. In June 1862, less than a year into his tenure in Nanaimo, Good had approached Ebenezer Robson about land on the Native reserve that the Methodist had secured for a school. Despite the fact that Robson had received permission to build on the site, Good wished him to relinquish it. 'He does not recognize me as having any equal claims with him,' Robson said of Good. '[He] looks upon his church as the only church & acts accordingly.'[57] There can be no doubt that Good craved special treatment by the government; the Catholics possibly felt that, when Good was allowed to continue his Nlha7kápmx mission after 1868, he had received precisely that. Seymour doubted Good's integrity but, ultimately, did not intervene.

Good knew that the Oblates were in Lytton before him. As in Yale there was no fixed mission, but Good was only one of several Anglican missionaries who documented, grudgingly, the strength of the Catholic hold. Visiting with Lytton's white population in 1860, Crickmer found the town 'wholly given to idolatry,' and suspected the same false faith of local Natives.[58] This latter concern was substantiated seven years later when Good received the first Nlha7kápmx deputation at Yale. Encouraged by his visitors' piety, Good was alarmed by evidence of Roman Catholic instruction. That the Nlha7kápmx had thus far been resigned to the 'undisputed sway of a foreign power' was intolerable, and called for action; in place of 'superstition, error, and ceremonial observances,' Good would offer the heathen uncontaminated Truth.[59]

While he acknowledged the Oblate influence on the Nlha7kápmx, Good divorced his summons from this prior missionary activity. He was happy, to be sure, to occupy, in Lytton, 'ground that was vainly supposed to be the undisputed possession of the Church of Rome.'[60] As Good

understood it, however, the Nlha7kápmx appeal to his church was uncon-
nected to their experience of Catholicism. In this Good was wrong.

In May 1867 the Oblates discovered that their Lytton mission was finished. The Nlha7kápmx had gathered in town to welcome Good (who
was not yet able to leave Yale), and as they awaited the tardy Anglican
an unknowing Oblate priest, Father Jayol, arrived. The Natives dismissed
him at once.[61] Yet it is clear that the Catholics considered Lytton their
mission field.[62] It is also clear that they resented Good muscling in. In
early June, around the time that Good finally moved to Lytton, Father
Léon Fouquet, who ran St. Mary's mission on the lower Fraser, complained
to Peter O'Reilly about Good's conduct.[63] The Oblate position was more
or less Robson's: Good disregarded the tacit law that no church interfere
with another's Native work.[64] And we should not underestimate the force
of this Catholic umbrage. When Father Adrien G. Morice, an Oblate missionary in British Columbia from the 1880s, wrote his *History of the
Catholic Church in Western Canada*, he described Good's assumption of the
Nlha7kápmx charge as the 'first and only serious check in the history of
the Pacific coast missions.'[65] This was a heavy blow.

How should we understand the Nlha7kápmx decision to reject the
Oblates and welcome Good? The most revealing incident occurred
towards the end of 1867. In the second week of October the Oblates
lodged another complaint involving Good. Governor Seymour received
word from Fouquet that a fellow priest, Father LeJacq, who was based at
Fort Rupert until the end of the previous year, had been assaulted at
Lytton. Asked by Seymour to investigate,[66] O'Reilly went to Lytton to
question the town constable. He was told that two Natives named Chillue
and Troppasa had assaulted LeJacq on 4 October. Confident that this information was accurate, the magistrate served both men with summons.[67]
The case went to court in Lytton on 5 November, and O'Reilly found the
accused guilty as charged. They were sentenced to pay $25 fines, in default
of which they would serve one month's imprisonment with hard labour.[68]
Bishop Hills, to whom the fines seemed excessive, recorded that they were
paid by a local merchant named Buie, who was, significantly, a close
friend of the Reverend John B. Good.[69]

The details of this 'assault' provide an invaluable window on the
Nlha7kápmx rationale for approaching Good. It seems that they turned
to him as their experience of Catholicism soured. O'Reilly learned that
the Oblates had worked with the Nlha7kápmx for some years, but that
the relationship had cooled significantly, to the point of hostility. The
locus of contention was a chapel on the Lytton reserve. According to
O'Reilly's official report, the Nlha7kápmx built this chapel in the early
1860s.[70] Reluctant to establish a permanent mission in Lytton, Oblate
priests gave services when they passed through town, which, judging by

the return period at Yale, was probably once every two to three months.[71] The Oblates regarded the chapel as their property, 'consecrated for the performance of the Roman Catholic worship,' but the Nlha7kápmx claimed it as their own and insisted that the key remain in Native hands.[72] The holder of this key, Sashiatan, was out of town when LeJacq arrived in the first week of October. As Bishop Hills tells it, LeJacq secured the key from Sashiatan's wife under false pretences and refused to give it back when confronted by Chillue and Tropassa – who subsequently took it from him by force. When LeJacq protested the constable advised the Natives to hand over the key on the understanding that the assault charge would be dropped. Chillue and Tropassa stuck to their side of the bargain (the key was returned); LeJacq evidently did not.[73]

As O'Reilly correctly surmised, Good's summons was tied to a complex politics of patronage. Under Roman Catholic tutelage the Nlha7kápmx had come to expect a steady commitment. They were let down. Oblate visits to Lytton, never more than sporadic, had almost entirely ceased by 1867. Such was the context of Good's call. 'The neglect of the Priests,' O'Reilly remarked, 'gave offence to the Lytton Indians, and caused them to invite an Episcopal Clergyman, the Revd Mr Good to become resident among them.'[74] Native allegiance had switched from one church to another; first Jayol was snubbed, then LeJacq. If the Oblates believed that the Nlha7kápmx abandoned them and Good deceived them, the Natives claimed that the Catholic Church was guilty of desertion.[75] This suggests that we should root Good's summons not in Native regard for English religion but in Native frustration with Oblate priests they had hitherto preferred. The Lytton reserve was a Nlha7kápmx space. The chapel was built by Natives, used by Natives, and proffered to missionaries whom Natives themselves chose. Once Catholicism had outlived its welcome, Yale missionary Good was the obvious replacement.

## Pragmatic Rationality and Practical Religion

> The LORD also will be a refuge for the oppressed, a refuge in
> times of trouble.
>
> – Psalms 9:9

While Oblate neglect probably explains Good's summons in 1867, the question remains why the Nlha7kápmx were interested in Christianity. From at least the late 1850s, and maybe even earlier, some Nlha7kápmx had adopted European religions in one form or another. It is quite possible that the Oblate impact was minimal – it almost certainly paled beside Good's sway – but we know that an audience for Christianity existed before the gold rush, before the onset of white settlement, and long before

Good. Indeed, there is evidence of interest in Christianity from the earliest stages of the European presence in Nlha7kápmx territory; not in Simon Fraser's day, perhaps, but when Hudson's Bay Company Governor George Simpson travelled through what would later be British Columbia in 1824-5, he received requests for religious teachers from several Native groups, including 'the Thompson River chiefs,' who appealed to Simpson for 'a Messenger from the Master of Life.'[76]

What was going on? To appreciate Nlha7kápmx inquiries about European religion we must realize that Native life was deeply spiritual. 'The basic element of all Amerindian culture and societal structure,' write Russell Smandych and Gloria Lee, 'is the spirituality of individuals and the collective spirituality of the society in general.'[77] As the linchpin of social life and individual conduct, spirituality must figure in any discussion of precontact Native worlds or, as in this case, Native responses to European intervention. If spirituality held the precolonial world together, it had to adapt in some way when Natives were faced with a new order of things. For ethnographer James Teit, a general animism was the essence of precontact Nlha7kápmx religion. His subjects believed in 'mysterious powers pervading all nature.' Mountains, trees, animals, and rocks were all possessed of spirits. Religious rituals, while less developed among the Nlha7kápmx than among certain coastal nations, were central features of this Native spirituality, and included prayers to the dawn and rain and ceremonial dances focused on sun worship. The sentinels of this spirituality were 'shamans' or 'medicine-men,' who had the power to intercede with the spirit world and both cause and cure disease.[78]

When Europe infringed on the Nlha7kápmx 'spirit-land,' as Teit called it, turmoil was inevitable. According to Olive Dickason, harmony is critical to Aboriginal spiritualities; rituals and taboos serve to keep the cosmos in tune and secure the individual's position within it.[79] Spiritual order was bound to be upset by social change, for the spirits were attuned to a condition of life that could no longer prevail in its previous form. It is possible that the Nlha7kápmx sought in Christianity a means to preserve spiritual order that might otherwise dissipate. This interpretation would broadly tally with the established literature on colonial conversion. This Weberian tradition holds that indigenous conversion is explained by the incongruity of Native belief systems in the context of an alien colonial modernity, which Christianity better befits. Conversion, then, is a rational response to an unfamiliar social matrix.[80] Robin Fisher's discussion of conversion in colonial British Columbia conforms precisely with this model: 'It was no accident that the establishment of effective missions to the Indians coincided with the beginning of settlement. As long as their traditional way of life remained intact, the Indians had no reason to adopt a new value system such as Christianity. It was only after the disruptive impact of settlement seemed to render old truths ineffectual that the Indians needed to turn to new ones.'[81]

This is a useful way to rationalize the fact that many Native peoples, among them the Nlha7kápmx, were open to missionary instruction. Yet the model has its problems. One is the implication that conversion entailed a strict break between Native spirituality and new faith. As Dickason makes clear, and as we shall see in Chapter 5, it was not always necessary to replace one religion with another to maintain spiritual peace. Indeed, in many cases Christianity, poached selectively, could help to rejuvenate indigenous spirituality that had lost some of its purchase. The encounter with foreign religion very often occurred as synthesis rather than conversion, and Natives frequently identified biblical characters with figures from their own spiritual world. For some, the cosmos could contain a broad range of spiritual beings, each invoked in particular circumstances and with specific needs in mind.[82] Teit intimated that the Nlha7kápmx were monotheistic[83] and reported at several junctures that his subjects regarded Christianity as reasonably compatible with their own beliefs. Learning from European religion did not necessarily imply abandoning spirits that had hitherto sufficed.

Another problem with the Weberian model of conversion is its assumption that the only reason for embracing religion is religion. This is patently not the case. If the Nlha7kápmx dilemma is reduced to a need to rationalize, spiritually, social life, we ignore the possibility that the appeal to Good was a form of pragmatic rationality, in the sense that missionaries offered assistance that was not only spiritual but worldly.[84] The arrival of Europeans and the implementation of a colonial regime required Natives to make extremely difficult choices. Should they fight back or submit? Should they deal with the colonial government alone or with the help of willing white advocates? These questions were of the greatest importance and were not easily resolved. When thousands of miners descended on Nlha7kápmx territory in 1858 and conflict broke out, the Native leaders had to decide whether to continue a fight that looked hopeless or to negotiate a peace with the colonial authorities. Some were ready to battle it out, but the great chief Spintlum (Cexpe'-ntlEm or Cixpe'ntlam) pacified them and spoke to the whites.[85] A renowned peacemaker, Spintlum hoped to guide his people through troubled times. If Christianity could reanimate a shaken spirit world, missionaries were desirable; if these Christians could help Natives to cope politically and physically, too, so much the better.

My own feeling is that the Nlha7kápmx deemed Christianity a source of spiritual replenishment – though by no means a substitute for traditional belief – and a practical means of facilitating life in colonial British Columbia. Disease was a major consideration. Teit reported massive

Nlha7kápmx depopulation from smallpox, influenza, and measles, with infant mortality especially high.[86] While the 1862 smallpox epidemic did not hit the Nlha7kápmx as badly as some other nations, it was not for Natives to spurn the aid of those who vaccinated them. Missionaries of various stripes were to the fore in this effort, as were government officials. When the Reverend Alexander Garrett accompanied Hills to the mainland that summer, he plied the lancet as the bishop preached near Spuzzum. In this way Natives were 'reminded of the value which the white man might be to [them].'[87] This observation was cruel but telling. The reality was that Europeans were best equipped to prevent European illness. This placed Natives in a predicament that missionaries exploited to the full. Early in 1875 an outbreak of measles among Good's charges gave him a useful leverage, for while his patients survived, many of those left to 'the tender mercies of the old medicine work' were not so fortunate.[88] It seems plausible that missionaries were entertained by Natives in part for the medical help they tendered.

The urgency of Good's summons may also have been tied to the increasing gravity of the land question in the late 1860s. Reserves were first set aside at Lytton in 1860, and by the time Good arrived in Yale European settlement had begun in earnest. A recently published oral history describes how the Nlha7kápmx were forced to give away land to appease aggressive white intruders.[89] Confronted by colonial officials who disregarded their land claims, the Nlha7kápmx needed spokesmen to articulate their anger. Missionaries seemed prepared to act as mediators; it is telling that Natives from Nicola Lake had asked Good to petition the government within months of his move to Lytton. There is some truth to Good's claim that in the encounter between Natives and Europeans, missionaries occupied an interstitial space.[90] Roman Catholics and Protestants of various denominations tried to publicize Native dissent. It should not be forgotten, however, that the Anglicans were Englishmen in a British colony. The Nlha7kápmx would surely have taken notice when, for the first time, they encountered missionaries speaking the same tongue as the surveyors and magistrates who coordinated and sanctioned the theft of their land. The decision to invite Good in place of the Oblates was perhaps consolidated by a belief that more effective arbitration would ensue. Only time would prove this assumption unfounded.

Although we cannot be sure of Nlha7kápmx motives, it is likely that they turned to Christianity for a number of reasons. They were not a homogenous people, and Good's value to one person was not his value to another. Yet it is vital that we emphasize the importance of Christianity as a practical religion, for in doing so we can cast doubt on the Anglican thesis that Nlha7kápmx wants were spiritual, and that they required Christianity and were damned without it. This singular narrative does not square with the facts as discussed in this book. Indeed, Good himself suspected the Nlha7kápmx of worldly incentive. It was not until three months into his mission that Good's charges first accepted spiritual as well as temporal advice.[91] Thus far they had embraced Christianity but overlooked its raison d'être. This was a disturbing realization, and left Good plagued by paranoia and distrust, typical symptoms of colonists who disseminate Western knowledge with no assurance that its acceptance is sincere.[92] Dubious motives unsettled mission work, and Good's anxiety about the authenticity of faith is evident in the long probation period he imposed on converts. Concerned that Natives would feign conversion to retain his advocacy, Good had his charges prove themselves before he baptized them. To baptize freely was to jeopardize his flock's purity, for 'they are ready to believe anything that may be told them on the strength of our own reputed authority.'[93]

As a result, Good was beset with ambivalence – another symptom of colonial fallibility.[94] On the one hand he witnessed consistent Nlha7kápmx abuse at the hands of colonial officials and an iniquitous land policy. Genuinely troubled by his flock's predicament, Good felt morally obliged to intervene. On the other hand he realized that representation of Nlha7kápmx grievances would leave him unsure of their sincerity; if he offered assistance in land disputes, the reality of Native conversion was not guaranteed. It was a nagging dilemma with no clear solution, and Good vacillated endlessly. His head told him one thing, his heart another. He maintained that to substantiate Native integrity, a missionary had to remain aloof from the worldly politics of colonialism; but he studiously ignored this injunction, affirming his own role in seeking redress for Nlha7kápmx loss of land.[95] This was just one of many contradictions of empire that John B. Good experienced.

# 2
# Redemption

For all have sinned, and come short of the glory of God.
                                                    – Romans 3:23

Most discussion of nineteenth-century colonial discourse has focused on its 'codification of difference.'[1] Scholars have charted the manifold ways in which Europeans distinguished themselves from non-Europeans, showing that such distinctions often buttressed and coloured colonial practice. Homi Bhabha offers a useful synopsis of these findings. 'The objective of colonial discourse,' he claims, 'is to construe the colonized as a population of degenerate types on the basis of racial origin, in order to justify conquest and to establish systems of administration and instruction.'[2] Although, clearly, colonial discourses were not all of a piece, most appealed to some form of racial hierarchy. Immutable and asymmetrical difference vindicated and explained imperial supremacy.[3]

Anglican missionary discourse does not correspond to this model. Although it turned (at one level) on the identification of differences between Christian Europeans and 'heathen' Natives, it did not, and could not, assume immutable difference.

Consider a picture that appeared in an SPG publication, the *Gospel Missionary*, in 1870 (see Figure 5). It purported to show Good at work in British Columbia. Usually, such an image would have delighted him. Like many of his colleagues, Good depended heavily on the munificence of the British reading public and therefore craved publication – for he knew that 'to be out of print is to be out of mind.'[4] But this picture troubled Good, and for the following reasons. A long day's ride to the northeast of Lytton was the town of Ashcroft, where Good had baptized a Nlha7kápmx chief henceforth known to the Anglicans as John Mahascut. Upon returning to Lytton Good wrote to the SPG with details of the conversion. His account of what followed, penned many years later, is revealing:

*Figure 5*   Image of Native baptism

When the account of the reception of this dear old man into the Household of Faith by Baptism went home to the Society for the Propagation
of the Gospel in London, and they were anxious to insert it in their little publication called the 'Gospel Missionary,' they were at a loss for an
illustration of my act of initiation[. It] happened that they had by them
a picture of some American missionary baptizing one of the Pawnee
Indians which they thought would just, as we say in this country, 'fill
the bill.' What stood for me, unless I unduly flatter myself, was a perfect
caricature, whilst my friend John Mahascut was represented with sharp
cut features, scalpknot, tomahawk hard by and altogether a most villainous individual, whereas John was the mildest mannered pleasing
specimen of his whole tribe. When that periodical was sent out to me, I
carefully kept it out of sight of our Indian congregation, for had they
seen it we at home would have been looked upon as woefully destitute
of knowledge.[5]

An eager metropolitan readership demanded illustrations, and a careless
editor, bowing to public pressure, had substituted a member of one Native
group for another. Good, aware that this switch violated Nlha7kápmx
identity and not afraid to bite the hand that fed him, contacted his sponsors immediately. He suggested that in future more care was in order,
adding that such unsuitable images were 'calculated to do incalculable
harm both here and at home – for it gives people an utterly wrong impression respecting the ancient inhabitants of this country.'[6]

It was not the picture itself that bothered Good but its inappropriate use. He was disturbed by the editor's assumption that any image of Native baptism could adequately represent this particular chief's conversion. The implication seemed to be that an Indian was an Indian; such stereotypes struck Good as distasteful. As Bhabha reminds us, stereotypes are, by their very nature, promiscuous, for their essential property is a 'repeatability in changing historical and discursive conjunctures.'[7] During the age of empire stereotypes were pervasive, with a few powerful images serving to caricature many different peoples. To Good's mind, this indiscrimination was injurious. He regarded the Nlha7kápmx as distinctive and was angry because the picture accompanying his report intimated that Mahascut was equivalent to other Native Americans. Feeling compelled to voice his concerns, Good criticized the SPG for fomenting popular misconceptions.

Yet if this image has some of the qualities of a colonial stereotype, it lacks others. Stereotypes generally seek to establish and authenticate an unchanging identity. As Bhabha describes it, the colonial stereotype is a representation of racial permanence: 'it connotes rigidity and an unchanging order.'[8] It was this fixity that the *Gospel Missionary* picture rejected. This may not be immediately apparent. After all, the chief's face is sunk in darkness while the missionary's is bathed in light; the differences seem as clear as night and day. In the active performance of the missionary, however, in his outstretched hands, lies the possibility of redemption, the enduring promise of change. The contrast between light and darkness is only temporary, for baptism will dissolve the divide between heathen and Christian.

As an ethnological portrayal, the baptism picture, as Good told his superiors, was fraudulent. But as an icon of Christianity's redemptive power, it was vivid propaganda. Anglican missionaries disputed the fixity inherent in most colonial stereotypes and instead preached conversion; in this respect they offered a distinctive discourse of empire.

The Anglican mission did not generate the essentialist rhetoric described by Edward Said and other theorists of colonial discourse. Analyzing nineteenth-century Western representations of 'the Orient,' Said contends that this imperial archive consists of 'tested and unchanging knowledge, since "Orientals" for all practical purposes were a Platonic essence.'[9] Such permanence contradicted basic theological principles. If identity was immutable and difference was abiding, the heathen were intractable – immune to what Good called 'the transforming power of the Spirit of God turning them into other men.'[10] The idea was absurd. The Anglican missionary agenda, as propagated by Good, could not be reconciled with more worldly discourses of empire; like the Methodist mission to the Solomon Islands discussed by Nicholas Thomas, it was concerned with transformation rather than subjugation. 'The dominant movement of colonial history in [the missionary] imagination,' Thomas writes, 'is not the establishment of a fixed hierarchical relationship but a process of conversion.'[11]

The discourse of the Anglican mission coexisted uneasily, even duplicitously, with the strict racial hierarchies of secular colonialism. Anglican missionaries borrowed the standard lexicon of empire but altered its signification. The Reverend John West, whose mission to the Red River Colony had enthralled a young Good, provides a typical example of this Anglican perspective. West identified 'human depravity and barbarism' among Native peoples, but whereas other colonists saw this barbarity as a racial defect, West denounced it as 'gross ignorance.'[12] Good made much the same case. In the mission field his chief antagonist was not an inscrutable racial other but the (as yet) 'ignorant savage.'[13] Both West and Good tied savagery to a lack of knowledge, not to a fixed racial taxonomy. For many Europeans an innate racial trait, barbarism was for Anglican missionaries a moral expression of spiritual dearth.[14]

The essential assumption of mission work was that this heathen ignorance could be cured. As Lillooet missionary Lundin Brown put it, 'wherever there is a human face, however disfigured by sin, is there not a human mind which can apprehend God's truth, and a human heart which is in need of it?'[15] To the extent that missionaries anticipated and enacted change, their representations of the colonized were mutable. The rhetoric of savagery authorized mission work but was obsolete once Natives converted. Barbarians before they encountered Christ, Natives were civilized through faith. In referring to these converts missionaries disclaimed discourses they had previously propagated; savagery was now a redundant trope. 'I really cannot sometimes attach the idea of "barbarian" and "savage,"' Good reported from Nanaimo in 1862, 'to the orderly, devout, and decently-attired assembly of Indians before me.'[16] This disavowal marks the caesura of Anglican missionary discourse, the point at which heathens become Christians, others become the same. Secular discourses of empire did not share this break between old and new – they turned on binding racial hierarchies and, as such, could not codify Anglican imperial intent.

### Human Unity and Catholic Faith

In 1867, the year that Good began his mission to the Nlha7kápmx, an anonymous contribution to *The Mission Field* detailed the broader demands upon colonial Christianity. The author stressed Anglican obligations to the 'heathen' – 'those who, if they differ from us in religious belief, are of the same flesh and blood, with like affections, like fears and hopes, and like capacities of knowing and loving Him who has revealed Himself to us for our loving adoration.'[17] My argument in this book is that such statements contributed to a discourse of empire but *not* of race. Peoples were distinguished from one another by religious belief, not by genus or skin colour. In the words of David Scott, 'it was not race but religion (or more properly, the lack of one) that constituted the discursive frame within which the difference of the non-European was conceived and represented.'[18] Europeans stood apart only to the degree that non-Europeans lacked Christianity; in all other respects, humankind was considered uniform. Of the same stock as their colonizers, the colonized were no more unworthy of God's grace and had an equal aptitude for worshipping Him.

This mission discourse posited Christianity as a catholic religion and traced its catholicity to St. Paul. Raised a Jew, Paul's conversion was tied to his refutation of national covenant. He maintained that God's salvation was at the hands 'not of the Jews only, but also of the Gentiles' (Romans 9:24). Since Jesus had died for all, the Christian community in turn should be inclusive. This charge was echoed in other early Christian writings – by the end of the Gospel of Matthew, for example, a religion originally directed at the Israelites had shed ethnic bias in favour of a potentially universal membership[19] – but it was Paul who laid the theoretical groundwork for an ecumenical Christianity. The Apostle held that God's truths were available to, and could be apprehended by, all peoples, and that mission was therefore a viable Christian project. Paul was as good as his word. The breadth of his vision was rivalled by his appetite for souls, and to this day the Pauline Church is renowned for 'the vigor of its missionary drive.'[20]

Paul has had a towering influence on successive generations of missionaries, and as we shall see in later chapters, his thought and practice inspired virtually every facet of Good's Nlha7kápmx mission. That Good's intellectual genealogy was Pauline is apparent in the bare facts of his career. His ordination took place in Newark Church in 1858 on 25 January – the Conversion of St. Paul – and his churches in Nanaimo and Lytton were both named in honour of the Apostle.

The foundation stone for the Lytton St. Paul's was laid in the fall of 1871. Bishop Hills organized his annual trip through the interior so that his arrival in town coincided with the date Good had chosen for the service: 18 October. Good had invited Hills to perform the ceremony, and both men would later recall the event with satisfaction, each dwelling on the symbolic implications of the consecration. Good thought it telling that the bishop had put aside a mallet and instead had used 'an ancient stone instrument of rare interest, value, and construction' for the purpose of planting the foundation block. This, Good claimed, was no ordinary stone: 'It was proof amongst many of the common origin of the human family, similar instruments having been found not only amongst the Chympseans in the north and the Delawarres in the east, tribes of the great Indian family separated by thousands of miles and by different languages, but also among the New Zealanders.'[21] Hills, too, recognized the symbolism of this implement, citing the same archaeological finds as 'proofs of a wide spread unity ... confirming so far the Scriptures which assert the derivation of man from one stock and that God made of one blood all nations upon earth.' The bishop also invoked the man in whose honour they had gathered: St. Paul, 'the great apostle who taught the catholicity of the Church breaking down the partition wall of prejudice.'[22]

The catholic basis of Christianity was a central theme of the Oxford Movement, which rejigged nineteenth-century Anglicanism. Starting with John Keble's assize sermon of 14 July 1833, this High Church revival, with protagonists dubbed Tractarians, had an explicitly Pauline agenda. Both Hills and Good subscribed to this position, although the strength of the bishop's views is unclear – one commentator said he was not High Church,[23] and yet the faith he advocated was clearly the 'golden mediocrity' that, according to the men of the Oxford Movement, could accommodate puritans at one extreme and Roman Catholic sympathizers at the other.[24] Most scholars would now accept that Hills was a Tractarian, if only a moderate one.[25] He respected the patristic scholarship that fuelled the Oxford Movement, and when embattled sought inspiration in Chrysostom, not Calvin.[26] From his perspective and that of other High Church Anglicans,[27] catholicity entailed realignment with the ancient and undivided church – the tradition of Paul and the other Fathers – rather than surrender to papal authority. Paul had taught Christians that as members of a universal religion, they belonged to an invisible fold of redeemed souls. The Tractarians took this lesson to heart, insisting that the Church of England, as direct heir of the Early Church, could be a truly Catholic institution.

As we saw with Paul, it is a short step from the belief that all people can apprehend Christ to the conviction that a Christian's duty is to help the 'heathen' turn. In her discussion of evangelism in the nineteenth-century Solomon Islands, Sara H. Sohmer ties the Anglican missionary impulse directly to this tenet of catholicity. Indeed, she claims that for those involved in the propagation of the gospel, mission represents tangible 'proof' of Christianity's universal substance.[28] Through the nineteenth century and beyond, many were the Anglican missionaries who believed that because their religion was universally relevant, the unification of humanity under Christ was a legitimate objective; they located the origins of this desire for unity in the Early Church, and in Paul in particular. 'The whole thunder of the Pauline message echoes around Christians corporately as well as individually,' maintains one apologist in a book on the Catholic theology of Anglican mission work.[29]

Underlying this modern rationalization of mission was the concept of human unity, which contradicted the thrust of contemporary racial theory. Such theory, to be sure, was relatively recent. Robert Young has usefully reconstructed European anthropological controversies over human speciation, demonstrating that for much of the age of empire, it was agreed that humanity reduced to a single species. 'The Enlightenment humanitarian ideals of universality, sameness and equality,' observes Young, 'reigned supreme.' In the mid-nineteenth century, however, this view was displaced by a racial doctrine of polygenesis (multiple species). 'From the 1840s,' Young reports, 'the new racial theories based in comparative anatomy and craniometry in the United States, Britain and France endorsed the polygenetic alternative.'[30]

Good dismissed this new scientific consensus. He insisted on the inclusive theory of monogenesis and even corresponded with the Anthropology Department at Berkeley in an attempt to intervene in prevailing debates.[31] He was, of course, only one among many Anglican missionaries, not all of whom shared his views. As an SPG man who largely ignored white settlers, Good dodged his sponsors' guidelines; other SPG missionaries, Alexander Pringle among them, were less disposed towards Native work, adamant that 'they came out to preach & elevate, first of all and foremost a white race.' Based in Yale in the early 1860s, Pringle was troubled by the small number of white 'agriculturalists and settlers,' and recommended the summary confinement of Natives on reserves.[32] For Pringle, the notion of a distinct racial hierarchy was perhaps not unpalatable.

Yet among the Anglicans such views were atypical. Most clergymen accepted a fundamental human unity. 'In the sight of God,' said John Garrett, brother of SPG missionary Alexander and commissary of Bishop Hills, 'the white man and the coloured man are of equal value.'[33] Hills, for his part, was keen to ensure that this gracious rhetoric was translated into a practical equality that (as much as possible) transcended prejudice. His sympathies surfaced in a dispute that divided white Victoria in the fall of 1860. The city's population included a number of African Americans who had looked to the British colony as a refuge from the bigotry they suffered in California.[34] Initially, their hopes of fair treatment seemed dashed. In the summer of 1859, a year after the first blacks arrived in Victoria, a disillusioned migrant wrote to the editor of *The British Colonist*. 'Have the colored people realized their fond anticipations in coming to Vancouver's Island?,' he wondered. 'I answer *no*.'[35] Even religious institutions proved illiberal. Under Father Demers, the Roman Catholics yielded to whites who threatened to withdraw their children from Catholic schools unless they were segregated.[36] The Congregationalists also segregated, albeit only after bitter infighting had split their ranks; the Reverend William Clarke, a Canadian, spoke out against slavery and welcomed blacks as equals in his church, but the Reverend Matthew Macfie, a racist Briton, ultimately won the day.[37]

Bishop Hills, on the other hand, decided that St. John's, his new church, would not be segregated, a contentious decision in a settler colony in which prejudice was a fact of life. The bishop often mused that this climate of intolerance was a product of an immigrant American mining society, but his fellow British colonists were not blameless.[38] Even for some of those who opposed segregation, 'race' was a de facto biological distinction. Hills spoke of one Briton who, while outwardly sympathetic to his new policy towards African Americans, 'evidently believes the race is a different species of man & spoke of them rather patronizingly with pity rather than honour & respect as of fellow immortals & equal in the sight of God.'[39] These attitudes worried Hills greatly, for racial hierarchies flew in the face of Catholicism. Yet the bishop stood firm. Supported by fellow Anglicans Edward Cridge and the Reverend Robert J. Dundas, Hills found strength and direction in Paul and resisted public pressure; he would not segregate church services, for 'there should be *no difference* in the house of God.'[40]

### Otherness: A Moment within the Same

In step with his bishop's example, Good also tried to be open-minded and therefore evenhanded. He claimed that his instruction of Natives and whites was identical.[41] Similarly, he chose not to discriminate within and between different Native groups. Even when his Nlha7kápmx mission began to produce results, he insisted that prospective converts would not be separated from the 'heathen' majority. I analyze this policy in some detail in Chapter 5; it suffices to note here that Good treated the Nlha7kápmx as a single social body. If the 'heathen' mixed freely with enlightened peers, they might learn by example – such was the crux of Good's mission philosophy.

This strategy drew on time-honoured mission principles that crystallized during the first few centuries of the church. Good's work can only be understood in the light of this patristic theology, particularly the thought of St. Paul and St. Augustine. More generally, Good appears to have favoured those Fathers who rejected the hermetism associated with certain forms of asceticism. On the grounds that exposure to the world was contaminating, some ascetics sought absolute isolation from everyday life. While this picture of lonely hermits is something of a stereotype – it admits neither the transformation of asceticism into monasticism, nor the ascetic bent of worldly men such as Ambrose of Milan and Augustine himself – it was the one familiar to Good. His chief nemesis was the Donatist movement of the fourth and fifth centuries. It was against Donatist thinking that Good propounded mission endeavour, so the shadow cast by Donatism serves to illuminate (by way of contrast) the mechanics of his colonialism. In the sense that they urged Christians to resist contact with pagans, the Donatists reinforced difference and discounted unity under Christ. Good knew that Donatism was introspective and, as such, anything but colonizing; he had no time for this stagnant Christianity. Good's taste was for Augustine, the Donatists' antagonist.[42]

But yet again Paul was lurking in the background. Indeed, Augustine was himself strongly influenced by the Apostle.[43] Besides its missionary drive, Pauline Christianity was perhaps most notable for its urbanity. It was, according to Wayne Meeks, 'entirely urban.'[44] This geography distinguished Paul's mission from Christian traditions that shunned the world, as did Anthony and the other Desert Fathers. Why this spatial contrast? One reason is that Paul rejected ascetic views on intercourse between Christians and pagans. In the cities of the Roman Empire, desert ascetics located a profanity that threatened to pollute Christian purity. Paul argued that this ascetic fear of the world was misplaced; morality could only be violated from within, he maintained, not by contact with pagans.[45] Thus, Paul saw the city not as a source of contamination but as an aggregation of nonbelievers in need of Christianity. His vast urban mission embodied his belief, somewhat unconventional in its day, that Christians should convert the Gentiles rather than repel their otherness.

Paul always saw in the outsider a potential insider. He was convinced that religious difference would yield to Christian unity and relied on proselytism to achieve this goal. In effect, Paul's mission mediated between sameness and otherness – the basic categories of nineteenth-century imperialism. As Elizabeth Castelli has argued, the Apostle indicted difference of any kind. 'Christians are Christians,' she writes of Paul's message to the Gentiles, 'insofar as they strive for the privileged goal of sameness.' Castelli's most profound insight is her identification of the 'colonizing potential' harboured by this Pauline Christianity.[46] Paul delimited otherness as that which was not Christian, but vowed to absorb that difference into the sameness of God's fold. This desire for mutual identity was a thoroughly colonialist gesture and has provided an enduring theological benchmark for the Christian mission. The vision of a newly united humanity was evoked with graphic intensity in the Pauline Letter to the Colossians, which envisioned a future in which 'there is neither Greek nor Jew, circumcision nor uncircumcision, Barbarian, Scythian, bond nor free: but Christ is all, and in all' (Colossians 3:11). Paul's quarry was paganism, and the dissolution of this otherness was the objective of the Catholic mission he commenced.

'Augustine's mystique of the Catholic Church,' described excellently by Peter Brown, appealed directly to this Pauline tradition.[47] Like Paul before him, Augustine envisaged a universal Christianity. But his contemporaries did not all endorse this prospect. Awarded the bishopric of Hippo in 395, Augustine entered a North African church riven with conflict. The chief dissenters were the Donatists, whom Augustine battled tirelessly in the early fifth century. This movement of protest preceded Augustine by almost a century, born in 312 of the nonconformist views of Donatus, bishop of Carthage. In some respects Donatism was a local phenomenon, and its extraordinary persistence in Southern Numidia (to 596) was, by all accounts, a function of regional Berber history. Yet the dispute with Augustine reflected more fundamental tensions within the church at large, and it was these key debates that animated Good's interest in Donatism.

Simply stated, the issue at hand concerned the position of the church in the world. The Donatist position was that the church comprised a union of the righteous, and that this elect body should be separated from the corrupt because sin was contagious. A religion of joyous praise, Donatist Christianity proclaimed the virtue of spiritual life. Martyrdom was encouraged and devotion to the Scriptures enforced. Contact with outsiders was avoided for it jeopardized the Christian's exclusive relationship with God. The Donatists, then, would separate good and bad before the Day of Judgment. The church was considered a place of refuge, a holy retreat from the worldly Roman Empire. This was an 'other' space reserved for the pious. And if some Donatists tempered the claim that their church had no sinners, they, unlike Augustine, would strive to purge their ranks of infidels.[48]

This division between the church and the world precluded precisely the growth that Augustine championed. It was impossible for the church to expand if, as the Donatists had it, paganism infected Christian purity. Concerned above all to police its borders, Donatism was at best a stagnant religion, at worst a regressive one. It was certainly not aggressive. It was constrained by neurosis or, in Brown's words, 'immobilized by anxiety to preserve its identity.' The same cannot be said of Augustine's church. Whereas Donatism held paganism at arm's length, Augustine vowed to swallow that other world whole. In the Old Testament God had promised a global faith, and in the New Testament Jesus had told His disciples to speak His name to the ends of the earth. Augustine's mission was to realize this covenant; he would reunite humanity under Christ. Instead of fleeing from the world, the church should consume its being and permeate its every pore. In the North Africa of his day, Augustine's vision challenged introspective Donatists. In the nineteenth century it gave European Christians an estimable rationale for empire, for the Catholic mandate was to seize the 'heathen' and reduce their otherness to sameness. 'This church,' says Brown, 'was hungry for souls: let it eat, indiscriminately if needs be. It is a group no longer committed to defend itself against society; but rather, poised, ready to fulfill what it considered its historic mission, to dominate, to absorb, to lead a whole Empire.'[49]

These Augustinian prescriptions were of lasting significance. Until the late fourth century, Christians had been deeply suspicious of the Imperial Government, which, to the Donatists as to their predecessors, represented the world that endangered steady faith. By the mid-fifth century, however, the church was fully allied with the Roman Empire, which now served as a conduit for the dissemination of Christianity. The conversion of Emperor Constantine had paved the way for this union, and Augustine hastened its consummation. Imperialism no longer represented mere Roman expansion; empire was now invested with Christian destiny. Ernest Barker suggests that the bond between imperialism and religion remained firm until the early nineteenth century – and even then it was only partly unsettled – and traces this symbiosis to Augustine. The debate with Donatism was a pivotal moment, for henceforth imperialism was Christian and Christianity was missionary. In Augustine's wake, Barker tells us, empire was 'charged with a deeper and far more sovereign content. Empire had never been mere power. It had always been a vessel carrying, and existing to carry, some great cargo or freight. From AD 400 we may say that it carries, and exists to carry, the freight of the Christian faith.'[50]

The salience of Augustine's teaching was evident to many agents of the nineteenth-century Anglican mission. In contrast to the Donatists, for whom caution and isolation ensured holiness, these modern English missionaries revived Augustine's conviction that expansion and confrontation were the true means of preserving moral fibre. 'Progression,' argued a review article in the *Church Missionary Intelligencer* of 1851, 'is the law of Christianity. Not to advance is to retreat: and the only hope of preserving the light for ourselves, is to let it shine, brighter, wider, more intensely, than any past era has witnessed.'[51] This rhetoric was positively imperial, and its roots were in the Early Church.

We can now return to our original question and ask why it was that Good refused to separate Nlha7kápmx converts from Natives still regarded as 'savages.' The answer is that Donatist-style division was inimical to the logic of catholicity. Segregation would entail inertia and partial conversion, which were not in Good's interest. Rather than accept lingering heathenism as inevitable, and best sequestered, Good maintained that Christianity could absorb otherness *in toto* by giving the lie to it. He insisted, moreover, that the most appropriate means of demystification was the new convert. Augustine argued that a good Christian does not hide from the heathen, but instead 'must coexist with sinners in the same community,' and 'must also be prepared, actively, to rebuke and correct them.'[52] Good envisaged exactly this role for his most successful Nlha7kápmx students:

I am more and more convinced that it is the true apostolic and primitive system for those who come out, and who are called out of darkness and begin to run well, to let their light shine amidst the wastes of their own dwellings and surroundings, until the little one shall have become a thousand, and the whole lump shall be leavened. The Donatist idea of separating the wheat and the chaff I never could understand. It seems wrong, unnatural, and productive of the worst consequences, to draw an arbitrary line of demarcation between what we may term the saved and the unsaved.[53]

As ventured by Good, the Anglican mission reconfigured a set of ancient Christian tenets – many of them Augustinian. Otherness, namely heathenism, could be subdued by a faith of universal substance, and Anglicanism was ostensibly that: a catholic religion. In a speech of 1860 the bishop of London spoke for all his High Church colleagues when he predicted 'one Church on both sides of the globe.'[54] This was an imperial prognosis driven by a powerful syllogism. The two essential premises were that sin was innate – 'As it is written,' reads Romans 3:10, 'There is none righteous, no, not one' – and that Christianity's redemptive force was in the gospel.[55] These propositions fed the conclusion that mission was not only viable but obligatory. In short, empire was a Christian duty because the need for the gospel was ubiquitous and the church controlled access to its redemptive power. Anthony Grant, a leading advocate of the Anglican mission, summed up this principle in an influential lecture series in 1843, noting that the gospel 'addresses itself not to this or that people, or condition of thought, or social state, or political organization, but to fallen human nature; and therefore it is designed of God to be universal; and the Church as the depository of this remedial scheme, the channel of its spiritual blessings, is evermore to expand.'[56] To any eye this was resolutely imperial stuff, and Good, as it happens, knew it well – Grant's Bampton lectures were his chief text during his final year at St. Augustine's.[57]

This mission discourse turned on shifting relations between sameness and otherness. The basic maxim was that of a common humanity. Sin was universal, as, therefore, was the need for salvation. While many Europeans had been justified by God's grace through redemption in Christ, the colonized generally had not; their otherness was religious and (most important) temporary. Missionary work could restore lost unity by introducing sinners to the universal household of faith. In this spirit the bishop of Oxford spoke of the Columbia Mission enhancing 'the indissoluble union of the Church of the Redeemed.'[58] We appear to have, in the theory of the Anglican mission, a discourse of *difference within sameness*. Human oneness was absolute but fractured, temporarily, by sin. If the mission enterprise was successful, Christianity would dominate and assimilate the heathen world it deemed other. This otherness, identified as savagery, legitimated empire but would not survive its fruition. The Other was a temporary break in the Same, a moment in its imperial history.[59] This moment was the definitive temporality of mission.

### Time, Space, and the People of God

If race was the 'organizing grammar' of secular colonialism,[60] time and space were vital surrogate languages. It is clear from the critical literature on European colonialism that discourses of history and geography often served to articulate racial difference. They did not reveal the nature of this otherness, just evidence of its location – *apart*. Otherness was somehow more apparent when rooted in a separate time and place. Identified as primitives and foreigners, non-Europeans were displaced from the here and now, their otherness accentuated by distance (historical and geographical) from the familiar and the everyday. In many cases the reference point for this othering was the modern West: other races were described as premodern and non-Western. More generally the construction of otherness assumed 'a denial of "coevalness" in time, and a radical discontinuity in terms of human space.'[61]

Temporal and spatial discourses demarcated empire's internal borders, placing Europeans in one time and space, 'savages' in another. Said first touches on these themes when he outlines the concept of an imaginative geography. He argues that only the notion of a strict spatial divide between metropolitan authors and colonial subjects can legislate a discrete imperial discourse such as Orientalism. 'Orientalism,' he claims, 'is premised upon exteriority.'[62] This detachment allows in turn the constitution of 'the Orient,' a distinctive foreign space. The difference of 'the Oriental' is consolidated by her distance from the West, and by the exotic nature of the space she inhabits.[63] Said maintains that this divisive spatiality is common to all European discourses of empire.[64] Imaginative geography helps the mind 'to intensify its own sense of itself by dramatizing the distance and difference between what is close to it and what is far away.'[65]

In an acclaimed study of his own discipline, Johannes Fabian, an anthropologist, shows that the othering of non-Europeans occurs through discourses of time as well as space. Assuming that the societies they study are not contemporary with the West, anthropologists have made 'traditional' culture the focus of their inquiry. This, Fabian argues, is a colonialist posture; Native primitivism automatically implies European progress. He adds that this temporal discourse functions in much the same way as imaginative geography – otherness is construed in terms of distance from a European norm, in this case a white modernity. Thus, 'anthropology's efforts to construct relations with its Other by means of temporal devices implied affirmation of difference as *distance*.'[66] Time, like space, distanced one people from another. And it is worth noting that these histories and geographies were intertwined, an imbrication captured in Anne McClintock's phrase 'anachronistic space.'[67] Her argument is simply that if peoples were separated by history and geography, then space was itself fissured by time. Travelling to the colonies, Europeans visited a bygone era; on returning, they went back to the future.

But many Anglican missionaries denied that time and space divided people in this manner. For obvious reasons, the High Church Anglican mission could brook no such obstacles to eventual Christian oneness. Although its agents did acknowledge otherness (or as they had it, heathen sin), they were wary of discourses that downplayed the potential for unity by fixing this otherness to distant times and spaces.

Consider, for example, Bishop George Hills and his rejection of this rhetoric of distance. His first impression of the Columbia Diocese in 1860 – its climate seemed 'thoroughly English'[68] – was not that of a man keen to distance colony from metropole. Quite the contrary, in fact. On a mission to absorb otherness, the bishop was interested in breaking barriers down, not erecting them – in taming 'savagery' rather than keeping it at bay. He enthused, therefore, about technology that gave the Anglicans quick access to virgin mission fields; Marx's 'annihilation of space by time' was an exciting concept for an imperialist church.[69] The bishop's voyage from England to British Columbia included a four-hour train journey across the isthmus of Panama, and the new railroad pleased him. 'Altogether,' he wrote in his journal, 'I felt deeply interested in this enterprise so successfully carried out and forming another connecting link of nations – and tending by bringing nearer together to promote the civilisation of mankind.'[70] Hills, clearly, did not visualize otherness through geography. Space was merely a physical obstacle, and its submission nourished Anglican destiny.

If contiguity replaced distance in this spatial imagination, what of the divisive histories discussed by Fabian? Again, Anglican missionary discourse tends to deviate from the typical colonial model. To use Fabian's own terminology, the contrast is between 'secular' and 'sacred' discourses of time. The former excludes on the basis of split histories, the latter accommodates (or appropriates) through simultaneity.[71] An otherness confined to the past contradicted the vision of a reunited humanity. Against this distancing, Anglican missionaries maintained the oneness of a common history.

'The history of Vancouver Island and British Columbia,' the Anglicans announced, 'may be said to commence from the summer of 1858.'[72] Indigenous peoples were not consigned to a prehistory equated with savagery. Instead, Anglican missionaries invoked a single history that bound God's children together. Natives belonged to the present, not the past, so precolonial history was immaterial. By denying British Columbia a heritage, the Anglicans inferred that Christianity gave Native existence a meaning it had hitherto lacked. Mission discourse constructed a present without a past; history began with the arrival of Christianity on foreign soil. The creation of the Crown Colony in 1858 was the focal point of this originary myth. When the Anglicans proclaimed just months later that 'We ... erect found make ordain and constitute' a colonial diocese, they secured the image of British Columbia as a *terra nulla* awaiting history.[73] The bishop of Oxford, speaking in London on the urgency of mission work in the new colony, noted simply that it 'should begin from the beginning.'[74]

This Anglican reading does not dovetail with other colonialist histories of British Columbia, though the myth of origins is common to most. As Daniel Clayton notes, the history of British Columbia has been given various different starting dates, 1858 but one among them; Clayton identifies George Vancouver's circumnavigation of Vancouver Island (1792), Fraser's exploration of the mainland (1808), the creation of the colony of Vancouver Island (1849), and British Columbia's entry into Confederation (1871) as others. While the colonialist narrative of origins is pervasive, the position of Natives in these histories varies significantly. If Anglican missionaries deemed Natives integral to empire, other commentators suggested that Natives belonged to a past that European civilization displaced. According to this scenario, Natives were obstacles to, rather than beneficiaries of, progress.[75] The Anglican mission also constituted otherness through a discourse of time, but its tactic was erasure, not distancing. The past featured only as an absence that the foundational rhetoric (erect found make ...) obscured from view. Michel de Certeau describes this absence as 'what we do not know, what is not endowed with a proper name. In the form of a past which has no locus that can be designated,' he goes on, 'it is *the law of the other*.'[76] Instead of using time to distance and consolidate otherness, Anglican historiography colonized otherness; it posited a shared history that prefigured Christian unity.

History and geography did not separate Christian from heathen, and yet unity was not yet at hand. Before the Word arrived in British Columbia, sameness was in abeyance and otherness prevailed. If neither time nor space framed this difference, was a more suitable register of distance available? The answer is yes; but this distance was in no sense worldly, and could be bridged through faith alone. The distance between saint and sinner was *moralized*, for it was religion, not race, that kept people apart, and earthly histories and geographies could not codify otherness of this order. Again, Augustine was edifying, for it was his thesis that moral virtue offered closeness to God; sexual sin, on the other hand, was experienced as alienation. Distance was a measure of moral worth. 'To be far from your face,' Augustine wrote in his *Confessions*, 'is to be in the darkness of passion.' If nearness to God was a function of morality, it was, likewise, sin that distanced one human being from another. Geography, at any rate, was dismissed out of hand. 'One does not go far away from you or return to you,' Augustine said, 'by walking or by any movement in space.'[77]

Such thoughts stirred Bishop Hills as he prepared to leave England for the mission field. Facing a long voyage to British Columbia, he was daunted only by the sin, not the geography, that separated him from the 'heathen.' 'Time and space,' Hills declared at his farewell sermon, 'do not separate the people of God. It is only sin that really separates us from one another, and from God. We may be one in Christ by a living faith.'[78] This was an astonishing statement, a pithy discourse on otherness and sameness as understood by Anglican missionaries of the bishop's persuasion. Faith would reunite a humanity divided, for the moment, by sin. It is surely significant that empire's racial exclusions, grounded in discourses of geography and history, were flouted. At the very least, it is clear that scholars who attempt to theorize *the* discourse of colonialism are being unduly ambitious and terribly reductive.[79] Anglican thinking on mission did not conform to a dominant set of ideas about cultural difference and the imperative of empire. These missionaries repeatedly distanced themselves from other colonial agents. To admit this is not to be an apologist for mission work: it is to insist that a reductive approach will not yield a better understanding of imperialism and its consequences.

### Discourses of Nation and Empire

The remainder of this chapter examines links between nation and empire in discourses of the Anglican mission. I have argued that for many Anglicans, the presumption of Christianity's catholicity enjoined mission practice, and that we should read the discourse of universality as a theology of empire. Yet as John S. Moir points out, a Catholic disposition entails a different set of forces for Anglicans, who belong to a specifically national church, than it does for Roman Catholics, members of an international religious and political body.[80] Is there a contradiction between the national basis of the Church of England and the universal pretensions of some of its clergy? Not necessarily, say those who have studied the place of catholicity in the theology of national churches.[81] The national element of Christianity has flowered in recent centuries, but though reacting in some cases against the tenet of universality, it has not supplanted it. While Christianity in its early, Catholic guise may not comfortably accommodate national identity, the two are not inherently hostile.[82]

In Anglican missionaries we can detect something of this duality, and it is clear that for those so inclined, universal designs did not preclude a nationalist sensibility. Good encouraged his charges to respect English authority and purred on hearing them sing his national anthem, yet his Catholic agenda remained to the fore.[83] Bishop Hills, similarly, assumed his message to be universal, but was known to lecture in mining saloons with a British flag draped across the wall behind him.[84] If Christianity was intended for all nations, the nationality of its emissaries was not in doubt, and was strongly felt. Indeed, I suspect that both Good and Hills would have approved of an 1849 article in the *Church Missionary Intelligencer* that yoked national pride to Catholic intent. 'Surely it is a lesson of all History,' it read, 'that the living, earnest, expansive Christian, who has a heart large enough to embrace the whole world, is the only true patriot.'[85]

How should we understand this relationship between imperial vision and nationalist sentiment? First, we must grasp that Anglican missionaries often struggled to reconcile them. Catholicity, as we have seen, implied willingness to overlook worldly difference, whereas nationalism, by its very nature, entailed a certain partiality. The conjunction of nation and empire was not always harmonious. As a bishop of the national church, Hills experienced this tension as intensely as any of his missionaries. He wrote tellingly of his anxieties when, en route to his diocese in 1859, he was asked to perform a funeral service at Colón in Panama. In this unfamiliar territory, his patriotism seemed to confuse his Catholic remit:

> In the service I remembered that I was not on British soil and that it was a Christian principle to pray for the authorities. It is a difficulty at most times in these theatres of frequent revolution to know who are the authorities. Just now this is a special difficulty here. So I prayed generally for all Christian rulers and omitted mention of Queen Victoria, though I included her in my heart. Perhaps if acting under the British Consulate my duty would have been to identify myself with England – but holding service as a Christian minister travelling through another land my duty was to pray only for the authorities of the land and so realise the Catholic character of Christianity.[86]

Even in British Columbia, a British colony, the relationship between nation and empire was not altogether clear. Anglican missionaries were Englishmen for whom empire was rightly British, but often, for political reasons, they were compelled to muffle their allegiance. When Hills arrived in Victoria he had to allay fears that the establishment of the Anglican diocese would jeopardize religious freedom. Many colonists seemed to think that the Anglicans intended a state church. The bishop countered: 'When I arrived, I found the papers full of warfare about the "attempt" to have a "State Church," the idea of an English Bishop being apparently inseparable from tithes, Church-rates, &c. In my first sermon I proclaimed for liberty, and told the people of the Church that upon them rested the burden, and that I did not dream of resting upon the State. This had the desired effect. The movement was crushed. There has not been a syllable since.'[87] Within British Columbia historiography the conventional view, first articulated by F.W. Howay in the early twentieth century, has been that the Anglicans did aspire to the status of an established church, but while some scholars still accept this account, others now argue that Hills wanted independence from the state.[88] What we do know is that the Church of England remained oriented to Britain in British Columbia long after having been Canadianized in the east.[89] My own impression is that Hills was an unqualified Anglophile, and that like Good, he coveted the symbiosis of colonial church and state that many domestic Anglicans, not required to mollify concerned colonists, advocated.[90] The bishop knew, however, that to stress his Englishness in British Columbia was to risk causing offence. 'Though I am a Protestant, I am a foreigner,' one miner told him, 'and I will never consent to come under the British flag.'[91]

Although the politics of empire could unsettle Anglican nationalism, such concerns were not disabling. Hills and Good, both defenders of Catholic Christianity, would remain patriots. That they coupled nationalist and imperialist sentiment suggests that links between nation and empire were central to Anglican missionary discourse. Indeed, the belief that imperial evangelism affected England as well as heathen nations was a sine qua non of this mission. The Anglicans tied English national virtue to the fate of those they evangelized. The imperative of mission was a discourse of both periphery and core; when they spoke of the fruits of mission work, the Anglicans evoked a centripetal flow that enriched England because heathen souls were touched. 'In gospel propagation,' said the *Church Missionary Intelligencer*, 'there is a wonderful re-action, and the more the divine element of truth is communicated to others, the more it augments in the influence it exercises on ourselves.'[92]

It is thus conceivable that Anglican discourses of empire were always discourses on the English nation at the same time.[93] Take the popular argument that only Christianity could save the heathen from the decimation that occurred with European colonization. The Anglicans maintained that the white impact on indigenous peoples was fatal unless mitigated by Christianity. The following is the opening refrain of a hymn sung at SPG annual services:

The heathen perish; day by day
Thousands on thousands pass away.
O Christians! to their refuge fly,
Preach Jesus to them 'ere they die.[94]

The bishop of Oxford addressed similar themes when he spoke at the Mansion House in November 1859. 'How cruel have been the wrongs they have suffered at our hands!' he noted of North America's Native peoples. 'Whole tribes' had been 'mowed down' by violent British colonialisms. 'Well, I say,' he concluded, 'England owes them a deep debt for past wrongs, which she is bound to repay.'[95]

The bishop's vision was certainly imperial. He authorized a foreign mission (in this case to British Columbia) by claiming that powerless Natives had capitulated to white might, and that only Christianity could repair this damage.[96] But the bishop also showed great concern for English national integrity. He clearly rejected Ruskin's characterization of England's past as 'a thousand years of noble history'[97] and described dreadful English crimes against other cultures. And when Bishop Hills returned to England in 1863 to raise funds for the Columbia Mission, he warned audiences that there would always be a 'blot upon the history of their Christianity' if these colonial wrongs were not redressed.[98] For both Hills and Wilberforce, the obligation to missionize turned on the shame caused by English misdoings, as well as on the need to convert those who had been violated. By helping the heathen, Anglicans hoped to expiate these national sins and repair England's tainted image. Mission discourse was therapeutic for Anglicans embarrassed by the national heritage.[99]

Anglican discourses of empire, therefore, were centrally concerned with a politics and poetics of nationhood. The temper of this Anglican nationalism needs to be carefully delineated, for it was not the post-Reformation patriotism that claimed England as an elect nation. Linda Colley thinks that this particular fallacy, disseminated in tracts such as John Foxe's *Book of martyrs* (1563), played a major role in consolidating British national identity; Britons came to see themselves as a chosen people, blessed with God's special care.[100] The notion of divine election, moreover, offered a fitting rationale for empire. 'If it really was the case that England was thought to be God's peculiar place, not just *an* elect nation but *the* elect nation,' writes Patrick Collinson, 'then we have unearthed in Protestant religious consciousness a root, perhaps even the taproot, of English imperialism.'[101] Perhaps. To my mind, however, Anglicans such as Good and Hills had no truck with this rhetoric, for the concept of election directly contradicted their theology. In denying an exclusive covenant between God and Israel, the Apostle Paul had discounted national privilege. 'Particularism, national limitation, in religion is abolished,' observes Stephen Neill of Paul's injunction, 'through the simple fact that Jesus Christ has died for all.'[102] Several discourses of the nation were harnessed to Anglican visions of empire, but none accorded the English special rights to God's care.

For Anglicans such as Hills and Good, England was not an elect nation so much as the hearth of an elect Christianity. These were very different propositions. The Anglicans held that it was not God that set England apart from other nations but truth.[103] Only Anglican missionaries preached a pure faith. In this spirit the Anglicans considered evangelizing the Roman Catholic nations of Europe as well as the heathen nations of empire.[104] Similarly, the decline of the Iberian empires was attributed to the corrupt creed they propagated.[105]

Why was England special? Because *its* national religion, and no other, was faithful to God's Word. Anglican missionary societies recognized that access to truth laid a heavy imperial responsibility on English shoulders, for the truth had to be promulgated[106] and churches that sullied it could not be trusted with God's mission. To the Anglicans it was self-evident that they, the English, were His most qualified servants. 'If our age is the era for Missions,' the CMS declared, 'no less plainly is our country the messenger-people to the whole earth. The Heathen cry, and they cry to us – to us Englishmen of the nineteenth century.'[107] In the Anglican imagination of empire, it was the concept of pure Christianity that gave mission work a nationalistic cast. If the indigenous people of British Columbia were savages, it followed that only England could save them from sin: 'although in a state of debased idolatry and superstition,' Hills said of them, 'they are nevertheless friendly disposed towards England, and they look to Englishmen to do them good.'[108]

In Anglican mission discourse nationalism and imperialism were indelibly linked. The strings that bound nation to empire were durable, if at times frayed. It is important to emphasize this connectivity, for it is now commonly held that nation and empire were incompatible under British colonialism.[109] This case has been well made by Benedict Anderson, who describes nineteenth-century English nationalism as a discourse of belonging. This field of thought, Anderson claims, demarcated an 'imagined community' excluding, among other people, the indigenous inhabitants of British colonies. Natives became *de jure* members of the British Empire upon colonization, but would never be English. This disjuncture constitutes Anderson's 'inner incompatibility of empire and nation.'[110]

It is easy to see how and why Anderson identifies this cleavage. His account is secured by a genealogy that equates the dawn of European nationalism with the 'dusk of religious modes of thought.'[111] His nationalism is both modern and secular.[112] Anderson argues that the secularization of postmedieval Europe entailed a fundamental shift in the conceptualization of human fellowship, as language replaced religion as the chief axis of social identification, and that with this transition came smaller imagined communities, for nationalism did not reproduce Christianity's universal designs. 'No nation imagines itself coterminous with mankind,' Anderson explains. 'The most messianic nationalists do not dream of a day when all the members of the human race will join their nation in the way that it was possible, in certain epochs, for, say, Christians to dream of a wholly Christian planet.'[113] In the nineteenth century, empire and nation deviated in the sense that one was totalizing and the other was not. An indiscriminate appetite fuelled empire, but as an imagined community that screened its membership, England rebuffed most of those it colonized; Anderson believes that this rejection occurred on many grounds, whereas other scholars reduce its rationale to racism.[114]

But what of Anglican nationalism? Anderson accords imperialism a pivotal role in the process of territorialization that eventually spawned nationalist sensibility. Early imperial forays, he claims, convinced Europeans that their own beliefs were not universal, and he uses Marco Polo's thirteenth-century encounter with Kublai Khan as an example. In Polo's subsequent description of Christianity 'as "truest," rather than "true," we can detect the seeds of a territorialization of faiths which foreshadows the language of many nationalists.'[115] This example is poorly chosen, however, for Catholic Christianity denied the relativism of modern nationalism. Compare Anderson's reading of comparative truths with this passage from the *Church Missionary Intelligencer* (1852): 'It is not merely that [Protestant Christianity] is the superior religion, so that there are others which are true, although this is more true; but that it is the truth exclusively, so that all other combinations of principles and opinions on matters connected with religion are false, and this alone is true.'[116] Here are radically different truth claims, one relative, the other absolute. If Anderson's incompatibility of nation and empire rests on the finitude of Englishness, what of nation and empire in Anglican discourse, which equated English Christianity with universal, not bounded, truth?

Nineteenth-century Anglican nationalism was of an entirely different order than the secular nationalism that excluded empire's unwanted. The most important distinction was between means and ends. David Bebbington argues that the concept of means was essential to the nineteenth-century evangelical mission.[117] We have seen that English Christians regarded their national religion as a medium for the dissemination of the gospel; their nationalism was a discourse of agency. By contrast, the contemporary rhetoric of national belonging was a discourse of ends; as posited by nineteenth-century educationists such as Thomas B. Macaulay, Englishness was the consummation of colonial subjectivity.[118] As secular entities nation and empire were incongruous, for, as Bhabha reminds us, there was a big difference between 'being English and being Anglicized,' residence in the British Empire never offering the colonized inclusion in the English nation, even for those who did conform to English ways.[119] As Anglican categories, on the other hand, nation and empire were compatible, for imperial ambition (in other words, universal conversion) could only be realized through investment in the national creed.

The sameness promoted by Anglican missionaries was not the normalized English civility that Anglicization policies proffered but withheld. The Anglicans intended a godly unity that would transcend national specificity; the nation, as expressed in its religion, was merely a tool to achieve this oneness, and Anglican empire was but temporary, held in trust until Christ returned to claim God's Kingdom for Himself.[120] What were the respective consequences of these distinctive constellations of nation and empire? Bhabha argues, convincingly, that in the case of official state colonialism, the incompatibility of nation and empire was manifested in colonial subjects who, while urged to mimic English ways, were denied the equality tendered by this rhetoric. Bhabha reads the predicament of being almost the same, but not quite – where to be Anglicized was not to be English – as being almost the same, but not white; racism determined partial mimicry to be the most appropriate form of colonial subjectivity. The result was a compromised 'mimic man' – told to be English yet refused the prerogative of Englishness – whom Bhabha finds in E.M. Forster, V.S. Naipaul, and other literature of empire.[121]

In Bhabha's view of things, the disjuncture between nation and empire required an agreeable Other, a colonial subject reformed but not quite equivalent. According to the Anglican mission, which fused nation and empire, 'appropriate' reform meant *complete* conversion, and equivalence would be in God rather than in the country that delivered His Word. Unlike Bhabha's colonists, concerned with racial boundaries and national identity and, in this spirit, intent on compromised colonial subjects, Good aimed to introduce to the Nlha7kápmx a 'perfect code of social and domestic reform and regimen,'[122] and English Christianity was the means at his disposal.

In its objective of absolute, as opposed to partial, sameness, this mission was colonizing to a fault, for if truth was singular, all other cultures were invalid, and would have to be disabused of their error. Such was the generic course of mission history; judged against a foreign Christian norm, Native societies were misconstrued, violated, and often ravaged. But in Good's case, as with other missions, there were limits to the process of normalization. He did not intend that otherness endure – the ground that separated him from his charges could be covered – but it did. This was partly because some Natives resisted change, but mostly because the Nlha7kápmx, not unlike Bhabha's 'mimic men,' had equality withheld by the colonial state, and in the struggle over sameness in the *secular* domain, Good ultimately proved impotent.

# 3
# Reproduction

In the early summer of 1860 Bishop Hills set off from Vancouver Island to visit the mainland portion of his diocese, covering some 1,300 kilometres, mostly on foot or on horseback, over the next three months. His only previous experience of the mainland colony had been a brief trip to its capital, New Westminster, in February, and he had little idea of what to expect in the unfamiliar territory beyond. What he saw in the way of religion, particularly white religion, clearly shocked and disappointed him, and on returning to Victoria he had this to say of his fellow colonists: 'The state of religion is as low as it can possibly be amongst civilized people. There is no recognition of it ... Morals I fear are as far from what is right as the case of religion. Some have acknowledged to me their dislike of the ungodly & immoral life which are common with those around them. With others, sin is a matter of indifference. They will speak of their acts, & disparage religion with the most unblushing boldness & without an effort.'[1]

Other Anglican missionaries, arriving from England tutored in Native, not white, ignorance, were as critical as Hills of British Columbia's immigrant population. The thrust of their (increasingly virulent) rhetoric was that the tension between civility and savagery did not reduce to empire's alleged racial cleavages. Instead, Anglican mission discourse identified a diverse field of sin, constituted primarily by Natives but compounded, and complicated, by ungodly whites. Most of the bishop's clergymen would have accepted *The Mission Field*'s judgment that 'the Missionary to the heathen who have been brought into contact with the white man has invariably to contend not with the sins of heathenism only, but with them, and the foul train of misery and sin breeding sin which have been added to them by the white man.'[2]

Gambling, drinking, and Sabbath-breaking were common complaints. When, at the first annual meeting of the Columbia Mission, the bishop of Oxford raged against gold miners 'risking all and endeavouring to gain sudden wealth by sudden luck,' he presaged a recurrent Anglican thesis that equated prospecting with gambling and denounced it as such.[3] Missionaries, moreover, felt that gambling went hand in hand with drunkenness, and SPG emissary Alexander Pringle's contention that miners preferred 'bad whiskey and gambling to anything more sober or intellectual' reflected a broader Anglican critique of colonial intemperance.[4] This reproach was also aimed at Natives – as when Good cursed the Haida for 'love of poisonous and villainous drinks'[5] – but whites received the more severe censure, if only for introducing alcohol to the colony and its peoples.[6]

Though Anglican missionaries battled many perceived sins, sexual evil ultimately tipped the balance between virtue and vice, Christian and 'heathen.' Anglicans considered life in the colonies (as elsewhere) a constant moral struggle and questions of sexuality pervade their moral discourse of colonialism. Prostitution was roundly condemned, as was consensual concubinage between white men and Native women.[7] Despite using varying euphemisms for the latter – the Reverend J. Reynard spoke of 'unholy bonds,' Good of 'irregular living'[8] – Anglican missionaries were united in denouncing such extramarital relationships. Much of this chapter considers their comments, which usually blamed white men for corrupting Native women. Insofar as they assumed white male guilt, of course, Anglican missionaries rejected Manichean discourses of empire that ascribe morality according to the sole criterion of 'race.' I hope to show that the Anglican mission offered a more complex moral taxonomy. Understandings of gender, nation, and class all contributed to Anglican representations of white vice, authorizing, together, a mission directed at colonizers as well as colonized.

Such moral discourses also reveal how missionaries viewed themselves and how they interpreted their own place in colonial society. Colonial identities were not pre-given, but were forever being reimagined and redefined in relation to a pertinent set of 'other' moralities. This point, central to the critical literature on European colonialism, has been well made by Tina Loo in relation to English settler identities in colonial British Columbia.[9] In the context of the Anglican mission, the most vivid dualism, contrived by the mission's own protagonists, was the contrast between self-denial and 'ungoverned passions.'[10] Missionaries laid claim to self-control to distinguish themselves from those they aspired to reform, and to this degree otherness, both white and Native, became characterized by unbridled sexuality. In their purported capacity for restraint, Anglican missionaries located a sense of exclusive identity. 'We learn by the practice of self-denial,' one claimed, 'to have power over our will and desires in little things. It follows that when, some day, we find ourselves face to face with a great temptation, our desires being used to give way to our strengthened will, we come off conquerors instead of being shame-fully beaten.'[11]

If it was restraint that Anglicans demanded of themselves – and any missionary who lapsed was asking for trouble[12] – then conversion to Christianity would also require the taming of passion. Anglican moral discourse contained strict guidelines for a better colony, and these directives (intended for whites and Natives alike) turned on the moral imperative of monogamous marriage. The assumption, in short, was that family life would serve to control desire and, by extension, improve moral standards. Such thinking, of course, was not exclusive to the Anglicans; many European interest groups, especially those of a didactic persuasion, made much the same case. Yet Good and his colleagues had their own take on these matters. Indeed, it was frequently in debates over morality that, in Ann Laura Stoler's words, different colonial agents 'confronted one another's visions of empire,'[13] and so it was in colonial British Columbia.

Family values dominated Anglican prescriptions for a moral colony, but families were structured by gender, and marriage partners figured to different degrees in this ethical agenda. Though they prized upstanding husbands and fathers, Anglican missionaries accorded women a far greater moral responsibility. 'To many men,' SPG missionary Lundin Brown once wrote, 'the Son of Mary still reveals Himself through woman, and through her puts forth His healing and civilizing grace.'[14] Coming from a man for whom practical Christianity reduced to a code of ethics, this was a considerable statement, for it implied a gendered politics of sexuality. As Brown saw it, women, as progenitors and custodians of morality, were the real brokers of his religion; without popular female collusion, he felt, the Anglican mission was impotent.[15] Such was the view of many Anglican missionaries, manifest in their work with both European and Native congregations. In this chapter I examine the femininity they had in mind.

### Colonial Moralities and Moral Identities

Protagonists of the Anglican mission often argued that the way to ensure the morality of colonists was to reproduce English society in the colonial setting. For these thinkers it was England's political, cultural, and religious infrastructure that underpinned moral standards at home; by extension, English emigrants would only maintain such standards if colonial society replicated its metropolitan equivalent. Thus, when the bishop of Oxford articulated his own vision of colonialism – of 'what it was indeed to be the foundress of a nation' – he argued that 'provision must be made by the founding nation for reproducing itself, in its own characteristic elements, and in its own special institutions, in the distant land to which it sends its sons.'[16] Wilberforce envisaged colonies with the same political constitution, social hierarchy, and ecclesiastical regime as England.

Bishop Hills focused more specifically on religion and emphasized the need to transfer Anglican administration and liturgy to the empire. 'We go from the bosom of the Church of England,' he said in 1859 of his imminent departure from Britain, 'to reproduce, in another soil, what heavenly mercy has planted and fostered here. We carry forth the blessed institutions of the Church, and the holy doctrines we have received.'[17]

When Anglicans spoke, as Hills often did, of 'the reproduction of England in our colonies,'[18] they offered their own rendition of a thesis central to contemporary colonial thought. Associated primarily with Edward Gibbon Wakefield, the concept of reproducing England overseas was in vogue in the mid-nineteenth century.[19] Wakefield's ideas were applied in many areas of the British Empire, among them British Columbia, most notably in the Hudson's Bay Company's plans for colonizing Vancouver Island.[20] And while issues of land provision and ownership were closest to his heart, and dominate his writings, Wakefield, like those Anglicans who borrowed from him, held that a strict form of religious governance (preferably a system of bishoprics) was essential to any colonial blueprint. 'When the theorists of 1830 had been sometime engaged in the business of colonization,' he wrote, 'they discovered, and some of them became deeply convinced, that it cannot be done satisfactorily, still less as well as possible, without ample provisions of a religious nature.'[21]

If the export of English religion was critical to the export of English morality, the Anglican Church reasoned that the poverty of its missions must be partly responsible for prevailing colonial vice. Again, Wakefield agreed; when he wrote *A view of the art of colonization* in 1849, he described the existing clerical presence in Britain's colonies as a 'sham provision.' Without improved ministration, he maintained, white prurience would continue to blossom.[22] The bishop of Oxford offered the same explanation for the decline of European morals in British Columbia. Speaking in London in November 1860, Samuel Wilberforce claimed that English religion and society were yet to be reproduced in the Pacific Northwest, and that in their absence, white sin was inevitable:

Well, then, withdraw suddenly all these influences together – the long-established tone which the prevalence of Christianity has created in the land; the long-established tone which the different ranks, and the inter-joining and interfitting of those ranks, into what we call society, has done for England; the way in which everybody almost has some eyes upon him, and the consciousness that he has some eyes upon him which will condemn his conduct if he falls below the line which circumstances have made the level of those among whom he has been educated; – withdraw all those influences ... and you may conceive what must be the effect [of] it.[23]

In the early 1860s the need to transplant the church and its dogma was clearly a pressing concern for the youthful Columbia Mission. It did not escape Anglican attention, however, that many white colonists, only some of them English, were quite happy with life in British Columbia and had little or no interest in an increased church presence.[24] These dissenters argued that a colony gripped by gold fever was simply not the place for Christianity, and they resented missionary efforts to impose a philosophical orthodoxy.[25] 'They appeared to think that religion was out of place in British Columbia,' scoffed Lundin Brown of these self-styled mavericks. 'Churches and church-going might be well enough in an old settled country, but they were quite unsuited for a new one, where men came to get gold, and were content, for the time, to worship no other god.'[26] That miners sought gold rather than God was apparent to Good, too, and he condemned this earthly theology. 'This world is their god,' he said of such men, 'it they serve, and from it alone they seek their reward.'[27]

Such impiety did not augur well for the Columbia Mission, but the Anglicans felt that their struggle to peddle Christianity could not alone account for the colony's wretched morals. Reproducing England in the colonies required more than introducing the national religion, and in British Columbia the process of replication was found variously wanting. In particular the immigrant population patently lacked the gender symmetry that Wakefield, and the Anglicans with him, deemed an 'essential condition' of a moral colony.[28] Those whom gold attracted were almost exclusively male. An 1860 Emigration Report put the colony's non-Native population at '5,000 men, with scarcely any women or children.'[29] The Reverend J. Gammage estimated that the total number of whites was nearer four than five thousand, of whom 98 percent were men.[30] The town of Douglas, according to Bishop Hills, contained 204 men and just 2 women, while New Westminster, with 30 women in a population of 290, was slightly more balanced.[31] These skewed gender profiles would dominate British Columbian demography for many years. In 1867 just 17 percent of the non-Native population was female, a fraction that diminished significantly in areas of sparse white settlement – 9 percent, for example, of the combined population of Hope, Yale, and Lytton.[32] Even by the time of the first national census in 1881, white men still outnumbered white women by a ratio of three to two.[33]

This asymmetry entailed a strange existence for female immigrants. While recent research shows that colonial British Columbia was not the male preserve assumed in earlier historiography, and that European women made a significant contribution to its society and economy (some were breadwinners supporting hapless miners),[34] it is clear that life for female pioneers could be very lonely[35] and that Anglican missionaries acknowledged their predicament. In the Fraser Canyon in 1860 Hills wrote of an Irish woman, married to an Australian miner, who seemed unhappy with exclusively male company. 'She was very lonely & had no female society,' the bishop observed. 'One other female there was, but her character was such that she could not associate with her.'[36] European women, unlike their male counterparts, seldom had (or desired) any contact with Native women, and most therefore lived an isolated life with scant opportunity for female friendship.[37]

Although he sympathized with this lonely Irish woman, it would be fair to say that Hills, like other Anglicans faced with this lopsided colonial society, was more concerned about male morality than female peace of mind. Visiting with Lillooet's white population in the summer of 1861, the bishop concluded that a lack of 'female society' was responsible for the town's poor morals: 'Men were uncivilised & immoral & reckless in the absence of such influence.'[38] Anglicans argued that colonial morality required gender symmetry, for only a sound, Christian femininity could bring men to heel. If the immigrant population was largely male, as in colonial British Columbia, men would follow the menacing natural instincts that missionaries wished to curb. 'Dissevered from the softening influence of women,' wrote Lundin Brown, 'men generally become more or less rough.'[39]

Anglican missionaries viewed much of the immigrant male population as carousers allowed free rein in a land where neither English demography nor English religion had been reproduced. They knew, furthermore, that many such men had found an outlet for their passions not just in drinking and gambling but in 'pernicious' sexualities: homosexuality and, more often, extramarital sex with Native women.[40] Back in England the bishop of Oxford was convinced he knew the problem. 'You must give the opportunity for home life to reproduce itself in the distant land, if you mean to take the commonest means possible to transform the distant settlement into an abiding colony,' he reflected. In British Columbia, Wilberforce maintained, 'moral abominations' abounded because 'an equality of the sexes' had not been achieved.[41]

In this young colony Anglicans confronted European communities quite unlike the English parishes they had left behind. Pringle, for example, was aghast at the immigrant population in and around Hope, briefly his station in the early 1860s. He observed that a 'decent & well ordered resident' was 'an exception to the general rule,' and, for him as for Wilberforce, a shortage of white women was responsible.[42] A similar predicament faced the Anglicans further up the Fraser at Lytton. From the very beginning of his mission to the Nlha7kápmx, Good was at loggerheads with white settlers, especially those intent on 'illicit connection' with Native women.[43] He endeavoured to shield these women and to restrain the men in question, but was only moderately successful.[44] Good never really got to grips with Lytton's whites. Indeed, repeated conflict with Europeans strengthened his resolve to focus on Native work, and by the mid-1870s he had abandoned all hope of reforming Lytton's 'so-called white civilized & Christian community.'[45]

Disheartened by faithless colonists but unsure of how to articulate the sins they perpetrated, Anglican missionaries turned to a vocabulary ordinarily reserved for Natives. In doing so they repudiated the purity of whiteness. 'White barbarism' was Good's blunt assessment of European demeanour in colonial British Columbia.[46] His bishop's judgment was of a piece; like Good, Hills represented heathen whites much as he did sinful Natives. Riding from Yale to Lytton during the summer of 1862, he came upon a Native man whose daughter had been seized and taken off by a white. The bishop's pursuit of the culprit was fruitless, his criticism sharp. 'Such outrages I regret to say are not unfrequent,' he wrote in his journal. 'I have had complaints frequently from husbands & fathers of the forcible abduct[ion] of their wives & children by the white savage.'[47]

Concepts of savagery and barbarity pervade European discourses of empire, but only recently have scholars acknowledged that both in Europe and in the colonies these labels tagged certain whites as well as non-European populations at large. This new research has shown that colonialist terminology, associated primarily with the representation of racial difference, has served at various junctures to differentiate Europeans from one another. Class consciousness, for example, has often been characterized as a racial property, such that a colonialist argot permeates the rhetoric of capitalism. From the birth of the industrial revolution, according to Ann Stoler, the British middle classes saw themselves as a race apart and likened working-class labourers to 'savages' in overseas colonies.[48] Other social groups have been similarly stigmatized. Tina Loo observes a racialization of criminality in nineteenth-century Britain and compares this discourse to the representation of Natives in colonial British Columbia.[49]

If middle-class Europeans used a racial grammar for whites with less cultural capital or different moral sensibilities, the Anglican critique of white savagery suggests a similar etiology – class relations, perhaps, expressed in a racial tongue. There is, however, one significant difference, best appreciated if we recognize, with Anne McClintock, that the English stereotype of the Irish as a degenerate race 'complicates postcolonial theories that skin color ... is the crucial sign of otherness.'[50] This observation is telling, for, in contrast to this apparent paradox, Anglican representations of white barbarism do not belie the idea that religious belief, rather than racial type, constituted otherness in missionary discourse. White savagery is possible, according to my argument in Chapter 2, because sin is not tied to skin. Indeed, Good used examples of

European vice to question contemporary theories of racial difference. When he cursed 'the depravity of those who profess to be civilized and evangelized representatives of a superior race,' Good rejected not only their civility but their belief that civility was a racial property.[51] In identifying white savagery he and Hills did not posit sinful whites as an inferior race – they used a language of empire to emphasize that savagery, like sin, could come in any hue.

Yet if not a racial discourse, 'white savagery' was certainly a colonialist discourse, and clearly tied to questions of class consciousness and cultural distinction. Most Anglican missionaries were working class, but this did not preclude middle-class airs and graces. While keen not to alienate low-income students, the CMS, for example, cherished its high-brow employees. 'Eighteen new candidates have been accepted during the year,' the society announced at the end of 1873, 'and while we rejoice that two of these are from Oxford and four from Cambridge, we rejoice also that our commercial and industrial population still continues to provide a succession of godly young men to be trained for the highest of all services.'[52] Self-improvement was a central tenet of the Anglican mission, and for those of the artisan class the mission field was a place to rise above one's station. When Good applied to St. Augustine's College, one of his referees observed that 'he has *no means* whatever.'[53] These were hardly middle-class credentials, of course, but class boundaries were fluid, and to become a missionary was to cross 'a bridge to the middle-class establishment and its values.'[54] Newly arrived in British Columbia and part of an immigrant society still finding its feet, Anglican missionaries felt that their education and piety distinguished them from other whites. Class was constituted afresh in the empire, and Anglicans used an imperial vernacular, savagery, to devalue uncultured colonists.

The nationality of these stigmatized whites should not go unnoticed, for Anglicans described white savagery as a largely American trait. 'We complain in England of the little hold religion has upon many of the Artisan Class in one large town,' wrote Bishop Hills in the summer of 1860, 'but I never met with anything at all approaching to the calculating & matter of course infidelity which prevails amongst many who have been trained in America.'[55] In Anglican eyes English immigrants were more civilized than those from south of the 49th parallel.[56] I do not mean to suggest that Anglican missionaries never criticized their own countrymen; Good, for one, often did.[57] For the most part, however, English and American moralities occupied antipodes. Hills was perhaps the chief architect of this dualism and was often criticized for the obstinacy of his views.[58] When he learned of white misdoings, he trusted that the offender was not English, and in instances where the reprobate was, thankfully, American, the bishop was pleased to see his convictions confirmed.[59] He essentially reduced white vice to 'an American element'[60] – a national bar-barism that accentuated the refined Englishness of Anglicans themselves.

Anglican missionaries placed themselves apart from those of a differ-ent nation and a different class. With an imperial lexicon at hand, they stereotyped American immigrants to British Columbia as lewd material-ists and contrasted their own self-images with these critical representa-tions. Set off against the unrestrained (and explicitly sexualized) white savage – the miner who 'compels the earth to unfold her secrets'[61] – we find the moral masculinity of the English missionary, whose nominal virtues, according to Gail Ching-Liang Low, were those of 'daring, endurance, self-restraint and honour.'[62] To my mind, the qualities most often vaunted were abstinence and resolve. 'Self-denial,' one Anglican clergyman said of his church's missionaries, 'is the discipline of their life,'[63] and here is how Hills imagined the intrepid missionary he would dispatch from Victoria: 'You will see a man with stout country shoes, cor-duroy trousers, a coloured woollen shirt, a leather strap round his waist, and an axe upon his shoulder; he is driving before him a mule or a horse laden with packs of blankets, a tent, bacon, a sack of flour, a coffee-pot, a kettle, and a frying-pan. He is a pioneer of the gospel.'[64]

In point of fact neither the reckless, degenerate miner nor the valiant missionary existed in quite the form conveyed by the Anglicans. These Christians reproduced, and were to some degree responsible for, the cus-tomary image of miners as bondless, immoral vagabonds, and though historians have yet to fully unpack this stereotype,[65] Averill Groeneveld-Meijer has shown that it does not begin to represent the hugely varied mining community that came together in colonial British Columbia.[66] Bishop Hills's vision of the daring English missionary taming the colonial frontier is equally misleading. The young Methodist Ebenezer Robson, a Canadian, claimed that most Anglicans arrived in British Columbia palpably green and unprepared for the harsh physical environment that awaited them. He expected few to make successful missionaries, though the one exception, interestingly, was Good, a man of 'considerable energy and talent' whose experience in Nova Scotia had made him 'more suit-able to mission life in [British Columbia] than some of his colleagues who have never been out of England until they left for this country.'[67]

It is also clear that missionary masculinity entailed an ambivalence that troubled some Anglicans. Leonore Davidoff and Catherine Hall suggest that this 'manly presence based on moral authority ... came dangerously close to embracing "feminine" qualities,'[68] and though their observation pertains to evangelical manhood in nineteenth-century England, it bears directly on manliness in the mission field. Effeminacy in any guise was unacceptable. Missionaries liked to be thought of as gallant, caring gen-tlemen, but also as brave colonists in a rugged land and hostile public sphere. At St. Augustine's, therefore, Good was reconciled to a masculinity that explicitly, but also anxiously, rebuffed feminine tendencies. A later warden wrote that the college trainee should cultivate 'a liking for manly games, and let the body be trained to habits of endurance' on the playing fields. 'Manly games, cricket and football,' the warden went on to say, 'have much to do with "keeping the body in temperance, soberness, and chastity." Effeminacy is repulsive in a candidate for the arduous work of the Mission Field.'[69]

In these Anglican constructions of maleness, which ranged from the prurient miner at one extreme to the virtuous (but not, God forbid, impotent) Christian at the other, we can detect an edge, but only an edge, of an Anglican moral agenda. To reproduce England in this foreign land, the Columbia Mission promoted English male morality as a vital constituent of English religion. As Good's experience with Lytton's whites suggests, this venture was not entirely successful; if anything, he had more luck with Nlha7kápmx than with white men, many of whom were openly derisive of church policy. It is important to emphasize, however, that for all Good's advocacy of the model husband and father,[70] Anglican hopes for a moral colony were pinned not on him but on the Christian wife and mother.

### Femininity, Domesticity, and Empire

One important aspect of the femininity advocated by Good and his peers was its spatiality: the moral influence of women began in the home. This accent on domesticity is apparent in church plans for educating the female children of white colonists. To improve colonial society, the Anglicans set out to regulate female morality as it took shape, during childhood. In 1863 plans were hatched for a girls' school in Victoria that would, it was said, be 'of no small consequence to the best welfare of the colony.'[71] The Girls' Collegiate School, later renamed Angela College (after Angela Burdett-Coutts, benefactor of the Columbia Mission), opened its doors in 1866, with Mrs A. Kennedy, wife of Vancouver Island's governor, laying the cornerstone. 'Exhibiting in [her] own accomplished home the example of a successful education,' she seemed to Bishop Hills to be a paragon of domesticity, and, as such, an appropriate role model for the next generation of colonial women.[72]

The girls' school was a means of training white women for their role in empire. Instruction would focus on motherhood, which for Anglican missionaries was a female colonist's greatest responsibility. Rosemary George explains why. 'The quality of motherhood,' she writes, 'was seen as directly affecting the quality of the "future citizens" (read "male children") – which in turn determined the vigor of the imperial race.'[73] Hills articulated this theory on numerous occasions, first in a paper written shortly after his arrival in British Columbia,[74] and then again at the inauguration of the Girls' Collegiate School. On the latter occasion he stressed that male progeny were a woman's chief contribution. 'Most important,' he informed his audience, 'is [girls'] training in its bearing upon the manhood of the future.' In an infant colony dominated by sinful men, a robust maternity would check further deterioration of male morality. A Christian manhood required the education of *female* desire. The bishop left no one in doubt as to the gendering of this strategy: 'Depend upon it, if you let your girls grow up into frivolous, vain and pleasure-loving womanhood, you have a generation of effeminate, selfish, shallow and unstable manhood, with consequences far worse to many. But if your girls, well trained, grow up into sensible, practical, well-principled women, with clear views of faith and duty, you will have a manhood vigorous, temperate, cultivated, high-principled and useful. We trust, therefore, the girlhood of our Province may acquire that good discipline and useful knowledge which may enable them to perform creditably the duties of life.'[75]

For Anglican missionaries, as for the English evangelicals discussed by Davidoff and Hall, 'the moral influence of mothers was the linchpin of religious regeneration.'[76] Christianity would flourish in British Columbia only if it was rooted in a suitable maternity. Schooled in womanly propriety and domestic management, graduates of the girls' college would set the moral tone for other colonial women, and thus for colonial society more generally. In this respect their charge matched that of the missionary's wife, perhaps the most storied model of colonial womanhood. In the early years of the Columbia Mission, any suggestion of using female missionaries sparked heated debate.[77] Besides the staff at Victoria's Girls' Collegiate School – primarily its principal, Mrs Woods, and the teachers Catherine and Ann Penrice – missionaries' wives would long remain the only female agents of the Anglican mission to British Columbia.[78] As Myra Rutherdale has demonstrated, the church had a narrow view of their role, 'intricately connected to the image of Victorian womanhood.'[79] While the missionary operated in empire's public sphere, his wife was to defend household civility and the morality of family life.[80] Such, at any rate, was Hills's rationale for sending the Reverend J. Reynard to William's Creek, in mining country, with his wife in tow:

It was thought by some that Cariboo was not the place to take a lady to, on account of the rough and unsettled state of society. The Bishop, however, was of opinion, that – given a lady courageous enough to endure the hardness of that life – her presence there would do incalculable good, not only in supporting her husband in a fight almost too great for any man, unaided by human sympathy, but also in affording an example of the order and beauty (even amidst manifold privations) of family life, in a place where virtuous women were, to say the least, excessively scarce.[81]

We should understand, however, that this discourse of domesticity does not begin to represent the full range of work performed by missionaries' wives. Good, for example, advocated a gendered division of public and private space – evangelization was manly work, women belonged in the home – but, to realize his ambitions with the Nlha7kápmx, relied heavily on his wife Sarah's assistance. Unfortunately there is insufficient evidence to reconstruct the details of Sarah's life in the mission field. It was not in her husband's interest to make public the extent to which he leaned on her. Such honesty would only have served to dilute his reputation with both peers and sponsors. His correspondence was in large part an exercise in self-promotion, and this imperative required the silencing of his wife. But we do know that she contributed. Not only did Sarah take on a share of Good's pastoral duties, assuming full control when he was away from Lytton, but she played the organ in church and worked closely with Native women – this in addition to caring for her husband and children.

There was a considerable fraud to Good's writing on gender roles in the mission enterprise. His rhetoric of separate spheres assumed male competence and bravado, but the reality of his mission was less impressive; Sarah's myriad toils bucked the domesticity to which she was theoretically confined, and, as we shall see in Chapter 7, Good struggled terribly when she was not there to help him. Peter Robin, Good's biographer, writes that 'Good stood tall as a practising cleric in the mission field, but to a very large degree he was standing on the shoulders of his wife.'[82] Other Anglican missionaries embraced similar contradictions. Pringle expected his wife, Mary Louisa, to manage their home *and* to help with teaching, but complained when he was himself forced to lend a hand indoors.[83] Mary Louisa, meanwhile, was aware of her principal duties. In a revealing letter of 1860 to her sister-in-law, she apologized for not having written previously, saying that Pringle had himself kept the family updated. She wrote now only because her husband neglected to include 'domestic intelligence' in his correspondence; this, she knew, was her domain.[84]

Yet college-trained women – 'the young ladies of the colony'[85] – and the wives of Anglican clergy could only do so much to lift moral standards. Their sphere of influence was minimal, to say the least. Anglican missionaries needed no reminding that many male immigrants lacked any kind of female company, let alone company endorsed by the church. 'Ladies bound for the upper country were rare birds, indeed,' recalled Byron Johnson of his days as a Cariboo miner. 'Even the homely laundress was raised by the scarcity of her sex into a goddess for the nonce.'[86]

The Anglicans knew that some colonists had formed relationships with Native women, but frowned upon such alliances. It became increasingly clear that the colony required more white women. To address this need a public meeting, animated by a letter that John Garrett, Hills's metropolitan commissary, had received from Lundin Brown, was called in London on 27 February 1862. Garrett said he had 'seldom read a missionary letter of more practical interest and value,' and opened proceedings by citing from it at length:

> Though this note is confidential, and not intended for the public ear, there is one thing which you may make public, nay, even proclaim upon the housetops. It is this – the cure for what, if let alone, will ultimately ruin Religion and morals in this fine country, I mean an emigration of white women from Great Britain. Dozens of men have told me they would gladly marry if they could. I was speaking one evening on the subject of the dearth of females, and mentioned my intention of writing to beg that a plan of emigration may be set on foot; whereupon one member of the company immediately exclaimed, 'Then, sir, I preempt a wife'; another, and another, and all round the circle of those listening to me earnestly exclaimed the same. Fancy the idea of preempting a wife![87]

This call for English women was not unique. It was self-evident to male Europeans in British Columbia that the colony needed more female settlers, and many articulated this concern in print. A New Westminster man, for example, wrote to *The Times* of London to tell readers that there was, perhaps, no better British colony in which to raise a family.[88] Another observer, Congregationalist minister Matthew Macfie, went further yet, claiming that no place on earth offered single women greater opportunities for marriage.[89] Brown's own feeling was that unless the colony attracted more women, the Anglican mission would fail. 'Churches may and must be built,' he admitted, 'our faithful witness must be borne for holiness and virtue, but where there is no wedded life, church-going must be difficult, because morality is almost impossible.'[90] This was, clearly, a dispirited Brown, but his conviction is illuminating; like other Anglican missionaries, he assumed family life to be the essence of a religious life.

Such overtures from British Columbia found a receptive metropolitan audience. Edward Wakefield, concerned about England's glut of young, unmarried women, had once described his country as 'the greatest and the saddest convent that the world has seen.'[91] Convinced, in any case, that colonization without women was folly, Wakefield implied that England's uneven demographics clinched the case.[92] Other commentators, feminists to the fore, maintained that high rates of female unemployment also favoured emigration. Emily Faithfull, representing the Society for

Promoting the Employment of Women, suggested that with women excluded from many jobs in England, it was logical to send them to the colonies, where advocates of female settlement stressed that domestic work, as well as marriage, was a viable option.[93] With women needed in British Columbia and, to some minds, redundant at home, emigration was an obvious solution.

Those Anglicans who gathered at the London Tavern to discuss Reverend Brown's letter considered, first, colonial morality, then the availability of colonial employment for women. But there was also a sense of national purpose. At the time concern was rife in Britain that some colonial populations were too cosmopolitan. For imperialists who held that British colonies should be settled by Britons, emigration was a pressing national imperative. In this light there was a special premium on female emigration: only British women could beget future British subjects. 'If the British population did not increase fast enough to fill the empty spaces of the Empire,' writes Anna Davin, 'others would.'[94] In the early colonial period British Columbia was home to Chinese, German, French, Italian, and American immigrants, with Britons constituting less than 20 percent of the total white population.[95] Metropolitan Anglicans were doubtless alive to fears, expressed by Pringle among other missionaries, that unless Britain peopled British Columbia with 'her own teeming populace,' the colony would follow a course determined by 'aliens & foreigners.'[96] If Anglicans could arrange for the emigration of women, they would help to fortify the British presence in the Pacific Northwest.

Such concerns, however, were secondary. Having read from Brown's letter, Garrett endorsed its contention that white women would improve the woeful morals of British Columbians. The bishop of Oxford spoke next and, like Garrett, summarized the potential moral fruits of female emigration. But where Garrett deferred to Brown, the man on the spot, Wilberforce had his own answers to the issues at hand and delivered them with his typical rhetorical flourish.[97] He argued that if British Columbia needed women, it made sense to send workhouse women who, in Britain, contributed least, suffered most, and placed the greatest demands on public spending. For the colony this emigration would provide moral reform; for the metropolis, social and economic relief. Women could be freed from privation, shipped off to British Columbia, and transformed 'into the characters of wife and mother.' Such was the bishop's intent. Like others, he saw domestic femininity as the answer to male vice, and as his words were drowned out by resounding cheers, his last thoughts on the subject of female emigration were with these white colonial men – 'you will have made morality possible, you will have made Christian homes a fact, you will have made the elevating influences of woman's society and of family life a healing blessing to those adventurous souls.'[98]

The meeting at the London Tavern was deemed a great success and led to the founding of the British Columbia Emigration Society. Garrett, as honorary secretary, wrote to *The Times* to clarify the society's aims and identify potential emigrants. Focusing on the moral value of female emigration, he claimed that 'it is an essential element in the sound growth of a new colony that the men who first open it out should be able to settle and surround themselves with the humanizing ties of family life.' He maintained, with Wilberforce, that emigrants should be drawn from the 'thousands of women whose hopes and prospects in this country are most dreary and painful beyond description.' Garrett had in mind young women from orphanages and workhouses, and stressed that although there were countless potential husbands in British Columbia, domestic work was available for women too young to marry.[99]

In the following twelve months over a hundred single women were sent to the colony of British Columbia.[100] Little is known of the first twenty, who left England in April 1862. The next contingent, numbering sixty, was the largest, and set off two months later on board the *Tynemouth*.[101] They finally arrived on 17 September. The local media had trumpeted this day for weeks, and with Victoria's businesses closed for the occasion, the women, who had already suffered rigorous supervision en route, now had to endure the scrutiny of hundreds of men. The newcomers did not disappoint. 'As a matter of course,' reported *The Daily British Colonist*, 'we went aboard the steamer yesterday morning and had a good look at the lady passengers. They are mostly cleanly, well-built, pretty looking young women – ages varying from fourteen to an uncertain figure.'[102] Four months on, in January 1863, a third group arrived on the *Robert Lowe*, the final thirty-six women charged with civilizing British Columbia.

These women were of diverse backgrounds. Few were from the workhouse population favoured by the bishop of Oxford, but English orphanages, identified by Garrett as another possible source, had provided many young girls barely into their teens. Others, primarily those who arrived on the *Robert Lowe*, were factory hands unable to find work in a depressed Lancashire cotton industry. The remainder were middle-class, educated women in their twenties and early thirties, mostly governesses representing the Female Middle-Class Emigration Society; these women had no official ties to the Anglican Emigration Society, but had wanted to travel with an organized party, and they arrived in British Columbia expecting neither marriage nor domestic servitude but paid employment.

Although the fate of most of these immigrants is unclear, some general comments can be made. It is unlikely that many, if any at all, of the men who had prompted Brown's letter ever saw the fruits of his labours.

Most of the women who wanted to marry, and were old enough to do so, found husbands within weeks of their arrival. One was courted as she alighted from the *Tynemouth* and was married three days later.[103] Most men confined to mining country far from Victoria would continue to live without white women. The demand for such women was great, and the immigration only modest. Still, Bishop Hills described it as 'a very great boon to the colony.'[104] He felt that it could not but raise moral standards and was quick to denounce any man who suggested otherwise – for there were doubters.[105] The Congregationalist Macfie, for example, while impressed with those who married, argued that some of the women were bad eggs.[106] The Reverend Edward Cridge, too, lamented that not all were virtuous, observing that 'some half dozen [had] fallen.'[107] One such woman came in for virulent censure in the local press, her crime an unsupervised conversation with a young, unsavoury man.[108] White women were expected to enhance social morality, and those who did not conform to a normative standard were criticized.[109]

As for the youngest arrivals, girls aged thirteen to sixteen who were, as yet, too young to marry, the Immigration Committee's efforts to place them in domestic service met with very limited success. Many of the girls disliked their new employers, while others proved unsuitable for the job. Some were dismissed in short order, one by Mary Moody, wife of Colonel Richard C. Moody of the Royal Engineers, for being 'too young, too small, and incapable of sewing.'[110] Another was sent packing, according to Bishop Hills, for being religious![111] Beyond this vague picture of a harsh introduction to colonial life, we know little of what happened to these women – virtually children, remember, far from home and alone in a strange place.

British Columbia would especially disappoint the twenty governesses. Few would find the work they were looking for. When, four days after the *Tynemouth* docked, local journalists visited the Marine Barracks that had housed the arrivals, they found that almost all the remaining women were governesses.[112] Women willing to marry or enter domestic service had found a position. The governesses had not. As Cridge would later observe, British Columbia did not seem the place for this 'educated class.'[113] Indeed, the idea that the colony needed governesses was, on occasion, mocked. Here is Alexander Pringle:

I hear that [John] Garrett has been advocating Vancouver Island & B. Columbia as a fine field for the settlement of 'decayed gentlewomen' – for Governesses ... Oh dear! who could have filled his Irish imagination with such ideas – For mercies sake, do all you can to stop such insanity[.] The market in Victoria is already stocked with ladies, employing themselves in needlework, keeping millenery shops – in fact grievously disappointed at the number of people who do *not* want governesses and ladies to do the work which we want to get out of a pair of hard hands & brawny arms.[114]

In one respect Pringle was right: white society in Victoria did not need governesses. But he was wrong about Garrett. When Garrett first wrote to *The Times* in April 1862, he made it quite clear that British Columbia needed working-class women, *not* 'women who have received sufficient education to place them in situations as teachers in families and schools at home.' Governesses, whom Garrett described as 'women who should depend upon the use of their brains alone for support,' should not consider emigrating to the new colony; on this point, at least, Pringle and he agreed.[115] Yet the governesses *did* emigrate and, clearly, they had a tough time of it. An English journalist in British Columbia said that they were 'in advance of the place,'[116] and his observation can be taken quite literally. Governesses would be required once colonists began turning out children to be educated, but with white women so scarce in the early 1860s, this was not yet the case. As the Anglicans repeatedly pointed out, the colony needed white wives and mothers, and only their imperial labour (reproduction) would provide employment for governesses.

They were also in advance of the colony in terms of their expectations. In addition to wives British Columbia needed domestic servants, and with the influx of English girls in 1862 doing little to reduce demand, colonists were left fuming that their own wives, ladies no less, had to perform menial household chores. Alexander Garrett captured this middle-class angst perfectly. 'Ladies,' he rued, 'are their own servants.'[117] Anglican missionaries were among the many European immigrants who sought domestic servants – to ease the strain on middle-class women and, perhaps, as markers of social status.[118] But governesses did not fit the bill, for women who would not deign to carry out domestic duties were of little use. This had been John Garrett's point, and Pringle's too; Cridge, in the same vein, said that 'cooks and washerwomen' should be the priority for future female emigration.[119] The consensus was that governesses were overqualified; too educated, too advanced for a fledgling colony. Sapper Richard Moody made this case emphatically in a letter to Maria Rye, leading light of the Female Middle-Class Emigration Society that sent the governesses to British Columbia. Rye's policy, he insisted, was fatuous. 'Household work is what is demanded,' he told her. 'Our wives, the ladies of the colony, from the highest to the humblest, have to labour in the kitchen, the nursery, and the workhouse.'[120]

Governesses shunned the moral imperatives of the Anglican mission and tendered labour for which there was no apparent demand. British Columbia had little to offer them, and they proffered little in return.

Theirs was clearly a 'status incongruence,'[121] to use Jeanne Peterson's apt label – the governess was neither the godly wife and mother anticipated by the church nor the domestic servant craved by the colonial gentry.[122] This status incongruence explains why the *Tynemouth* governesses had little success; it also explains the quarrel between Rye, patron of female middle-class emigration, and the likes of Moody and Pringle. Indeed, this dispute reflected a broader cleavage within British colonialism, identified by Julia Bush as a mismatch between 'the colonies' demand for wives and domestic servants, and the female emigrators' prioritisation of distressed "ladies."'[123] This mismatch must have been painfully clear to the governesses who arrived in British Columbia in 1862. As the other female immigrants rapidly joined colonial society, they were left holed up in Victoria's barracks, facing a difficult, even intractable choice. Either they married, or they accepted domestic work they would ordinarily spurn.

In short, then, two options awaited the women who arrived on the *Tynemouth* and the *Robert Lowe*: marriage or domestic service. Jean Barman claims that even those who first worked as servants were ultimately expected to marry; as far as Anglican agendas were concerned, she is probably right.[124] But the vital point, surely, is that either as wives or as servants, these women would be dependants lacking the social and ecnomic independence valued by the governess. To that extent it is immaterial whether the colony wanted wives or servants, for both implied subjugation to the master of the household. Davidoff shows that in Victorian England most girls moved 'from paternal control, in their parents' home, into service and then into their husband's home – thus experiencing a lifetime of subordination in private homes.'[125] Those who emigrated to British Columbia followed a similar trajectory, a life of repeated domestic constraint – interrupted for some by a brief period of factory work in Lancashire. The women were sequestered en route, cooped up in Victoria's barracks, and only released once a suitable home had been found. Their lives were socially and spatially compromised by the church's reliance on a circumscribed femininity to correct abject colonial morals. In Stoler's words these women were to act as 'custodians of family welfare and respectability, and as dedicated and willing subordinates to, and supporters of, colonial men.'[126]

It is hardly surprising that the Anglicans placed women on unequal terms with the men they were supposed to civilize. Just as European contract theorists had long insisted that men rule women – for Hobbes it was a political right, for Locke and Rousseau the order of nature – so European Christianity had established male dominance as a God-given fact.[127] Indeed, the Anglican mission was rigorously patriarchal – during his first address at Lytton in June 1867, Good lectured the Nlha7kápmx on 'the man honouring the woman as "the weaker vessel," and the woman obeying her husband.'[128] Yet Good and his fellow churchmen regarded such codes as anything but repressive. To illuminate the civility of Christian family life, they argued, as did many agents of empire,[129] that gender relations were considerably less just in Native societies. This was Samuel Wilberforce's insinuation when he spoke of Natives as accustomed, 'under their heathen system, to a low, "squaw" estimate of women.'[130] Similarly, the Reverend Reynard claimed that Native women failed to resist abusive white men because they had been reared to accept servitude.[131] To the degree that Native men oppressed their women, argued the Anglicans, Christian patriarchy was manifestly liberal. Which begs the question: would the *Tynemouth* and *Robert Lowe* women have agreed?

Unfortunately, we will never know – as Jackie Lay has noted, we understand the male motives for this female emigration but not the women's own thoughts on their prospects and experiences.[132] And though some of the emigrants doubtless resented their lot, others may have treasured it. If any linking theme has emerged from the burgeoning literature on white women and European colonialism, it is that there is no linking theme.[133] Racism and sexism combined in different ways in different places, and white women sometimes assumed positions of power, sometimes not. Surveying this recent scholarship, McClintock emphasizes that 'white women were not the hapless onlookers of empire but were ambiguously complicit both as colonizers and colonized, privileged and restricted, acted upon and acting.'[134] For some such women, domesticity was stifling, for others, empowering.[135] A member of the Canadian Women's Club in early-twentieth-century Victoria, Nancy de Bertrand Lugrin, eulogized the English female pioneer for her 'love of her mate and the guarding and rearing of her young.' Convinced that orderly households sustained the vitality of male colonists, Lugrin placed domesticity at the heart of the triumph of empire.[136] Some of the women dispatched by the Columbia Mission may well have shared her zeal. If so, it would be ironic, for the essence of this imperial pride was a spatialized femininity fought tooth and nail by English feminists of the day.[137]

### Marriage and the Morality of Sex

This emigration provides a window on Anglican moral intent, but it did little to alter the social landscape of colonial British Columbia. Based in Victoria, Hills was privy to the town's affairs and could assess the women's local impact. His active missionaries, on the other hand, stationed away from the capital, would go about their business much as before. They still traversed a land where almost all whites were men. They still found the general moral climate repugnant. And, most importantly, they continued to encounter white men living in sin with Native partners. As far as these missionaries were concerned, nothing had changed.

Commentary on concubinage pervades the archive of the Anglican mission. All Anglican missionaries protested extramarital relations between male colonists and Native women, and most considered this to be the worst colonial evil. It would be easy to interpret this intolerance as racism. Relationships between white men and indigenous women sparked intense debate in many European colonies. The question of why officials felt compelled to judge these alliances, and why their response was so often negative, has drawn varied answers, but most scholars point to concerns about racial boundaries and the hierarchies of rule.[138] Where colonial authority was firm and European supremacy seemed undisputed, interracial unions were tolerated or even encouraged. Ties with local women would keep male colonists from prostitution and homosexuality, and would also foster permanent settlement. But where political rule was vulnerable and European identities fragile, miscegenation threatened to blur the distinctions that sustained imperial power – between white and coloured, colonizer and colonized, civility and savagery. Mixed relationships were discouraged or banned in these troubled moments, as fears of cultural contamination and racial degeneracy called for the strict policing of European borders. Occasionally promoted, otherwise condemned, miscegenation raised essential questions about biological purity and cultural distinction. Located at the hub of colonial contact, it sometimes inspired arrogance, sometimes anxiety, but always, it appears, prejudice.

Thus, it seems only natural to identify racism when we read the Reverend Lundin Brown denouncing white men for their 'degrading concubinage with native women.'[139] It is clear that Brown, and other Anglicans with him, blamed such mixed relationships for the dissolution of social morality. But to impute racism is to privilege one possible motive for Anglican criticism and exclude all others. We cannot overlook the possibility that it was not the unions themselves that worried Anglican missionaries but the conditions under which they were conducted. Most importantly, was it interracial sex or extramarital sex that angered Brown? Or was it a combination of both? These are crucial questions.

Recalling his days in Lillooet some years after leaving British Columbia, Brown told the story of a young Native woman named Kenadaqua, a sixteen-year-old orphan who had gone to live with her uncle after her father was murdered. When a 'wild and reckless' miner offered money for Kenadaqua, her 'mean and sordid' uncle handed her over. Brown met Kenadaqua some time later when she visited her kin in Lillooet. Her arrival in town coincided with one of his lectures and, as she stopped to listen, she heard his diatribe against interracial concubinage – 'the prevailing social evil.' His criticism implicated Kenadaqua herself, and she would probably have heard the same thing from any other missionary.

But the Reverend Brown was not finished. 'If any white man wanted honestly to wed with an Indian girl,' he added, 'that was another thing.' This was a considerable caveat. Kenadaqua had been bought and quite possibly mistreated, but when, having listened to Brown, she asked if she should leave her partner, she was told that, rather, she should ask him to marry her. Apparently the miner refused and Kenadaqua returned to her village, but the point I want to emphasize is that marriage was 'another thing.' It was recommended even in circumstances – like Kenadaqua's – where the missionary *must* have had concerns about the relationship in question.[140] The sin, to Brown, was concubinage, not the fact of a white man and a Native woman being together. Skin colour was immaterial because ethics belonged above and outside history; marriage was a moral law, and dogma could not defer to worldly particulars. This was, however, a colonial society. In granting married couples moral impunity, Anglican missionaries risked consecrating the abuse of Native women.

Upon moving to Nanaimo in 1861, Good was concerned to find many of the town's white men living with, but refusing to wed, Native women.[141] Had they married, Good would have been satisfied; several mixed couples received his blessing, both in Lytton and, albeit not initially, in Nanaimo.[142] Anglican criticism of concubinage was fuelled by an unyielding moral dogmatism rather than a concern for racial purity. Thus, when Adele Perry argues that the Columbia Mission advocated female emigration from England because the presence of white women might 'deter white men from wedding aboriginal women,' she is wrong.[143] Anglican missionaries actively encouraged marriage between these parties (see Figure 6).[144] Mixed relationships clearly vexed Lundin Brown and almost certainly provoked his call for female emigration, but he was bothered by concubinage, not colour. European men were reluctant to marry their Native partners, even with considerable goading from the church,[145] and Brown, for whom marriage *was* morality, felt that male colonists were more likely to wed white women.

Marriage was the linchpin of the Anglican moral mission. It was a pivotal contract for other mission churches, too, and also for colonial civil society, but the morality of matrimony could vary greatly. Indeed, Stoler says that for some colonial governments 'it was not interracial sexual contact that was seen as dangerous, but its public legitimation in marriage.'[146] Quite the opposite was true for British Columbia's Anglican missionaries, whose marital ethics were colour blind and for whom wedlock defused, rather than aggravated, sexual sin. In a sense this Anglican moral stance is more intelligible than many secular positions, for while the former posited marriage as a universal imperative, the latter often coupled sexuality to 'race' and ethics to place. In the summer of 1860, for example, Bishop Hills met a Scottish resident of Hope who lived with, but had not married, a Native woman, and who maintained that, for a number of reasons, metropolitan moral codes did not apply in the colonies. While acceptable in British Columbia, concubinage, he told Hills, would be a sin in Scotland. 'There were Churches in Orkney & white women,' he explained. The bishop pointed out the error of the man's ways: 'I showed him that the sin was the same here as in Britain.'[147] Hills appealed to a morality transcending 'race' and space; his antagonist's morality was contingent on place and people.

This disagreement was doubtless mirrored at many levels of colonial society, as competing moral visions jostled in the attempt to define ethical norms and impose them on the colony. Anglicans were not the only critics of interracial unions. Other missionaries were equally outspoken. Some, such as Methodist Thomas Crosby, agreed with the Anglicans that marriage could put right sinful relations between European men and Native women.[148] Others were less generous. When the Congregationalist Macfie warned of a 'commingling of races so different in physiological, psychological, intellectual, moral, religious, and political aspects,' he used a racial grammar that would have unnerved most Anglicans; yet even Macfie suffered mixed couples if they married.[149] Secular commentators

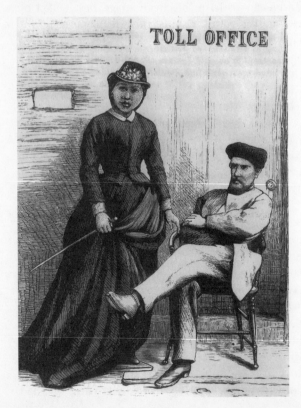

*Figure 6* Settler pictured with his Native wife

had other views on the subject. The colony's senior lawyer, Attorney General Henry Crease, was ambivalent despite his conviction that miscegenation could ruin colonial society. He longed for a white colonial future, but realized that if male colonists did *not* take up with Native women, there might be no colonial future at all. 'How is the Country to be peopled if this sort of thing goes on? or doesn't go on?' he wavered.[150] Crease was himself a staunch Anglican, but his moral agenda, undecided and riven with racial anxiety, was not that of clergymen like Good.

There was also considerable debate around the question of whether marriage should always take place in church. The Church of England firmly resisted the secularization of morality in Victorian Britain,[151] and in colonial British Columbia its missionaries strictly opposed nonreligious marriage. There was a local precedent for this critique as well as a tradition of church thinking at home. One reason why the Hudson's Bay Company lacked a chaplain west of the Rocky Mountains until 1836 is that George Simpson, its governor, worried that the fur trade custom of marriage *à la façon du pays* would be misunderstood. His fears were well founded; the first such chaplain, Herbert Beaver, denounced all relationships between company men and Native women.[152] Some couples were not married, and those that were followed rites peculiar to the fur trade. As Sylvia Van Kirk has shown, missionaries of various stripes deemed traders' 'wives' concubines and held that only a church ceremony could vindicate such relationships.[153] This resistance to secular marriage carried over to the colonial era. Good identified the 'bad effects' of private weddings,[154] and Hills told Attorney General Crease that since the 'happiness & stability of society' depended on the 'sacredness of the marriage bond,' a 'religious ceremony' was indispensable.[155] To allow lay marriage was to encourage moral abandon:

> Moralists of various denominations in the States of America complain of increasing laxity in reference to marriage, and great frequency of divorce for trivial causes. Much of this sad result may be traced to abandonment of sacred principle in respect of marriage. Let us Clergy and Laity in this British country take warning and keep up the sanctity of this great contract of society. Let the marriages be always solemn, in the face of the Church, in the house of God, at sober hours, and never in private houses except from such necessity as great distance from a church. So may we guard our own people at least.[156]

In Anglican eyes the morality of marriage transcended worldly divisions, but in a world of increasingly secular ethics it was important to distinguish between a moral marriage and a meaningless one. The most essential of moral contracts, marriage was of no moral value unless endorsed by the church. While debates on 'race,' sex, and morality were clearly salient in colonial British Columbia, this particular breach in the philosophy of morals was, for the Anglicans, the most critical concern of all. 'Morality without religion,' one wrote, simply yet profoundly, 'has been called morality without motive.'[157]

## A Theology of Gender

On some counts the Anglican missionary's moral agenda appears strangely inconsistent. Consider, for example, one aspect of Good's own policy. Highly critical of interracial concubinage, he denounced white men as the 'least excusable' partners, the chief felons in this carnal crime.[158] Yet in dealing with mixed couples he focused on the morality of the women. 'If the mother is a steady woman & faithful to the man she cohabits with I generally advise them to marry. But where the woman is drunken ...,' Good stressed, 'I do not like to offer such advice.' If a marriage was to take place, Good's priority was to attract the woman, not the man, to his mission.[159] Thus, while men were assumed to be responsible for sexual sin, correcting sexual morality entailed educating women.

Why this disjuncture between male problems and female solutions? Having singled out male vice, it seems odd that Anglican missionaries did not privilege the moral reform of men. There was, however, a weighty mandate for the Anglican, and more generally Christian, emphasis on female sexuality. 'And God said, Let us make man in our image, after our likeness' (Genesis 1:26). According to Rosemary Radford Ruether, Western Christianity has traditionally gendered this decree, and speculated that if man is created in God's image as a transcendent ego, woman represents a material, bodily nature.[160] The patristic tradition of Paul and his successors consolidated the femininity of the body, and thus of passion, blaming Eve for the Fall and equating sin, which was female, with sexuality; a mortal humanity required sex to survive through procreation.[161] Peter Brown's remarkable study of celibacy among early Christians, *The Body and Society*, shows that the epistemology of sex was intrinsically gendered; in pondering the ethics of sexuality, Christian men used women and their bodies 'to think with.'[162] To the extent that it has been considered innate, male sexuality has been overlooked. 'Preoccupation with forms of manliness,' write Davidoff and Hall of early evangelicalism, 'was never as central and overt an issue as forms of femininity for Christian preachers and writers, since man's nature was seen as in God's image while woman was defined as "other."'[163]

Anglican missionaries focused on women's sexuality because, with maleness fixed, female morality determined the moral health of society. Yet this dualism was plainly contradicted by the male sin that Good and others identified – the colony's 'white savages' were evidently *not* made in God's image. Still, some Anglicans disregarded this male vice and, in keeping with received wisdom, sought female scapegoats. Visiting Lillooet in October 1869, Reynard judged that Native women 'whose custom it is to have their fill of vice before marriage' were responsible for the town's ills. 'Respectable young men,' he wrote, 'who for years kept away from this habit of society, have at last given in, and now are among the worst.'[164] To Reynard's predetermined mind these men *were* God's kind: innocent victims of unbridled female sex.

For most Anglican missionaries, however, male morals were clearly problematic – which makes their focus on femininity all the more striking and dogmatic. They knew that men were sinners, but convention said that female sexuality, not male probity, dictated the moral tone of social life. As godly wives and mothers in charge of Christian households, women could ensure decent family life and a moral colony. In Anglican hopes for female emigration and in their plans for schooling white girls, we have seen this obsession with domesticity. It is also evident in plans for Native girls' schools, where the church hoped to secure the female virtue that would buttress indigenous Christianity. The Reverend W.S. Reece, based at Cowichan, claimed that such institutions, 'conducted by godly women, sisters and servants of the Church,' and teaching faith and deference, constituted 'the main hope ... of evangelizing the natives.'[165] Without female morality, he implied, all was lost. Significantly, not only Anglicans felt this way. Missionaries of many denominations, in many parts of the world, believed that to convert young Native women was to convert their people. No one put it better than a Presbyterian missionary in Wisconsin, Isaac Baird. 'If we get the girls,' he said, 'we get the race.'[166]

Missionary Anglicanism could well be described as a theology of gender.[167] The Columbia Mission recruited women to tackle the moral problems of society at large and assigned them domestic roles that, presumably, were often deeply resented. That missionaries placed such stock in female morality, all the while criticizing male behaviour, seems counterintuitive, and prejudiced. Some Anglicans, however, were sensitive to the contradictions, though not Good or Hills, nor Pringle, Garrett, or Reynard – indeed none of the main characters of this book. In New Westminster's *Churchman's Gazette* of April 1884, an Anglican named A.E.V. Bewicke wrote a scathing review of Christianity in British Columbia. His main criticism was that, to date, his church had done little enough to raise *men's* moral standards, and that

God has been but too often represented as
'He that should be served
Only by women, and whose laws were made
Merely for girls to keep.'

Bewicke claimed that too many Christians imposed moral burdens on women and turned a blind eye to male iniquity. This, he said, had to stop, and though his moral agenda would strike many modern readers as puritanical, his contention that 'the virtue of purity is alike binding upon men and women' is perhaps not entirely unreasonable.[168]

# 4
# Space

The adoption of another people's gods always entails the
adoption of their space.

— Henri Lefebvre[1]

On 22 December 1864, the Reverend John Sheepshanks, rector at New
Westminster and chaplain to the bishop of Columbia, gave a lecture in
Brighton, England, on the progress of the Columbia Mission. Having
described the penury of the colony's Natives, he spoke of two Anglican
strategies for improving their lot. 'The first,' he announced, 'is to send
instructors to pass through their country from time to time, and teach
the Indians as much as possible in short visits; to tell them the primary
truths of Christianity; to exhort them to temperance and morality; and,
more than aught else almost, to lead them to desire more complete
instruction in the way of the truth.' The alternative Anglican approach
to teaching Natives was 'To establish defined settlements among them,
so that the young as well as the adults may be educated and brought up
as Christians.'[2] Sheepshanks envisaged two different geographies of Christian colonialism: itinerant missions based on intermittent forays into
Native territory, and fixed mission stations offering perennial access to
Native society.

In this chapter, concerned primarily with Good, I argue that the spatial organization of mission work was a central Anglican concern. Where
to send missionaries? For how long? In what numbers? At one level these
were questions of supply and demand. The Anglicans saw considerable
demand for their services but, underfunded and undermanned, could not
realize their full ambitions; they sought to maximize their reach while
minimizing expenditure. Yet Anglican geographical strategy did not
reduce to the neat logistics of spatial economy. According to Roberta L.
Bagshaw, funding was one of three factors that determined Bishop Hills's
placement of his missionaries, the others being the master plan he

brought with him from England, and the colony's difficult physical and human geographies.[3] I examine the bishop's original formula – which Good endorsed – and ask where it came from, what obstacles it faced on the ground in British Columbia, and how the Anglicans, and Good in particular, responded to such challenges. In that Anglican strategy assumed a tension between itinerant and permanent ministration, Sheepshanks offers a useful framework for interpretation, and I situate Good's experience in terms of these contrasting mission geographies.

First, however, there are the spaces of Anglican administration. A single diocese, established in 1859 and encompassing the twin colonies of Vancouver Island and British Columbia (both before and after their union in 1866), was the principal spatial matrix of the Columbia Mission, but it would not stand the test of time. Anglican missionaries were staggered by the size of the Columbia Diocese. Good spoke for all of them when he marvelled at its 'magnificent distances.'[4] From his seat in Victoria, Bishop Hills had to coordinate Anglican operations not only on Vancouver Island (almost as large as Ireland) but also in a mainland territory stretching east to the Rocky Mountains, and north to Russian America. The bishop recognized the futility of the task. In response to charges that he favoured the island at the expense of the mainland, he replied, quite reasonably, that the size of the diocese made it 'impossible to give that attention to all localities, which is most important in the early stage of planting and fostering the institutions of Christianity.'[5]

Over the years, the Columbia Mission introduced various administrative expedients intended to devolve Hills's powers and enhance administration of the diocese,[6] but the basic problems of distance and isolation remained. A geographical predicament demanded a geographical solution. The most obvious answer was to divide the Columbia Diocese into a number of smaller dioceses, each with its own bishop. In 1863 Hills proposed that Vancouver Island be made one diocese, and British Columbia another, but his plans met with dogged opposition from Frederick Seymour, governor of the mainland colony. On his first trip to the mainland in January 1860, Hills, meeting with Sheepshanks, had been told of intense rivalry between the two colonies and had learned that many on the mainland wished him to move to *their* capital, New Westminster.[7] This rivalry[8] troubled the bishop, and throughout his office he tried to be evenhanded. Separate dioceses, he thought, might solve the problem; the colonies had always been hostile, so why keep them together?[9] But Seymour was suspicious, first because Hills insisted that the seat of the episcopate remain on the island, and second because the planned split did *not* mirror colonial boundaries: the northwest section of the mainland colony would be annexed to Hills's new Vancouver Island diocese, robbing the mainland of William Duncan's Metlakatla, clearly the jewel in the mission crown.[10]

When these issues came to a head in 1866, the opposition won the day, but the Columbia Diocese was now living on borrowed time. In 1879 the mainland was divided into the Dioceses of New Westminster and Caledonia, and a separate diocese was established on Vancouver Island (see Figure 7). Supporters claimed that by 'narrowing the fields of labour' and increasing the number of mission operations, this new division would help to boost the struggling Anglican Church.[11]

In the meantime, however, Anglicans focused on the local administration of their mission. Hills envisaged a diocese comprising independent church districts, each managed by a resident missionary, and his preference was for a comprehensive network of Anglican parishes closely resembling the English parochial system. 'May our brave seamen, as they come here from their village homes in Britain,' he wrote, 'find the "Church-going bell," and the sights and sounds within the walls of this future sanctuary, a blessed and grateful likeness of what they have left behind in their loved and distant home.'[12] Reproducing Anglicanism in the colonies entailed replicating its geography, as well as its liturgy and ecclesiastical hierarchy. In calling for a parish system in British Columbia, Hills assumed close ties between spatial order and social morality. As we saw in Chapter 3, the bishop often accused American immigrants of low morality, and felt that superior English ethics were attributable, in

*Figure 7*   British Columbia, showing the three dioceses, 1879

part, to the country's national religion; a single faith encouraged moral conformity. If America lacked a national religion, he pointed out, it also lacked a common unit of religious and community life, such as the English parish. Hills maintained that the parish system gave society a structure and consistency conducive to good living, and that exported to British Columbia, it would serve as the infrastructure of a moral colony.[13]

To introduce Christianity to British Columbia, Hills delegated power to clergymen in their respective parishes. In this respect the Anglican mission's spatial form patterned its exercise in the same way that the distribution of juridical power, according to Tina Loo, conditioned the scope and efficiency of colonial law. From 1858 the colonial government sought to transform a fur trade society, with its own disciplines and regimen,[14] into a colonial society in which Natives, settlers, and miners could coexist. Missionaries were part of this colonial agenda, but maintaining order would also be the job of local justices of the peace, serving at once as gold commissioners, Indian agents, and magistrates. From cruel spectacles of colonial might, such as the 1864 execution of five Chilcotin, to the more peaceful settlement of everyday disputes, law was vital to the European colonization of Native land; its techniques have been charted in some detail.[15] My interest in Loo's work is her observation that, just as Hills had to confront his isolation from much of his diocese, so the legal system had to bridge the distance between Victoria, seat of the colonial government, and the mainland mines where order was lacking. As Loo shows, the deferral of extensive powers to local courts and resident magistrates was the chief solution to this problem.[16] While Anglican objectives and tactics were, clearly, quite different, a parochial mission represented a comparable geography of power.

Missionaries had to impose themselves on the colony by ordering its space. This would be no mean feat. In a speech delivered in London in 1862, John Garrett spoke of how British Columbia resisted all efforts to be domesticated and claimed that it had taken the Anglicans four years to make any real impression. In response to allegations that the Columbia Mission was too costly, Garrett defended Hills by saying that 'when we began, the whole place was utterly unknown. The very name and position of the colony were unknown. An entirely new machinery had to be organized over the whole country; thousands and thousands of miles had to be travelled several times over, and information had to be given, as well orally as by printing and advertising. The machinery,' he went on to say, 'is now working.'[17] Good's view was that clearly circumscribed parishes, with every nook and cranny known to their incumbents, were essential to a successful mission. Garrett's 'machinery' required spatial structure, in other words, and Good used the phrase 'parochial machinery'[18] to indicate that he, like the bishop, favoured a parish geography.

By dividing British Columbia into independent church districts, the Anglicans would know it, tame it, and embrace its peoples.

Based in Lytton from 1867, Good made every effort to dominate the charge he was assigned. He mapped his parish (see Figure 8) and, to facilitate the administration of those who inhabited it, kept an exhaustive parish register; Figure 9, showing the name, address, and date of baptism of each of seventeen male charges, is typical of this inventory. By the fall of 1872 Good doubted whether his parish contained a single settlement, or even a single residence, that had eluded him.[19] Yet I am sceptical about his sway. This parish was huge, covering somewhere between 4,000 and 10,000 square miles (Good's estimates varied wildly),[20] and the Natives who lived there spoke a language it took him years to learn.

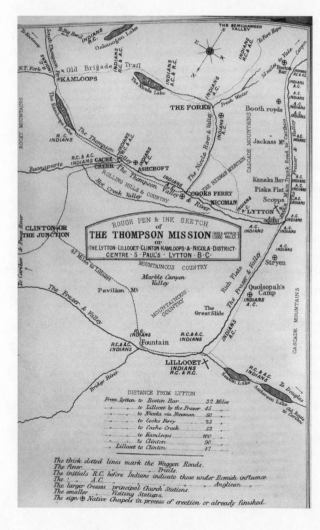

*Figure 8*  J.B. Good's sketch of his mission territory

*Figure 9*

**Male catechumens at St. Paul's Mission**

| Name | Residence | When baptized |
|---|---|---|
| Senaquia | Lytton or Nicola | – |
| Shako | Lytton or Nicola | 11 June [1870] |
| Commiltum | Lytton or Nicola | 1 June 1872 |
| Commeanken | Lytton or Nicola | 1 June 1872 |
| Nalee | Lytton or Nicola | 1 June 1872 |
| Mahaskut | Sklalet | 1 June 1872 |
| Nil-këy | Shemikaltsee's House | 1 June 1872 |
| Shemikaltsee | ? | 1 June 1873 |
| Spintlum | Lytton | 1 June 1872 |
| Kowkan | ? | – |
| Quolsopah | Fosters Bar | ? |
| Poonah | Kanaka Bar | 1 June 1873 |
| Pahlaek | Yale | – |
| Ne Nowchean | Lytton | – |
| Komâte Kane | Lytton | – |
| Meshall | Lytton | 1 June 1873 |
| Sahtok | Neky Yah | [4] Feb 1868 |

*Note:* After the Lytton Mission Register, BCA, Add. mss 1495.
? indicates illegible entry
– indicates not baptized
[] indicates probable entry

In this difficult environment parochial machinery was erratic. In the colony at large, the Columbia Mission's sparse regional geography did not approximate to England's dense patchwork of parishes. The essence of parish religion was a vicar familiar with his parishioners – it was this bond that Anglicans accused Calvinists and radical evangelicals of disrupting[21] – but while Good and other missionaries tried to know all their charges, the enormity of colonial parishes made intimacy impossible. The Columbia Mission, quite simply, had too few missionaries; it would achieve neither the social dominance of the Church in England, nor the comprehensive spatial order of the English parish system.

In 1870, when the Anglicans claimed to have 5,000 Natives under instruction, the geography of Hills's mission read something like this: Reverends Cridge, F.B. Gribbell, and Percival Jenns joined the bishop in Victoria, as dean of the cathedral, principal of the Boys' Collegiate School, and rector of St. John's respectively; Venerables Reece and C.T. Woods were based at Cowichan and New Westminster, as archdeacons of Vancouver and Columbia respectively; Good was at Lytton, Holmes was down the canyon at Yale; Reynard was still in the Cariboo; Duncan, at Metlakatla, and Reverend R. Tomlinson, at Kincolith, continued Anglican work on the north coast. All other Anglicans were on the island: Mr W.H. Lomas at Cowichan, Reverend H.B. Owen at Comox, and Reverend J.X. Willemar and his catechist Mr H. Guillod at Alberni (see Figure 10). That this organization scarcely resembles England's parish geography does not diminish Hills's conviction that to manage colonizers and colonized, order had to be imparted to the space they shared.

## Pauline Strategy and the Urban Pastorate

'The plan then we propose in this mission,' Bishop Hills announced at his farewell sermon in London in 1859, 'is, first, to take in hand the European population by occupying the towns as they rise up; already there are, I believe, twelve towns marked out, and in a state of rapid formation, in each of which we ought at once to place a faithful pastor.' Although Hills also appealed for men to cover less populated regions of British Columbia, the burden of Anglican ministration to white colonists would be on these twelve urban missionaries. The bishop assumed that a similar strategy would serve for the indigenous population: 'With regard to the natives we propose to have Christian settlements in the neighbourhood of heathen villages.' The basis of the Columbia Mission would be a network of resident missionaries, each stationed in a centre of white or Native settlement. 'I trust that by these means,' Hills concluded, 'we

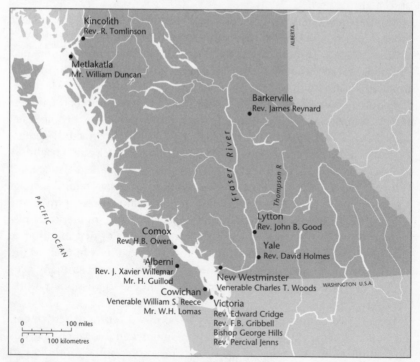

*Figure 10*   Locations of Anglican missionaries in British Columbia, 1870

may be able to cover the land with a religion which may bear testimony for Christ.'[22]

The bishop's vision was that of many missionary societies of the day, and, as with so many aspects of mission policy, was modelled on St. Paul's quintessentially urban mission. Between the years 45 and 61 AD, Paul made four extensive missionary journeys through the northeast Mediterranean basin.[23] He introduced Christianity to Philippi and Thessalonica, to Ephesus, Corinth, and other metropolitan centres of the Roman Empire. The Apostle's tactics were not always the same. In some cities, civic officials allowed him to lecture in bustling public spaces. Where the political climate was less tolerant, Paul spoke in a less conspicuous forum: a rented town house, perhaps, or a friend's villa.[24] But while the detailed geography of his evangelism varied from town to town, Paul's broader mission geography remained constant. Stephen Neill describes it thus: 'It was Paul's custom to settle for a time in one of the great cities of the empire, and through his younger helpers to radiate out from that centre to the smaller cities of the region ... As soon as a church had taken root and showed signs of being able to stand on its own feet under its local leaders, Paul felt free to move onwards towards a further fulfilment of his plan, that all the Gentiles might hear the word of the Lord and so the end might come.'[25]

Anglican missionary societies took Paul's lessons to heart. For the ancient cities of Gentiles and Jews, they substituted the 'heathen' settlements of British colonies. In both cases, they argued, Christian missionaries had the odds stacked against them. But Paul had prevailed, and so, if they imitated his modus operandi, could modern missionaries. The CMS maintained that entering the mission field was akin to going into battle undermanned: missionaries were hugely outnumbered by the people they hoped to convert, and their only chance of victory was tactical genius. In Paul's judicious deployment of his helpers, the CMS saw an almost military precision. Certain that rigid Pauline strategy marked a successful mission, the society described mission work in language reminiscent of Clausewitz: 'When a General has an arduous duty before him – the subjugation of a difficult country, and that with forces numerically disproportionate to the work which is to be done – it is of first importance that he be skillful in the disposition of them, and address himself to the occupation of commanding points, from whence, as from so many centres, he may advance to further conquests. It is just so in Missionary work. Missionary work is a grand strategical operation.'[26]

The essence of Pauline strategy was to occupy a centre of settlement, introduce Christianity to that population, and, when a local church was up and running, move on. As the CMS realized, the initial foothold had to be carefully chosen; it was not enough to select a town on its own merits alone. The size of its population was certainly important, but so was its location with respect to other settlements. This was what the CMS meant by 'commanding points.' Missionaries should not direct their attention to isolated settlements but to places giving easy access to other towns. Good had an excellent understanding of this dynamic mission geography. He knew that a 'concentrated effort' was vital when starting out, but that myopia was debilitating. Unless the original locus of evangelism was understood as 'a stepping-stone to further work beyond,' rather than as an end in itself, mission success would be short-lived.[27] The CMS envisaged an unbroken chain of linked missions: 'The positions occupied ought to be such as shall command influence, and introduce us to further conquests. It is desirable that our initiative and primary operations should be directed, not to points of a terminable nature, on the attainment of which, after much expenditure of valuable elements, we find our further advance in no wise facilitated, but to such as shall prove doors of access to the countries beyond.'[28]

Such a mission strategy was clearly at play in plans for the Columbia Mission. While Victoria would long remain the hearth of Anglican colonial operations, many missionaries doubted its value as a stepping-stone. The city had large white and Native populations, but was detached from the bulk of the colony. To some missionaries, New Westminster seemed a better base of operations. Not only did it have many settlers and, as the Reverend Holmes pointed out, Natives 'congregated round a common centre,' but, situated at the mouth of the Fraser, it was an obvious springboard for mission work in the territory beyond. As archdeacon of Columbia, Woods had more interest than most in promoting the city, and spoke enthusiastically of 'what a blessing it would be if we had an efficient Mission working from New Westminster as a centre, and sending our priests and lay agents into all places.'[29] Yet although this was precisely the Pauline strategy that Anglicans favoured, New Westminster never became a premier centre of Anglican work – perhaps a reflection of Hills's alleged bias towards the island, but more likely of the sway of Roman Catholicism on the mainland.[30]

In any case, the Anglicans arrived in British Columbia with a clear idea of how they would go about their work. Hills had clarified this policy in his farewell sermon and reproduced it a year later in a letter to Governor James Douglas;[31] Good established his own preference for Pauline missionary strategy in an early letter to his sponsors, penned during his brief stay in Nova Scotia. He saw no reason why Paul's tactics could not be applied in the colonial mission field.

This I believe was the Apostolic mode of establishing the Church of Christ. They seized upon the most important town or spot in a province or country; the very stronghold it might be of superstition, idolatry, or vain philosophy: and there they planted the Church: there they erected her gates ... there was the light housed – the city set on a hill which could not be hid, and which should gradually diffuse its light around as time rolled on whilst they themselves moved on to establish the Church on a similar basis in a new territory.[32]

A striking feature of Pauline mission strategy, one stressed by nine-teenth-century Anglicans, was its exclusive urbanity; as Wayne Meeks argues, 'the mission of the Pauline circle was conceived from start to finish as an urban movement.'[33] Tied to this urbanity was a specific relationship between power and space, an aspect of Paul's mission that needs to be clearly spelled out. According to Anglican missionaries, Paul observed a strict spatial formula, based largely on the size and relative location of different cities, and they themselves assumed an extant urban network. Imagining the mission field that awaited them, they pictured a series of towns to be possessed and saturated with Christianity one by one. Where Hills hoped to convert nonbelievers by 'occupying' their towns, Good spoke of the need to 'seize' commanding points in heathen territory. Both men advocated a derivative mission geography, one dictated by the existing social landscape of the colony. Arguing that settlements lacking Christianity could house its emissaries and digest its message, they inferred that suitable social spaces were in place. In British Columbia, however, towns hardly existed, and Anglican presumptions were rapidly undone. The Columbia Mission found few discrete settlements waiting to receive Christ; instead of simply occupying colonial space, missionaries would have to create it.

To understand the resulting geographies of the Anglican mission, it is worth probing Paul's strategy a little further and thinking more closely about the modality of power it entailed. Michel Foucault is of some help here, especially in his writings on Christian governance, systems of instruction and surveillance he refers to as pastoral power.[34] His thinking was stirred by his reading of Church Fathers who, like Paul, were urbanites. One of Foucault's biographers notes his penchant for Augustine,[35] Bishop of Hippo and author of *City of God* – a man dedicated to urban life. In his essay on pastoral power, Foucault invokes Chrysostom, Cyprian, Ambrose, and Jerome.[36] Their biographies are revealing. In the 370s, John Chrysostom spent two years as a hermit in the mountains of Syria, but eventually returned to Antioch as a deacon and then as a priest. 'The city,' writes Peter Brown of this one-time ascetic, 'had claimed him for herself.'[37] Cyprian, bishop of Carthage in the mid-third century, was also a city man, as was Bishop Ambrose of Milan, 'firmly anchored in his city' from 374 to 397 according to Neil B. McLynn.[38] Even Ambrose's contemporary Jerome, advocate of desert asceticism, was by all accounts an urbanite who 'knew little of the desert about which he wrote.'[39]

When Foucault observes that 'the pastorate of souls is an especially urban experience,' he is thinking of the pastoral regimes of these Christian leaders.[40] But his comments are also relevant to Paul's mission, itself thoroughly urban. What is the significance of this urbanity? Foucault argues that Christian teachers manage people rather than space, and that this concern distinguishes pastoral power from governance based on territorial jurisdiction. Most importantly, the unmediated social relations of the Christian pastorate contrast with the more detached sovereignty of a power exercised in the first place over a territory, and only indirectly over the inhabitants of that space. Foucault maintains that ancient Greek political philosophy and Machiavelli's *The Prince* both make power over space the bedrock of social authority, and that both therefore differ from Early Church theory, which posits the relationship between sheep and shepherd as the principal axis of pastoral power. The shepherd manages a flock, then, not the land it grazes.[41] Foucault's observation is suggestive, but at odds with the evidence from the Columbia Mission; if we begin to question this discrepancy, the seeds of an answer lie in the urbanity of Foucault's Christian pastorate.

Cities provide the essential raw material of a pastor's flock: people, in abundance. St. Paul worked exclusively in urban areas, which offered him a ready pool of souls – often recalcitrant, but always there. These were high-density environments in which public space abounded and privacy was rare. Given the right catalyst, people would gather in a flash.[42] Witness Paul's mission to Antioch, where, just one week after his arrival, 'came almost the whole city together to hear the word of God' (Acts 13:44). While important differences hold between Paul's urban pastorate and those of Foucault's Christians (most obviously Paul's missionary status), Foucault's claim that 'the shepherd's immediate presence and direct action cause the flock to exist' also seems appropriate to Paul.[43] When Paul occupied a city, he entered an arena comprising prospective mission charges, for a flock was latent in the social fabric and could, in theory at least, emerge at his behest. Even if a sceptical reading of Acts is in order,[44] and we question the speed and scope of Paul's urban impact, the fact remains that the social space of his mission invariably preceded him. In Foucault's terms, Paul could tackle people rather than the geography they inhabited, for the Roman city provided prolonged access to a myriad of souls.

As Stephen Neill points out, Paul's urban emphasis was entirely reasonable, for the Roman Empire *was* a world of cities.[45] But British Columbia in 1858 was not. Armed with Pauline strategy, Anglican missionaries arrived in a place where it had little purchase. In most parts of the colony, they found a sparsely settled land, and their presence seldom drew the flocks they envisaged. Even where the population was dense, it was mobile, and certainly not urban. As the Anglicans endeavoured to adapt to the conditions at hand, power and space interacted in different ways. The management of space became essential, not ancillary, as it was for Foucault.[46] The reason is clear. Anglican missionaries regarded the pastorate of souls as an urban experience, but British Columbia lacked the urban geography that, in the tradition of Paul, they anticipated. The Columbia Mission could not rely on prior command points, for few existed. In short, the colony was without an obvious space for Christianity. To manage flocks Anglican missionaries first had to generate them, for all they found in British Columbia were scattered sheep. The obvious way to gather a flock was to give it a land to graze.

**Intractable Geographies?**

The Anglicans were ill-prepared for British Columbia, where they found a harsh terrain through which travel was arduous. Access to the colony's inhabitants was hugely difficult. William Reece complained that he could not reach settlers in the Cowichan area, largely due to unpassable rivers.[47] Hills said that even in the lower Fraser Valley, not a challenging region, settlers were scattered and isolated.[48] The farther Anglicans ventured inland, the greater the obstacles to their mission. Steamers could navigate the Fraser only as far as Yale, beyond which river travel was virtually impossible, and the brigade trails of the fur trade provided only a patchy network of usable interior routes. When the Columbia Mission began in the late 1850s, there were no wagon roads on the mainland. Although transportation slowly improved,[49] and the church did its level best to place missionaries in suitable locations, most Anglicans accepted that 'distance and rough travel' would always prevent a comprehensive mission.[50]

The colony's social geography was no less problematic. First there was the white population. Victoria was the only town of any substance, and even there the population was seasonal, a 'state of stagnation' descending on the city in the spring when the hordes of miners who wintered there returned to the interior.[51] This itinerance seemed to pervade the colony, and it vexed the Anglicans. How could they civilize white settlements that were there one minute, effectively gone the next? It was in these terms, for example, that Good understood his predicament at Yale. He cursed the rapid turnover in Yale's white population. Of those Europeans who settled in the town, few ever stayed; most left long before the Anglicans could win them over. The church's problems intensified when gold fever shifted north to the Cariboo, for Yale became a stopover – miners flooded through the canyon one way in the fall, the other way in the spring. This transience confounded Good; he was not idle during his year in Yale, but it disheartened him that should he manage to raise the town's morals, a short while later he might have an entirely different clientele on his hands.[52]

Such mobility confused Anglican plans. When Hills claimed that a dozen resident missionaries would provide for the immigrant population at large, he had towns in mind. But Good's experience put paid to this illusion: miners, the dominant component of white society in early colonial British Columbia, only periodically lived in towns. The geography of mining life went against the grain of Anglican strategy, which required the occupation of fixed colonial settlements and the introduction of parish churches to these communities. Migrancy was inimical to this pastoral vision. When Hills saw that miners were so 'unsettled' and 'restless,' he understood the threat they posed to a parochial mission. 'They feel no spot their home even for a while,' he worried, adding, as if in fear of conflict, that they 'will not identify themselves with the institutions of the neighbourhood so readily.'[53]

Hills had expected stable Native villages as well as secure colonial towns. Indeed, when he submitted his plans at his farewell service, he explained to his London audience that using resident missionaries was apropos in British Columbia, for the colony's Natives were 'more settled and less roving' than indigenous peoples in other British colonies and elsewhere in British North America.[54] There was some truth in what he said. As early as 1824 John West had written that Natives of the Red River colony had 'no settled place of abode,' and had appealed to his fellow Anglicans 'to visit those parts of the country where [Natives] are stationary, and live in villages during the greater part of the year.' Such conditions prevailed, he maintained, west of the Rocky Mountains.[55] Hills would have known West's views, and while indigenous population geographies varied greatly in British Columbia, and had shifted to varying degrees since contact with whites, in many areas the winter village was a basic component of Native settlement geography.

Yet Hills and his clergy would be as disappointed by Native as by white human geographies. Some Native communities were, as expected, relatively stable, but settlement was seasonal, and European intervention, manifested in new sites of trade and employment, appeared to have amplified Native migrancy. Alexander Garrett blamed this mobility for the fact that mission work was 'slow, small in apparent result, and trying to faith and patience.' Vancouver Island had initially seemed a bounteous mission field, but, Garrett claimed, 'the fact of the tribes being not resident, but migratory, causes the pupils to be continually changing, so that a very small opportunity is afforded for making anything of a permanent impression upon them.'[56] The Reverend Xavier Willemar gave the same explanation for his travails at Alberni. Natives were close at hand for most of the year, but in the summer moved west to trade and fish in Barclay Sound. Aware of no obvious means to quash this migration, Willemar predicted a bleak future and could but hope that 'seals and codfish would leave Barclay Sound and the neighbouring coast to go somewhere else.' This was nonsense, of course, but Willemar understood the root cause of his problem: his mission geography was out of synch with his charges' migrancy. The only way to revive the Alberni mission was to reconcile these discordant geographies. 'If Alberni could be removed thirty miles closer to the Pacific Ocean,' Willemar fancied, 'then it would be an almost perfect situation for a Mission settlement.'[57]

Faced with similar difficulties, other Anglicans pondered more realistic solutions. Their quandary, essentially, was this. Pauline strategy was unsuited to British Columbia, where potential Christian communities consisted only of ephemeral white towns and seasonal Native villages. Having envisaged more appropriate settlements, the Anglicans suddenly felt compromised and were forced to make some important decisions: they could either adapt to the population geographies at hand, or modify them to suit their preferred strategy. The first option would entail itinerant mission work, a fluid clerical geography attuned to social mobility. The second option was to cling to Paul, retain his mission's spatial form, and seek to replace existing social spaces with a more accommodating human geography.

If pragmatism encouraged an itinerant mission, Christian tradition did not, and dogma was hard to resist. Fundamental issues were at stake. Travelling through the colony in search of starving souls, missionaries could certainly introduce their creed to the people they encountered, but true conversion would require more than the passing word. Only sustained, systematic pastoral care could effect real change, and because an itinerant mission offered no such consistency, it was unlikely to bear genuine fruit. For this reason, Anglicans quickly silenced moves for mobile missions. Alexander Garrett, as one example, was confident that resident missionaries *could* cope with miners and Natives, and warned that to discard Paul would be rash. Having toured the Cariboo in the summer of 1865, Garrett thought intently about how his church should tackle the men who mined there. He acknowledged their mobility, but refused to accept that an itinerant missionary was appropriate. He told fellow Anglicans that 'However well the migratory character of the mining population may seem to justify a migratory mission,' this would be the wrong course of action. Many miners still returned to Victoria at the end of the mining season, but some now wintered in the Cariboo, and these men, idle during the off-season, could be readily courted by a resident Anglican, who 'would then have an opportunity of gaining a hold upon the whole population.' A resident missionary, Garrett argued, could do much more with miners than a mobile one.[58]

Garrett's broader contention was that Anglican strategy should not yield to alien local conditions – missionaries should stick with their seasoned principles. Even Native migrancy did not justify a drastic rethinking. Although Natives were not sedentary and were difficult to regulate, Garrett maintained that their mobility was not always negative. More specifically, he claimed that in Victoria, where several Native migrations converged, order could be distilled from apparent chaos: since various groups passed through at one time or another during the year, there would always be a significant pool of Natives in the city. To Garrett's mind, the aggregate of these migrations was a perennial flock (a whole greater than the sum of the parts). In April 1859, for example, some 2,835 Natives, according to the *Victoria Gazette*, lived in the Victoria area,[59] more than enough souls to pique Anglican interest. The following year Garrett followed his instincts and approached the Colonial Secretary for funds and for a site on the reserve for a school and a church. 'Victoria,' he wrote, 'must ever be of prime importance, as a centre from which to operate beneficially upon the aboriginal Races of the Colony.'[60] Garrett saw Victoria as the cornerstone of the Columbia Mission, not on account of year-round Native settlement but because Native migrations intersected in the city and thus vindicated a resident Anglican missionary.[61]

In a sense Garrett's were lazy responses to the problem of itinerance. He acknowledged migrancy but resisted its full implications and tried to persuade his peers that it was not inimical to Pauline strategy. Garrett argued that the Anglican mission could thrive with few changes to initial policy and with no direct intervention into the geographies of · colonial life. Time would show him the error of his ways. The Reverend Reynard, dispatched to the Cariboo to take up the position recommended by Garrett, had little success with the region's miners,[62] and Garrett himself eventually failed as a resident missionary in the colonial capital. By the fall of 1863 his Indian School, but two years old, was in dire straits, largely because Garrett had misconceived Native itinerance: the discontinuity of his flock was disabling (he could not 'civilize' Natives who attended his school only periodically), and a summer of discontent, capped by the departure of the Songhees to their traditional fishing grounds, presaged the gradual demise of the Victoria mission.[63]

The Columbia Mission spawned many reflections on the problem of Native migrancy, most of them decidedly sober: for those Anglicans who appreciated the gravity of the matter, Garrett's bare faith in resident missionaries was unwarranted. Yet if they rejected Garrett's naïve optimism, they agreed that an itinerant mission was undesirable. What, then, was the answer? The most popular approach was to try to check Native mobility. With Garrett, it was held that resident missionaries were preferable; but against Garrett, that such missionaries were worthless if Native itinerance persisted. In sum, many Anglicans, Good among them, chose to alter Native rather than mission geographies, in the hope of producing settled peoples to be converted, if not at the missionary's leisure then at least in the knowledge that with a flock securely in place, one day's work would carry over to the next.

**Producing a Space for Christianity in the Fraser Canyon**
When Good left Yale in 1867 having been courted by the Nlha7kápmx, his first decision was where to establish his new mission. Lytton was the obvious choice. Not only were Good's initial suitors from the Lytton band but he suspected that the town site, known to Natives as Hecumshin (Kumcheen or Klick.Kum.Cheen),[64] was central to Nlha7kápmx society. This was true, yet Good, who identified the junction of the Fraser and Thompson Rivers as a Native meeting-place chosen for its propitious geography,[65] did not appreciate the full significance of the spot; many years later, James Teit would learn that Hecumshin was the centre of the Nlha7kápmx world.[66] While unaware of its spiritual significance, Good did know that Lytton was the place to strike.

Other factors also worked in Lytton's favour, not least a church on the town's main reserve, dating from the intermittent Nlha7kápmx affair with the Oblates. But Good could not ignore the fact that Lytton was now a settler town – a mission there would be a mission to Natives abutting whites, contact scarcely encouraged by the history of the Columbia Mission to date. William Duncan's work on the north coast had seemed fruitless until the Tsimshian could be lured from Fort Simpson.[67] Good knew this, and could also look to his own experience in Nanaimo, where he had opposed Native proximity to white settlers and had approved Hudson's Bay Company plans for establishing reserves.[68]

Yet Good was not dogmatic on the need to shield Natives. He did not deny that the moral abandon of 'heathen' whites could disrupt Anglican evangelism, but denied that this was always so and refused to overlook Lytton as a possible site for his new mission. Others might have questioned his logic, but the decision was Good's to make, and he insisted that sound teaching would mitigate the dangers of association. 'I do not deprecate as strongly as some persons the practice of the white and native element being placed in juxtaposition,' he wrote. Penned towards the end of 1868, a year after he had decided to reside in Lytton, Good's letter reads as an apology for his own strategy, and it came embellished with caveats. Missions to Natives living by whites were suitable, he claimed, 'so long as the propinquity be not too close, and there is found some other superior and controlling power placed over both, and sufficient strength and capacity to keep each party under moderate restraint, and so deal out even-handed justice to all alike.'[69]

In this way Good sought to offset the negative commentary that this method had attracted, but his argument was not entirely defensive. While some Europeans had defiled their Christianity, others had remained true, and Good argued that these solid Christians were valid models for Natives. Proximity to pious Christians could only expedite moral reformation. 'For whilst an Indian may become undoubtedly "two-fold more the child of hell" by imitation of the worse side of his new neighbours,' Good pointed out, 'he may also derive immense benefit in innumerable ways by copying their better parts.'[70] This rationale was to the fore when, in 1867, Good installed his mission in Lytton, and for some commentators the comparison with Duncan was irresistible. 'To understand how real are these Indians,' wrote Archdeacon Wright of Good's charges, 'it must be remembered that they are not taken away from the world and trained day by day in a pattern village, but they live in the midst of white men, trade with and work with white men.'[71] The success of Good's mission seemed all the more impressive because it did not replicate Duncan's Metlakatla.

Wright's point is moot, however. By 1877, when the archdeacon toured the Fraser Canyon with Bishop Hills, Good had long since reconsidered his initial position and had, *à la* Duncan, sought to isolate his charges from Lytton and its whites. Only shortly after arriving in Lytton Good began to regret basing his mission there. He had assumed that Lytton's darker side could be contained and that a central mission could flourish, but had misjudged his own influence. Many whites slighted him, and lax behaviour, concubinage in particular, remained rife. This was no environment for a serious mission. When 'One of those vile institutions in which white men and the worst class of Indian women meet' opened hard by his parsonage, Good finally accepted that he had been wrong. It was time to quit this 'unhappy spot.'[72]

But Good had no intention of leaving the Lytton area altogether. Regardless of the burgeoning white presence, the river confluence retained its significance among Natives; it would have been foolish to look elsewhere. Instead, Good sought land on the outskirts of the town – within reach of Lytton's Natives and of the few Europeans who attended his services, but removed from the immediate vicinity of sinister types. In the fall of 1868 Good found what he was looking for: a piece of land on a hillside overlooking the town. He contacted the Lands and Works Department to obtain a lease,[73] and rejoiced that he could soon escape Lytton to his 'little Zoar on the hill.'[74] The lease, approved in the early days of 1870,[75] was in Good's hands by May,[76] and by year-end he had left Sodom behind and occupied his new Zoar (see Figure 11). It was a

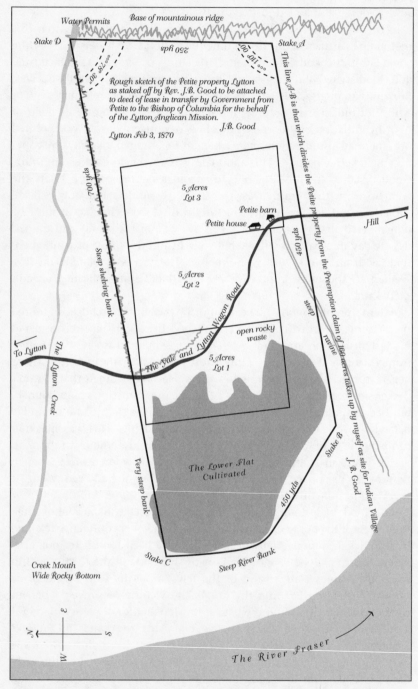

Water Permits    Base of mountainous ridge

Stake D                                         Stake A

250 yds

S 87° 30'                    110°

Rough sketch of the Petite property Lytton
as staked off by Rev. J.B. Good to be attached
to deed of lease in transfer by Government from
Petite to the Bishop of Columbia for the behalf
of the Lytton Anglican Mission.
                             J.B. Good

Lytton Feb 3, 1870

This line, A-B is that which divides the Petite property from the Preemption claim of 160 acres taken up by myself as site for Indian Village  J.B. Good

700 yds

Steep shelving bank

5 Acres
Lot 3

Petite barn
Petite house

Hill

450 yds

steep

ravine

5 Acres
Lot 2

The Yale and Lytton Wagon Road

open rocky
waste

To Lytton

The Lytton Creek

5 Acres
Lot 1

Very steep bank

The Lower Flat
Cultivated

Stake B

450 yds

Creek Mouth
Wide Rocky Bottom

Stake C        Steep River Bank

N E
   S
W

The River Fraser

Figure 11   Rough sketch of site of St. Paul's Mission, after J.B. Good, 1870

pivotal moment in the history of the mission. Good described his new premises as 'most romantically or rather gloriously situated,' and contrasted this superior geography with the 'dungeon state of social existence' he had suffered in lowly Lytton.[77] Having fled to the surrounding hills, Good now frowned on the town from his moral high ground.

Not only poor morals had frustrated Good's work in Lytton. He had moved to the town because he recognized its location at the heart of Nlha7kápmx territory, but it soon dawned on him that centrality did not imply stability. Many Nlha7kápmx, to be sure, lived near the confluence, but this residence was seasonal and did not give him a sedentary flock. It troubled Good that even those Nlha7kápmx whose 'proper home' was Lytton resided there for just four months a year.[78] His observation tallies with Teit's claim that the precolonial Nlha7kápmx wintered from late November into March, the Lytton band near the river confluence and other bands in dwellings spread far along the Fraser, Thompson, and Nicola Rivers.[79] Good's concern was that his access to Natives diminished in the spring, when many left the valleys and exchanged pit-houses for tents made of bark or rush mats.[80] A fixed mission assumed concentrated, sedentary charges, but such was not the basis of Nlha7kápmx geography. Dispersion and seasonal itinerance struck Good as its main characteristics, and in this light he rued 'the scattered nature of our native charge.'[81]

We should bear in mind, however, that Good, like many other missionaries, was apt to exaggerate Native migrancy. The Nlha7kápmx were not sedentary, but neither were they the 'nomadic race' identified by Good.[82] His sweeping critique belied the true nature of Native geographies. On account of a large fish diet, villages on the Thompson and Fraser were occupied for longer periods, and by more people, than Good would have us believe, and this remained the case for the entire duration of his Nlha7kápmx mission.[83] Furthermore, Good provides no information about regional variation in Native settlement patterns. According to Teit villages south of Lytton were more stable than those to the north.[84] He did not mean that some bands were steady, and others erratic. Natives moved within very well-established subsistence rounds, which gave life a predictable routine and ensured consistency from one year to the next; there was nothing unstable in this. Teit's point, presumably, was that southern Nlha7kápmx villages were inhabited for more of the year. The canyon is severe towards Spuzzum, much steeper than near Lytton, and Natives in that area were probably more reliant on fish.

Such distinctions were lost on Good, who mistook methodical, seasonal movement for aimless roaming. Fall saw a concentration of activity along the rivers, for this was when the salmon ran, but except for a few roots found in dry valleys, other food sources were in the mountains. Teit observed that the Nlha7kápmx knew the exact harvest time of various roots and berries, and which feeding grounds deer frequented at different times. Moving between root-digging and deer-hunting grounds on mountain slopes, Nlha7kápmx men and women were highly mobile, but in no sense nomadic.[85] If this, after Teit, was the general form of pre-contact Native geographies, had smallpox and measles epidemics, mining, and a decade of European settlement led to any major changes? In principle, no; although the Nlha7kápmx were being forced onto reserves in the late 1860s, and were told to farm them, very little agriculture was possible, and the Nlha7kápmx continued to hunt, gather, and fish.[86] There is some evidence that the Fraser's salmon harvest dwindled in the early 1860s (perhaps due to placer mining),[87] and the lower Fraser canneries possibly took their toll in Good's day, yet salmon remained the Nlha7kápmx staple. And while some villages may have taken on new residents and assumed a greater dominance as disease ravaged smaller ones,[88] these larger villages, increasingly located on reserves,[89] were not sedentary.

The fact remains, however, that Good's charges were not the nomads he suspected them to be. Nevertheless, many lived far from Lytton, and the Lytton band only resided in the town in the winter. In the manner of Paul, Good had occupied an obvious command point, but his command over the Nlha7kápmx was minimal; they were seldom at hand. Unlike the unmediated pastoral power that he associated with Paul, Good's connection to his flock was riven by language, culture, *and* geography. Lytton was not the social space on offer to Paul, for as a Native space, Good claimed, it was only periodically social. If Paul had managed subjects while taking their spatial setting for granted, Good could not do the same, since Nlha7kápmx geographies were so clearly problematic for his purposes. The upshot of Native dispersion and mobility was this: Good's presence in Lytton had not given him a settled flock, and the Nlha7kápmx would remain sheep without a shepherd unless something could be done.

Moving away from Lytton was Good's way of solving this problem. From the inception of the new mission, which he named St. Paul's, Good's priority was to fashion a space that would hold his charges and allow him to secure a stable flock. He pursued this agenda on several fronts. One plan (unrealized) was to introduce boarding-schools for Nlha7kápmx boys and girls from seven to ten years of age. This would serve many ends – not least to sever Native youth from 'heathen' society – but Good emphasized the importance of *year-round* superintendence.[90] He intended for instruction and supervision to be constant. And to ensure that Nlha7kápmx visiting his mission remained within his grasp, Good planned to dig pit-houses on the new premises, where Natives could bed down in peace, isolated from the seedy town nearby.[91]

Whether these pit-houses were ever built is unclear; what is clear is that Good wanted the Nlha7kápmx within reach. His principal means to ensure Native residency at St. Paul's was to offer his charges land for cultivation, and he was delighted to secure 150 acres for this purpose.[92] While other evidence suggests that the lease was actually much smaller,[93] we know Good's intent. 'I shall have to exert all my powers of persuasion,' he confirmed shortly before occupying the new grounds, 'to induce all the Indians properly belonging to Lytton, to settle in that neighbourhood upon land which I have preempted on their behalf and to cultivate the gardens I am about to offer for their acceptance.'[94] Good did not envisage this cultivation as a modest diversion for Natives otherwise occupied, but as the essence of their subsistence and labour. It is also evident that Good hoped to attract Natives from afar, not just from Lytton; by May 1870, months before he moved, Good had divided up the lower flat of the new property between Natives under Sashiatan, of Lytton, and those who followed Spintlum, a great Nlha7kápmx chief and the man Good appointed leader of church affairs for villages above the confluence.[95] The Nlha7kápmx would be able to live off the produce of this land, Good argued, and perhaps even sell any surplus. If he could provide Native subjects with a means of subsistence, as well as a place to sleep, then maybe he would establish the flock he craved.

There were other reasons for Good's emphasis on agriculture. It was a general tenet of the age that farming was virtuous toil, and Good was keen to propagate a serious work ethic. With 'the Gospel of Salvation,' he maintained, 'we would preach also the Gospel of Labour.'[96] Cultivating the soil for six days a week would edify Natives while checking their migrancy. In the belief that farming was worthy labour, Good packaged his offer to the Nlha7kápmx as their only chance of realizing 'an honest and reliable means of subsistence.'[97] In a colony still dominated by mining, which the Anglicans regarded as gambling, this was no empty rhetoric, for Good painted miners and Natives with the same brush: each lived according to nature's whim, while agriculture offered a more dependable living, earned on the back of hard work, not luck. Some years later Good announced that his charges had exchanged 'the certain produce of labour and cultivation' for their former 'precarious subsistence,' a shift he tied to their conversion.[98] More generally, Anglicans equated colonialism with agricultural settlement; and while missionaries elsewhere opposed agrarian bliss to urban blight,[99] the wilderness, not the city, was chief antagonist in Anglican patronage of a pastoral British Columbia.[100]

If there was a morality in agriculture, there was also a civility in the sedentary life it entailed. Like many other missionaries, Anglicans linked morals to the spatial constitution of social life; they held to a set of what we might call, after Felix Driver, 'moral geographies.'[101] In particular,

Anglican missionaries coupled migrancy to sin, and argued that to convert the heathen one had to curb their itinerance. If agriculture could settle Natives down, it would serve to improve their morals – not only because cultivation was itself a moral economy but equally for the stable geography it enjoined. In his work in the Red River colony, John West confronted migrant Natives (likened to roaming animals) and spoke of his desire to 'civilize and fix them in the cultivation of the soil.' To fix them *was* to civilize them.[102] As we learn from Carol Devens's *Countering Colonization*, this concept of moral geographies was often taken to extremes. In 1638, for example, a French Jesuit wrote from New France that 'it is the same thing in a Savage to wish to become sedentary, and to wish to believe in God' – a remarkable statement.[103] Anglicans in British Columbia did not go quite this far, but they did hold that a settled life was potentially one given over to Christ, and advocated settlement more vigorously than their Roman Catholic and Methodist counterparts.[104]

Such concerns were not far from Good's mind when he offered land to the Natives. Yet his abiding anxiety, both before and after moving in 1870, was that with many Nlha7kápmx beyond his immediate reach, his flock was 'not properly shepherded.'[105] As a resident missionary with mobile charges, he was acutely aware of his impotence. Migrancy militated against close surveillance and constant care, which for Good were two essentials of mission work. By settling Natives down, agriculture would allow him to watch them. That supervision was Good's main concern is certain, for this was precisely his problem with Native mobility. 'It will I think be readily understood,' he wrote, 'how very difficult it is to exercise an efficient oversight over a body of Indians so independent and nomadic as ours, divided up into so many small families or settlements, and so widely scattered throughout so extensive a range of country.'[106] If Good could assemble his charges in one spot by turning them to farming, a more effective vigil was possible.

Good's mission was not unique in this respect. Reverend David Holmes, Good's successor at Yale, complained of the Stó:lõ as Good did of the Nlha7kápmx, and he too turned to agriculture. By dividing land at Hope into sixty allotments and offering these to his Native charges, Holmes hoped to enhance supervision. 'The farm induces the Indians to settle down to one place,' he explained, 'so that a permanent hold may be gained upon them.'[107] Willemar tried similar methods on the island, albeit with limited success,[108] and Anglican missionaries urged the Haida, who left their Queen Charlotte villages for up to six months each year, to cultivate potatoes, turnips, and hay.[109] Most Anglican missions encouraged agriculture in one form or another, and the reasoning was often Good's: that a flock could not be supervised unless it came together in one place. Other denominations have followed a similar logic, in British Columbia and elsewhere. George Lovell provides one example among many, that of Roman Catholic missionaries pursuing the *congregacion* of indigenous Guatemalans so as to monitor their every move.[110]

The important point is that Good placed the production and government of space at the heart of his mission strategy. His would not be the classical pastoral power of the Roman city, nor indeed the intimate pastorate of the English parish, for his charge was vast and his flock scattered. St. Paul's was the fulcrum of his mission, and he knew that to succeed he had to fortify this headquarters. 'My first and main object,' Good admitted, 'has been to make our central position strong.'[111] Without a solid base, he could tour Nlha7kápmx territory and tell listeners of his faith, but this was unlikely to produce converts. If Foucault's Christians had exercised power over souls rather than space, Good acknowledged that his own flock required a defined local pasture. He tried to provide it, and to persuade Natives to stay; with agriculture his means, Good sought a truly *pastoral* pastoral power.

Little can have come of Good's grand plans for Nlha7kápmx farming. As any one who has visited the Lytton area knows, it is a parched, abrupt landscape with thin, sandy soils. There was little water for irrigation, and that was soon controlled by white settlers. The land Good occupied was hardly fertile; indeed, Peter O'Reilly, assistant commissioner of Lands and Works and no friend of Good's, agreed to the lease partly because he knew the land was worthless.[112] Furthermore, Good himself wrote little of the fate of his venture. He did claim, as we have seen, that his charges exchanged a reliable arable economy for their former means of subsistence, but this boast does not square with the facts: that most Nlha7kápmx continued to eke out a living from traditional sources; that these Natives, assigned poor land with no water, were largely unable to farm; and that much to Good's chagrin, most of Lytton's Natives remained in the town in the hope of finding paid work.[113] It is ironic that while Good waxed moral on the agrarian work ethic and denounced mining as gambling, he did not dissuade Natives from prospecting for gold and selling their finds,[114] and even accepted $100 from Hills for his charges to purchase mining tools.[115] If seeds were sown on the land he tendered, they appear to have failed, and Good's support for prospecting suggests he learnt a lesson familiar to others – that a missionary was unwise to rely on agriculture.[116]

An agrarian economy never materialized, and no Natives came to live on his grounds, but Good's mission blossomed. His dream of a settled flock remained wishful thinking, and yet the early 1870s were Good's most successful years, during which he procured a faithful Native following and, with it, a glowing reputation among his peers. It seems that despite his failure to reorient Nlha7kápmx settlement, Good's accent on a superior mission headquarters paid dividends, for while St. Paul's did not become the social space he had intended, it was from this base that he administered the Nlha7kápmx – still scattered, and still beyond his immediate clutch.[117] It is significant that although Good's mission was not a Metlakatla, since its subjects were not resident, neither was it an itinerant mission. Services were held at the same time every week. The Nlha7kápmx understood that St. Paul's was where they could find Good, and that it was the place to learn what Christianity offered them. Native mobility did not cripple his mission as it did others.

Good's Sunday services attracted Nlha7kápmx from all points of the compass, even a young boy who came six miles on all fours and a blind man who walked from twice that distance.[118] These Natives came to hear Good preach, to seek medical advice, and to request aid in the land disputes that embroiled them. Bishop Hills's annual visits drew as many as 800 to the mission. While Good was unable to supervise his charges as he would have liked, he did his best to overcome the problem. Most significantly, as discussed in the next chapter, he employed Native watchmen to monitor behaviour in the villages and to inform him of sinners. In addition, he periodically left St. Paul's in other hands (either those of his wife or his catechist Silas Nalee) and set off to tour his parish, reminding sceptics of their failings and converts of their duties. Travelling on mountain trails and wagon roads (see Figure 12), he covered prodigious distances. On one journey he baptized three children, riding forty-seven miles to reach the first, twenty more to the second, and another hundred miles to the last – only to face a seventy-mile ride back to Lytton for his

*Figure 12*   Road along the Fraser River

Sunday appointment in church.[119] Figure 13 shows that while most of his instruction took place at St. Paul's, Good gave services from Hope to Ashcroft, and from Lillooet to Kamloops. St. Paul's Mission eventually became the Anglican stronghold in the British Columbia interior, a region long dominated by Roman Catholicism. From it Good reached out to his charges, and to it, for some years, they flooded.

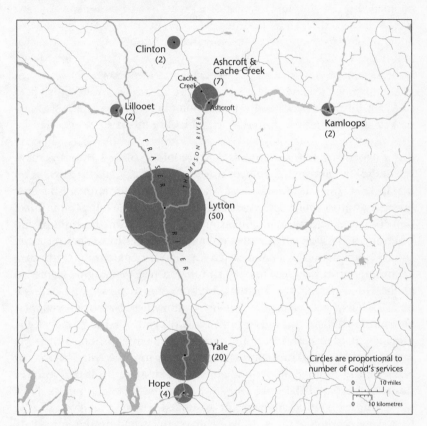

*Figure 13*   Services given by J.B. Good, 1876

# 5
# Conversion

For the kingdom of God is not in word, but in power.
– 1 Corinthians 4:20

'Long ago I was very wicked,' said Chil-lool-uk, 'now I repent & have my desire for baptism.' These words were uttered at St. Paul's Mission on 2 May 1874, as Chil-lool-uk stood before Bishop Hills, affirmed his conversion, and became a Christian.[1] By 1877 some 450 Nlha7kápmx had been baptized,[2] many after similar appointments with the bishop, and when the first Canadian census was conducted four years later, the entire Nlha7kápmx nation was enumerated (by Good) as practising Anglicans.[3] In little more than a decade, English religion had seemingly taken hold of the Nlha7kápmx, yet neither these bare statistics, nor Chil-lool-uk's words, tell us what conversion entailed, or how these Natives viewed their new faith. The latter question must remain open, for the ethnographic evidence, if illuminating, is thin, but from Good, Hills, and others we can discern the Anglican instruction that prepared the Nlha7kápmx for conversion. Behind Chil-lool-uk's absolution lay months, if not years, of spiritual and moral training.

An impressively deliberate air attended Good's mission to the Nlha7kápmx. He knew that Native conversion would not be immediate and steeled himself for a long haul when he set about teaching them. In this respect Good observed a heady tradition of Christian scholarship on reserve in communicating religious knowledge. As a graduate of St. Augustine's, Good was steeped in the writings of the Tractarians, who held that imparting Christian doctrine demanded tact, patience, and perseverance. Nonbelievers could not grasp the whole Truth at once, so had to be fed morsels, followed, eventually, by more weighty spiritual sustenance. When Good wrote that with the heathen 'it can only be line upon line and precept upon precept, here a little and there a little, first with milk, and then with strong meat as they are able to bear it,' he followed to the letter the Tractarian injunction to emulate Christ's apostles.[4]

*Figure 14*   J.B. Good pictured with his 'flock' at St. Paul's Mission

The Tractarians derived this doctrine of reserve from the Early Church, but their thinking was also influenced by evangelical philosophies of the day. High Churchmen looked askance at popular new methods of evangelism, which by Good's day had made their way to the far corners of Britain's empire. That some preachers expected to win converts by simply laying bare Christianity's innermost truths, the likes of John Keble, a leader of the Oxford Movement, could not credit.[5] The idea seemed even more absurd in the colonial context, where abstruse biblical sermons can have meant little to those without English. Inclined towards the Tractarians and the Church Fathers they patronized, Good shied away from modern evangelical quirks and resolved that rather than hold forth on intricate scriptural dogma, he would cautiously reel in his prey, feeding them milk, then meat, converting them 'by degrees.'[6]

This emphasis on reserve was also tied to Anglican teaching on baptism. As W.S.F. Pickering points out, most Protestant denominations refrain from baptizing adults until a clear change in the individual is apparent, whereas Roman Catholics, 'believing in the grace present in the church viewed as an organic body, and therefore an instrument through which a person can be helped, administer baptism relatively early on.'[7] This distinction generally holds for Anglican and Roman Catholic approaches in British Columbia. Good argued that all missionaries were tempted to hurry their work,[8] but maintained that while he and other Anglicans had retained their poise, the Oblates had not. This was part polemic, of course, and thus although Roman Catholics do appear to have baptized quickly,[9] we should be wary of Good's quip about 'manufactured converts'[10] and of Hills's claim that one Oblate priest gave baptisms at $2 à piece.[11]

As Chil-lool-uk and others discovered, it would be a long time before their fidelity to Good was rewarded. Baptism was often denied to Natives who claimed to have converted; some waited five years as members of St. Paul's before their conversion was acknowledged.[12] This policy raised eyebrows among both the Nlha7kápmx and English observers of the Columbia Mission. Hills had to placate a Cook's Ferry chief who, perhaps quite rightly, interpreted Good's reserve as a sign of distrust,[13] and one reader of *The Mission Field* wondered why Good delayed so long when evidence from other missions suggested that baptism was appropriate after as little as a week.[14] But Good stood firm. He suspected some Nlha7kápmx of embracing his mission on dubious grounds; *ficti*, or feigned conversion, was a very real concern.[15] If insincere converts were accepted, they would be 'profaning the Holy Sacrament of Baptism,' a risk that Good was not prepared to take, and he thus sought proof of faith in 'outward changed conduct and general course of living' before inviting an individual to join God's flock.[16]

In this way Good negotiated a set of thorny theological debates around questions of faith, morality, and conversion. On one side of the debate were nineteenth-century children of Reformation thought, who inherited Luther's doctrine of *sola fide* and argued that faith alone ensured salvation. On the other side were those convinced that, with God's grace, good works would take one to heaven. Most British evangelicals preached justification by faith, and while some stressed the importance of human works after faith, and thus were not antinomian,[17] Good favoured the more moderate theology of justification associated with the Oxford Movement. While they accepted God's grace as the essence of salvation, the Tractarians, and Pusey in particular, stressed the urgency of good works.[18] Good was scrupulously true to this moral directive – as we shall see in Chapter 6, his assessment of an individual's conversion was based upon 'the *exhibition of character* as well as upon professed belief.'[19]

Since grand discourse did not seem the way to convert, Good depended on more furtive persuasions. Suspicious, again, that he had been solicited for reasons not immediately connected with religion, Good tried to use this to his own advantage. As one example he offered to the Nlha7kápmx his modest medical expertise, having taken several courses in doctoring at St. Augustine's.[20] During his tenure many Natives fell sick, often with measles, and Good assumed that they would warm to him if he could help. In this respect, at least, mission medicine was a means to an end, in Good's words 'a wedge for reaching the inward secret defilement and sickness of the soul.'[21] He knew well enough the high regard in which Nlha7kápmx 'medicine-men' were held and fought a constant battle to break their authority. He lost. Many years later James Teit reported that all the Nlha7kápmx still believed in 'the power of the medicine-man,' and many resented the fact that Good and his successors tried to depose Native healers without providing a white doctor in their place. Of Teit's many observations on the *fin de siècle* Nlha7kápmx, one is critical to our assessment of Good's mission: that although they conceded white medical skills and would have used a white doctor had one been available, these Natives still trusted the 'medicine-man' with 'diseases of the soul' – the missionary's true field.[22]

While Good relied on medicine to win over sceptics, he was also concerned about Native material well-being. In his position as a colonial missionary, Good arrogated to himself many different roles. One, to be sure, was the deliverance of lost souls, and it is notable that the Nlha7kápmx identified Anglican teaching on redemption, with its emphasis on the selectivity of salvation, as the single greatest distinction between white theologies and their own.[23] Yet salvation was also a worldly concern, for Native mortality was high and the Nlha7kápmx imagined themselves doomed to extinction.[24] Adamant that ungodly white colonists were responsible for Native depopulation, and that only Christianity could help,[25] Good aimed to save bodies as well as souls and was committed to improving the general well-being of his flock. He tended to physical maladies, promoted European ideals of health and cleanliness, and, as we saw in Chapter 4, sought to provide Natives with a secure means of subsistence.

To Good's mind, then, his mission offered salvation in this world and the next. This was clearly a peculiar colonialism – if not always at odds with other white interests, very often ill at ease. Few other colonists had Native welfare in mind, still fewer made it the kernel of their calling. Good intended nothing less than the maintenance and improvement of Nlha7kápmx life. How should we understand this distinctive colonial power? Following Foucault we can contrast the role of a shepherd with that of a monarch. 'Who provides mankind with food?' Foucault asks. 'The king? No. The farmer, the baker do. Who looks after men when they are sick? The king? No. The physician.'[26] Farmer and physician are both shepherds in Foucault's estimation, for among the shepherd's many jobs are feeding and caring for the flock. The king, on the other hand, does not sustain the flock entrusted to him. If Foucault borrowed this distinction from Cyprian or from Ambrose, he could equally have done so from Augustine, who, in the *City of God*, writes of Christian leaders as those who give orders 'not with pride in taking precedence over others, but with compassion in taking care of others.' In the manner of Foucault after him, Augustine classes such teachers as 'shepherds of flocks' rather than 'kings of men.'[27] For him and Foucault both, Christian government is pastoral in the sense that father to novice is like shepherd to sheep.

James Bernauer and Michael Mahon have described pastoral power as a 'permanent concern with the total well-being of religious subjects,'[28] which stands as an apt summary of Good's bearing on his charges. His principal business was with Native faith, but their security and health could not, and should not, be set apart. Pastorship was an art of government, and it was to rigorous paternalism, as evoked by Foucault, that Good aspired.[29] It is difficult to know how the Nlha7kápmx interpreted this fatherly devotion. While some will have resented the intervention, it is clear that many embraced their putative guardian. With great pride Good recalled an early convert who thanked him heartily for his vigilance, and who noted not only 'how few sick there were amongst them, and how seldom a death occurred,' but 'how little want this year, and how changed for the better everything was connected with this people since my arrival.'[30] If these were Nlha7kápmx words we should, however, assume a loose translation; Good faced many obstacles and his pastoral care was not comprehensive. Because his flock was scattered, and because the assistants he needed never arrived,[31] Good's supervision of Native life was piecemeal at best. He could not provide food, nor land fit for cultivation, and one suspects that his medicine was crude. His was a certainly a pastoral power, but its exercise was imperfect.

**Pastoral Power**
There is good reason to listen closely to Foucault, as his discussion of pastoral power lends itself to consideration of Good's mission. We can begin with Foucault's contention that pastoral power is individualizing,[32] for Good emphasized that each of his charges had to be individually known. His parish register told him who belonged to his mission, and each member's age upon enrolment; it showed whether a person had been baptized, and if so the Christian name taken; it recorded the sins of sinners, and the punishment exacted in each case. To complement this inventory, Good issued certificates to adherents at each stage of their conversion – one upon joining St. Paul's, another with baptism, and two more after confirmation and communion.[33] Together, these documents distinguished Good's Nlha7kápmx flock as individual sheep. The system was not foolproof; some Nlha7kápmx men periodically changed their names, thus incommoding Good's endeavour to know them.[34] But in theory these records chronicled an individual's encounter with Christ, tied that person to his or her new Christian selfhood, and thus constituted a discrete religious subject. A convert named Sarah is one example:

> You might ask Sarah as a matter of curiosity and interest to let you see and examine her parchment roll so carefully protected by an outer covering of native workmanship, and wherein she carried her Church Certificates which would tell her Christian standing in the great Congregation. One would state when she joined the Anglican mission, and

the next when enrolled as a Catechumen, the third would note her Baptism then her admission to Holy Communion, and lastly the solemnization of her marriage, thereby sanctifying her union with her husband. Now unroll the parchment which may be some two feet in length, and there you will see a record, after her own native fashion, of her whole career as a disciple of Christ.[35]

It will be clear from this that a sacramental theology structured Good's mission. That he privileged baptism, confirmation, and communion again demonstrates Good's allegiance to the Tractarians who, influenced by nineteenth-century Romanticism, had revived sacraments denigrated by the rationalism of the previous century; Anglican evangelicals were less interested in the sacraments and many actively opposed what they regarded as High Church ritual. But Good was no evangelical. He held to the Tractarian view that with baptism, a convert entered a heavenly community of fellow Christians. John Henry Newman, architect of the Oxford Movement and eventual convert to Roman Catholicism, captured this thinking as follows: 'Baptism admits, not into a mere visible society, varying with the country in which it is administered, Roman here, and Greek there, and English there, but through the English or the Greek or the Roman porch into the one invisible company of elect souls, which is independent of time and place.'[36]

Converts affirmed their membership of this community in Holy Communion. The Eucharist was central to Tractarian thought,[37] was emphasized by Anglicans who offered a Catholic theology of mission,[38] and was fully indulged by Good. This practice put considerable distance between Good and Anglican evangelicals who maintained that personal faith was all, and that the Eucharist was a dangerous corporatism verging on Romanism. By contrast, communion was an essential component of Good's mission; as the shared performance of a mutual Christian identity, it represented the climax of colonization, the dissolution of otherness into the singular body of Christ. This is a vital point, to which we shall return. For now, we should be aware that this ethereal union did not gainsay Good's efforts to differentiate his flock. A Christian selfhood had to emerge before it could be renounced in communion. Good knew that to convert his charges, he had to know each one in detail, for unless he baptized according to individual faith and works, his would be a motley communion of believers and infidels, of the true alongside the fickle.

If the Christian shepherd must know all members of the flock and be ready to meet each one's individual needs, so every charge must know his or her self and be prepared to acknowledge past sin. Augustine's *Confessions* epitomize the rigorous self-examination that many Christian pastors, Good among them, require of their sheep. In this text Augustine quarries his deepest emotions and doubts, and exposes them to intense scrutiny and criticism. He calls on God to act as 'physician of my most intimate self.'[39] Good expected the Nlha7kápmx to be equally unsparing. From him they could learn doctrinal truths and moral etiquette, and he would do his utmost to enforce observance; but faith was ultimately an inner predicament, and Good could not access the recesses of the soul. He urged Natives to open their hearts to God and to disclose the secrets thus revealed.[40] The historian cannot gauge Native enthusiasm for this introspection, but we do know that some Nlha7kápmx took Good at his word; Spintlum, leader of the nation and for some time the missionary's confidant,[41] warned his people against sin and told them not to judge others' faults, but to 'search their own hearts and scourge themselves.'[42] Good's liturgy began with his congregation invoking God and inviting His exacting inspection. This was the appeal:

1. Try me O God.
2. Search the ground of my heart.
3. Prove me.
4. Examine my thoughts.
5. Look well if there be any way of wickedness in me.
6. Lead me in the way of Everlasting Life.[43]

An intense personal encounter with God was the crux of this Christianity, notwithstanding Good's role as an intermediary. Each Native was encouraged to seek the Lord's forgiveness and to trust in the value of steady faith and a clear conscience. But the pastor's influence should not be underestimated. We must remember that Good's flock was new to this foreign creed. As Foucault remarks, the Christian pastorate is 'a complicated technique which demands a certain level of culture, *not only on the part of the pastor but also among his flock.*'[44] Leaving aside for now issues of linguistic difference and the problems of translation, Foucault implies that redemption is meaningless if its meaning is lost on its subjects. Did Good's charges know wherefore they repented? Were they aware of God's supreme grace? To fuss over the different theologies of mission is in one respect an intellectual conceit, for the specific shading of Christianity was doubtless immaterial to most Natives, many of whom were bemused by strife among churches that worshipped the same God.[45] If some Nlha7kápmx did convert to Christianity, a fact for which we have to rely on the Anglicans themselves, Good was instrumental. He needed not only to guide his charges through the intricacies of the Bible[46] but to persuade them to accept him as both tutor and custodian.

In a sense this was a straightforward task, for since the Nlha7kápmx initially knew little about Christianity, and less about its various rituals and regulations, they were willing to allow Good complete dominion over church affairs. Whether their primary interest in him was spiritual or worldly is an other issue altogether, and by no means clear;[47] but for one reason or another, they followed his lead. This compliance should not be viewed as a mere aid to instruction, for it was much more than that. Obedience was a precondition of pastoral power, and it structured the very nature of Native conversion. If we recognize this, we can begin to efface what Gauri Viswanathan aptly calls the 'humanist script' of 'traditional conversion narratives,'[48] by which she means conversion understood as self-determined religious change. In taking up Christianity, Nlha7kápmx individuals certainly exercised personal volition, but we cannot remove this agency from the context of obedience to Good.

The scope of this obedience needs careful accounting. Some Nlha7kápmx had no time for Christianity and remained aloof.[49] But those who identified a use for this faith were willing to heed Good's lessons. They did so, presumably, for many different reasons – perhaps to resolve spiritual malaise, perhaps to secure Good's aid in land disputes. We do not know. Once they had pledged allegiance to St. Paul's Mission, however, they followed his will because it *was* his will, not because his rules suited their tastes.[50] Take, as an example, baptism, generally performed during Bishop Hills's visits to Lytton. In June 1872 the bishop baptized twenty-six Natives, all adult, and mostly men. As part of his rubric Hills checked that they did, indeed, seek baptism, but he was unprepared for the majority response, which can best be described as puzzlement: 'why do you ask such a question,' they wondered, 'are we not your disciples'? As they understood it, discipleship entailed conformity, which in turn meant obedience: 'you must tell us what to do not ask us what we wish,' they told the bishop, 'of course we wish for Baptism because you tell us it is right.'[51] If we return now to Chil-lool-uk and his desire for baptism, we can shed new light on the type of testimony he offered. It is true that the decision to convert was ultimately the individual's. But it is also true that this decision was often no more than obedience. Where this was so, baptism signified entente, and perhaps not enlightenment.

**The Limits to Power**

We have already seen that Good struggled. His charges were spread over a vast space, and he could visit them only periodically. Although many came to see him at St. Paul's, they often arrived in such numbers that Good, alone throughout his years in the canyon, was overwhelmed. By the beginning of 1870 he had 2,000 Nlha7kápmx under instruction (by Teit's era no more than 2,000 remained),[52] and as more filed in from 'all quarters' of his parish, Good, according to his wife, was 'driven to his wits-end.' In February he was obliged to turn down dozens of new candidates.[53] It was increasingly clear to Good, even at this early stage, that the Native demand for Christianity was greater than his capacity to provide it, and later that year he told his sponsors that the 'living instrumentality' of his mission fell 'sadly short' of what was required.[54]

As Foucault describes it, pastoral power turns on a direct exchange of dues between the shepherd and each individual sheep, the former offering edification and care, the latter, in return, deference. But as mentor to so many, Good could not provide such immediacy, for even if he knew every charge individually, he had neither the time nor the wherewithal to give each soul the attention it required. As a result, his mission structure could not reduce to a simple duality with him as instructor and all others as students; he needed a more efficient pedagogy, preferably one that retained the hierarchy of the pastoral model, but lightened the shepherd's burden. The use of English teaching assistants, subordinate to Good but senior to his charges, would have satisfied both criteria, but Good's constant solicitations fell on deaf ears. Instead he turned to his Native pupils, and asked those who converted quickly to disseminate Christianity in their respective villages.

It is unclear, however, if Good's appeal to indigenous help was due more to force of circumstances than to prevailing mission theory. The size and dispersion of his flock certainly encouraged the devolution of power, but the evidence suggests that Good had this policy in mind from the start, or at least before the extent of his mission was fully apparent. Within months of arriving in Lytton, he felt that some pupils were already nearing the stage where evangelism was within their purview;[55] if this was rather optimistic, it does support the view that Good planned for Native teachers all along. Many nineteenth-century Protestant missions used indigenous instructors, whereas Roman Catholics generally did not.[56] We should remember, too, that St. Paul himself had depended on assistants, a fact not lost on Good.[57] The CMS, and its leader Henry Venn in particular,[58] actively encouraged the promotion of indigenous church leaders, and while Good was not a member of this society, he cherished the earnest acolytes it envisaged: 'A son, a brother, hears the truth. It is brought home to his conscience, and he yields himself to its convincing power. He confesses Christ before relatives and friends, and bears patiently with the reproaches and injuries which are heaped upon him. He is willing to renounce father and mother, and all that, in an earthly sense, is dear to man, rather than abandon that Gospel hope which he finds to be more precious than all the world.'[59]

Often Good elevated Native chiefs, such as Sashiatan, leader of church matters among the Nlha7kápmx, and Spintlum.[60] He also identified pupils of his boys' school, opened soon after the move from Yale,[61] as possible future aides.[62] But Good's principal sidekick was a Native named Silas

Nalee, one of his first converts and his only catechist. When Good left Lytton to preach elsewhere, or, as in 1874, to return to England to raise funds, Nalee, in tandem with Good's wife, took charge of St. Paul's. His influence on his peers seems to have been significant. Towards the end of his mission to the Nlha7kápmx, Good claimed that many had benefited from 'the presence among them of our native Catechist, Silas Nalee, whose quiet salutary influence I can perceive in innumerable small matters which would escape the attention of the ordinary observer.'[63] It is likely that this comment was pointed, however, for by this stage Good had run afoul of Acton Sillitoe, his new bishop, who clearly disapproved of Nalee and would later strike the catechist off the list of New Westminster's clergy.[64]

Good relied on Nalee and other auxiliaries, all of them baptized, to propagate Christianity where and when he could not. 'I have now multiplied my indirect influence so to speak a hundred fold,' he said of their exertions, 'in as much as they are all missionaries amongst their various homes and encampments.'[65] There was a very obvious advantage to these Native proselytes – they spoke the same language as those as yet unenlightened. If Good's mission had many ends, it aimed above all to convert, and for Good this meant nothing but 'the pure unadulterated Word of God.'[66] With non-English speakers this clearly posed a significant problem: how could Good impart the gospel to those who could not understand him?

His first response was to learn local dialects, and he studied relentlessly not only at Lytton but also during his time at Nanaimo and Yale. On the island in the early 1860s, Good focused on Chinook, a fairly simple trading language, and, Alexander Garrett aside, he was one of the more proficient Anglican linguists.[67] Yet Good was quite dissatisfied with Chinook, for it was an inflexible trading pidgin that could not begin to accommodate the complexity of the Scriptures. He lived to preach the pure unadulterated Word of God,[68] but the Word *was* adulterated when Chinook was its medium. Good knew this, and the poor translations he mustered ashamed him. In his reminiscences he gave a telling example. The occasion was Bishop Hills's first address to Good's Native congregation at Nanaimo: 'Lifting up his hands and speaking with great impressiveness he poetically apostrophized them thus, "Children of the forest!" Now all the Chinook at my command, as interpreter to his Lordship, would only render his metaphorical address into something like this, "Little ones walking amidst big sticks!" I never dare tell the Bishop what a come down my rendering of his words must have been in their hearing.'[69]

This anecdote touches on a concern shared by all Christian missionaries to non-European peoples: the uncertainty of translation. Forced to convey intricate biblical truths in an unfamiliar language, missionaries feared the fruits of their incompetence. As Homi Bhabha argues, there was no assurance that a translated text carried the same meaning as its original. 'The process of translation is the opening up of another contentious political and cultural site at the heart of colonial representation,' Bhabha tells us. 'Here the word of divine authority is deeply flawed by the assertion of the indigenous sign ... The Word could no longer be trusted to carry the truth when written or spoken in the colonial world by the European missionary.'[70] This was a considerable worry, of course, for conversion required the Truth, which translation evidently could not guarantee. Vicente Rafael is therefore right that 'translation defined to an important degree the limits and possibilities of conversion.' His observation pertains to Catholic missions to the Spanish Philippines, but has a more general relevance. As Good's anecdote intimates, the use of pidgins or Native vernaculars altered signification and thus gave hearers 'the possibility of dodging the full weight of the missionary's intent.'[71]

These hazards seemed to spur Good rather than dishearten him, and he plunged into the local tongue once he was established among the Nlha7kápmx. His initial assessment was that the language would comfortably receive translated Scripture,[72] but his learning curve was painfully shallow. His first translations were clumsy, if not entirely redundant.[73] It is doubtful whether his early converts had anything more than the most skeletal understanding of their new faith, and perhaps not even that. There is no evidence that Good even realized that significant differences separated dialects north and south of Lytton.[74] It would be a decade into his Nlha7kápmx mission before he had at hand tolerable translations of church rites, which he printed on a press donated by the Society for the Promotion of Christian Knowledge.[75] Until this time, one can only guess at the confusion and misunderstanding that must have reigned. One example will suffice. Good later confessed that it took him 'years of study' before he found a way of translating the single word 'forgive' into the language of his charges.[76] In the early 1870s, by his own admission, Good could not convey this concept with any real conviction. This of course begs the question: how real were converts who were unfamiliar with God's forgiveness?

Before his translations were complete Good relied heavily on his Native assistants. Indeed, the mission's Nlha7kápmx texts would themselves never have seen print without endless advice from Nalee. He and others played a pivotal role in Good's success. They spread the Word to those whom geography and language isolated from Good. When Sashiatan first approached Good at Yale in 1867 they spoke in Chinook, and it was only with the arrival of the second deputation that Good found an English speaker to act as interpreter.[77] For the next sixteen years Natives with English were invaluable. Good's mission would have been sterile without them. On one occasion he slept while his interpreter spent a long night answering questions from fellow Natives. To such aides Good was deeply indebted, and he acknowledged that their responsibilities were 'almost as great as my own.'[78]

## Discipline and Punish

Good co-opted Natives to police as well as teach one another, for Nlha7kápmx dispersion precluded a solitary vigil. His main helpers were the village chiefs, or at least those he recognized as chiefs;[79] in addition he appointed headmen, captains, and watchmen, thus spinning a web of surveillance over Nlha7kápmx village life. In large settlements such as Hecumshin (at Lytton), which had an estimated 270 residents, more than a dozen men were commissioned. At Stryen, where a little over 100 dwelt, there were half as many church officials: one chief, three headmen, one captain, and two watchmen. Kluukl, the smallest village with only twenty-three residents, had just a chief and a watchman.

These men were to observe the conduct of their peers and report back to Good, the chief on those officials beneath him. This hierarchy of surveillance was introduced early and survived the entire duration of the mission. Good expected his officials to take some initiative: to remind converts of their vows and perhaps to warn those who erred. They were also to introduce to Good any Natives who expressed an interest in Christianity, but who had not yet visited St. Paul's.[80] Rewards were offered for work well done; in 1873 twenty watchmen received special badges from Bishop Hills.[81] But support for this supervision was not unanimous, and villages were often torn. In one, the majority opinion endorsed Good's plans, but a handful of 'bad characters' vowed to kill the watchman if one were appointed; presumably the dissenters were appeased, for the village ultimately got its guardian.[82]

While we know little enough about village administration beyond this bare outline, it is clear that Good was able to cull valuable information on his charges. To the Reverend Brown's observation that the watchmen were 'mighty agents for good,'[83] we can add that they were mighty agents for Good – without them, the conduct of his sheep would have eluded him. This hierarchical surveillance closely resembles the Oblates' so-called Durieu system, described for Shuswap villages by Elizabeth Furniss,[84] yet it was *against* Catholic missions, especially those in what is now California, that Good conceived his mission philosophy. To Good's mind the beauty of his own system was its deferral of power. He reserved sharp words for missionaries who subordinated all their pupils, a mistake he associated with the Franciscans. It was hardly an original critique – one could argue that it originated with the great conservative writer Robert Southey, in his discussion of the infamous Jesuit reductions in

Paraguay[85] – but Good provided his own slant. He saw the concentration of power not only as impractical but as disposed to servile and thus disaffected subjects. By devolving responsibility to superior students, Good hoped to ease his own workload and satiate his flock. 'The Missionary must organize, organize, organize,' he said, 'remembering order is heaven's law, and not forgetting Exodus xviii.18, *govern them through themselves*.'[86]

This was a significant theory of mission, with a basic premise that self-government was good government. Good believed that only strict discipline would keep his charges on the road to Christ, and he promoted supervision to ensure an ordered environment. His working assumption was that 'we need to have enrolled under strict surveillance and discipline for a given time the avowed adherents of our teaching.'[87] This conviction was based on Good's understanding of the role of the church in conversion. Although he granted his charges the final decision to convert, Good maintained that not only did these neophytes require help with the interpretation of Scripture but that the church should anchor personal volition in firm social discipline. In this aspect of his work, Good borrowed selectively from the Church Fathers to whom he so often turned. Most obviously Augustine had advanced this view of conversion and, in doing so, had turned aside the humanist tradition that came before. Against his predecessors, Augustine held that serious ecclesiastical discipline should prepare the way for conversion.[88]

Yet Good's view of discipline was not strictly Augustinian. When Good claimed of his mission that 'We do all by moral suasion & cooperation & nothing by coer[c]ion & armed force,'[89] he echoed the young Augustine of *De Vera Religione*, who said of Christ: 'He did nothing by force, but all things by persuading and admonishing.'[90] Augustine, however, would not remain true to this dictum. Initially opposed to coercion on the grounds that forced conformity would often entail feigned conversion, Augustine ultimately changed his mind. The crucial factor was the development of his understanding of grace and predestination. Now that he invoked an omnipotent God, the mature Augustine no longer saw *ficti* as cause for concern. To worry about feigned conversion was to impute limits to God's power where none existed. Why doubt God's ability to 'seek out His own among the multitude who had conformed with a bad grace to the Catholic Church'?[91] Where previous Christians had rejected coercion because they saw freedom of choice as the essence of religion, Augustine placed self-determination in the greater context of divine power and advocated discipline that did not exclude force.

Good's position lay between the humanist and the antihumanist. He too would enforce discipline but, not a fatalist, was terribly troubled by *ficti*, and saw no need or place for coercion – as is evident from the instructions he gave to his watchmen, many of whom were initially unsure whether the discipline Good encouraged implied physical intervention. In 1873, when Hills was at St. Paul's, Matthew Meshall, a great Nlha7kápmx leader, put this question to the bishop. If gentle persuasion did not discourage sinners, should he and other sentinels resort to force? The answer was no, which appeared to please a zealous Native by the name of Timothy Shemakaltsee. 'Very good the Bishop's word,' he confirmed. 'So I understand. Meshall was asking for strong remedies, but such strong measures are not belonging to the Bishop's pastoral advice. Jesus [Christ] did not advise so. He did not pain his followers but used soft measures – not far from this advice of yours. I do not want to have any such painful powers.'[92]

Neither Good nor Hills sanctioned coercion as a means of conversion, yet Good's claim that his police maintained order 'without in any way invading the proper civil rights of those over whom they thus kept watch and which we were always most careful to respect' belies the true nature of this pastoral power.[93] The concept of civil rights was a misnomer. Its singular deception was to displace the site of legitimation of power onto Good's charges themselves. To invoke civil rights was to appeal to an abstract theory of social contract: Good protected his flock in order to defend their inalienable rights to equal treatment and freedom from servitude. This was the theory, at any rate. Foucault has shown that subjects ostensibly acting out a contract are in fact objects of social discipline, and so it was with Good's mission. The rhetoric of rights disguises rather than discloses the true exercise of power. The scholar's task is to distinguish between ideas and practices, and thus extricate 'mechanisms of discipline' from the misleading 'principle of right.'[94]

Good spoke of civil rights, but his mission was disciplinary, and its backbone was a hierarchy of surveillance. But how did this discipline actually function? To answer this question we have to return to the sacramental theology that structured Good's mission. As we have seen, conversion was an incremental process. It effectively began with enrolment in St. Paul's, and led through baptism and confirmation to communion. At any given time, Good had charges at each of these levels, from novice to full communicant. In other words, differentiation among Natives was the inevitable fruit of his mission. Further still, Good tried to ensure that this distinction was readily apparent. One means was to segregate his charges when they came together as a flock. Thus, when he formulated plans for a new church on relocating in 1870, his main concern was with its internal space. He described his flock as in 'the variously progressive stages of advancement from downright Paganism to that of prepared full membership,' and sought a church that would accommodate this hierarchy of rank.[95]

His wish was fulfilled, and partitioning became a hallmark of church services. Communicants were placed around the altar and nearest the chancel, and the other ranks were distributed in rows down the length of the church; behind the communicants were the baptized, then came catechumens, hearers, and finally penitents, all guarded in their respective divisions by Good's watchmen.[96] When Bishop Hills visited St. Paul's in May 1874, he was witness to this meticulous segregation. As Hills called on the newly baptized to join the congregation, they entered one by one the church's west door and filed down the aisle past lesser ranks to gather in a space left vacant near the chancel, thus joining the previous converts, who stood as one.[97]

Because status was not fixed, neither was one's place in the house of God. Rank was both manifest and fluid: catechumens could see the baptized before them, and the baptized, in turn, saw a higher rank and thus every reason to remain true. All charges were afforded the same goal of conversion to Christianity, but each week they were reminded that some had advanced further than others; the context of conversion was palpably social, and religious spirit was fused with a worldly incentive to match or better one's peers. But the mission punished as well as promoted, and it was through rank that Good exacted discipline. If his assistants informed him that one of his flock had violated church rules, this individual would be summarily punished, which normally meant exclusion from the fellowship, worship, and sacraments of the church.[98] This generally took place on Sundays when, in front of all other charges, offenders faced Good and received their punishment,[99] having the option of leaving the church before they were officially excommunicated.[100] During the same service, those who had served time outside the fold, but who had shown new consistency, were returned to their former status.

This weekly exercise of discipline was much closer to the Early Church rite of *exomologesis* than to the private confession that later dominated the Western Church.[101] As with the patristic ritual, Nlha7kápmx confession took place within a public ceremony. Another parallel was the content of a confession that did not involve a detailed litany of sins committed but a simple admission that sin had occurred. Discipline was administered when subjects committed quite specific public crimes, such as idolatry and adultery; this was not an ongoing private confessional through which subjects traced the slightest fluctuations of desire and ill will. The Church Fathers, who promoted exclusion from fellowship and sacraments as the most fitting punishment, provided Good with this model of discipline. Private confession, which came later in the history of the church, was strictly against Anglican policy until the time of the Oxford Movement, and while Newman and Pusey were advocates, many other Tractarians continued to frown on the practice.[102] Hills was among them and advised Good to discourage confession as a private form of penitence.[103] St. Paul's relied instead on a weekly ritual of public discipline.

'Rank,' Foucault writes of disciplinary power, 'in itself serves as a reward or punishment,'[104] a maxim to which Good's mission conforms. Faith and true conduct were rewarded with graduation, while transgression led to exclusion. The penance Good proposed did not involve physical pain,[105] but he admitted that the discipline was severe[106] and that many of his charges kicked against it.[107] He infused the process of learning with powerful dualisms: belonging and exile, enlightenment and ignorance. Power operated in and through a social body. We could say that this mission was *normalizing* – for some scholars the chief disposition of a disciplinary power.[108] By way of the sacraments, Good guaranteed distinction in the same moment that he preached conformity. Faith was the elixir tendered to one and all, and conversion its common product; it is only an *apparent* paradox that difference was the means to secure this sameness. If Natives had not been distinguished by progress and discriminated by rank, would they have toiled to convert? And without the prospect of exclusion, would they have observed Good's rigorous moral codes?

Normalization was nothing more than colonialism in practice. As we saw in Chapter 2, Good held to Augustine's vision of a Catholic Church and contrasted the will to unity with the Donatist preserve of a superior moral elect. Good was a colonizer in the classical sense: he reached out to others and sought to subsume their difference into sameness. This singular identity was the body of Christ, and its consummation was in communion. Through the hierarchy of rank, Good negotiated the transition from savagery to salvation. He insisted that this procedure was not the Donatist policy of 'separating by man's judgement the chaff from the wheat,'[109] and he was right. The Donatists segregated good from bad to prevent bad from soiling good; Good, on the other hand, separated in order to unite. Rather than school Natives as common subjects, he individualized, for uniform treatment seemed destined to produce nominal converts.[110] By treating every Native as one, and placing that one in relation to others, he trusted that, ultimately, all would converge, each energized by the conversion of another.

Normalization turned on a dialectics of individuality and totality, difference and conformity, hierarchy and homogeneity. The 'true way to spread the gospel,' Good once claimed, was 'to enrol all volunteers into a probationary army; to let them continue to live amidst their old surroundings as good seed amongst the promiscuous grain, and so that both should grow together – *with and yet not the same.*'[111] This statement encapsulates the philosophy of Good's mission, the machinery of his colonial intent. The debate with Donatism is pivotal because it was against Donatism that Good sharpened his strategy. He denied the impulse to shield good from bad and thus rejected not only the Donatists but also contemporaries such as Duncan and Robert Tomlinson.[112] The Nlha7kápmx would remain one, for it was the tension between good and bad that, in theory, inspired the bad to good. Scattered among converts, nonbelievers were with and yet not the same: of the same flesh and blood, they would commune in the same body of Christ, but, for a moment within the same, they were other, heathen. 'In a sense,' Foucault writes, 'the power of normalization imposes homogeneity; but it individualizes by making it possible to measure gaps, to determine levels.'[113] It was this power that braced the conversion of Good's charges – individualizing, ranking, and segregating, but ultimately imposing homogeneity.

### The Reality of Conversion

Some readers may doubt the wisdom of appealing to Foucault on two separate fronts: his discussion of the Early Church pastorate, and his more familiar work on techniques of discipline in modern Western society. Ostensibly, we have here two distinct modalities of power, and two very different Foucaults. Yet a strong case can be made for viewing Good's mission through both lenses. Three points in particular need to be clarified. First, Good was a man of eclectic tastes. As we saw in Chapter 2, Anglican missionary thought was a strange hybrid, at once modern and premodern: in some respects it fitted within prevailing discourses of empire, in others within the seasoned theology of the Church Fathers. Good was in his element with Augustine, whose pastoral model is more or less the one Foucault recounted, but he was also a child of his age, and as a product of nineteenth-century Europe he knew its methods of discipline; indeed, his own training at St. Augustine's entailed a life of rigid order and regularity.[114] In the mission field, Good drew inspiration from both patristic study and personal experience, and yoked disciplines of the day to a pastoral power of old.

Second, Foucault makes no secret of the fact that, to his mind, the origins of disciplinary power are in ancient and medieval Christianity. In the years after *Discipline and Punish*, Foucault's lectures and writings turned increasingly to Christianity, and one can read this shift as (in part) an effort to uncover the genealogy of the modern powers he had exposed. In these later years he addressed questions of confession, ethics, and sexuality. Some authors have challenged Foucault's effort to root modern institutional discipline in early Christian tradition, but his argument has not been discredited.[115]

Third, there is no logical reason to distinguish pastoral and disciplinary power. Although he generally analyzes them separately, Foucault never makes them mutually exclusive. In fact he infers that pastoral power is *itself* disciplinary, in the sense that a power dedicated to the well-being of its subjects requires formal strategies of order. This theme emerges in Foucault's later work. At one point he writes that 'a power whose task it is to take charge of life needs continuous regulatory and corrective mechanisms,'[116] and at another that 'discipline was never more valorised than at the moment when it became important to manage a population.'[117] His broader point is that discipline has never been confined to the institutional setting to which some critics reduce it, but saturates any power exercised over a flock and concerned to ensure its welfare.

Good's pastorate rested on hierarchical surveillance and normalization, which, for Foucault, are the twin pinions of disciplinary power.[118] But we must stay with Foucault further yet, for his contention that observation and classification merge in examination, the quintessential ritual of discipline,[119] casts more light on Good's mission. The examination of Good's charges normally occurred during Bishop Hills's annual visit to St. Paul's, a significant occasion for all involved. Good described it as the year's main event,[120] and Hills, mired in a fractious rift with Cridge during the glory days of St. Paul's, was pleased to put his back to such troubles and get on with the work of conversion. The bishop's visit also stirred the Nlha7kápmx. While Sunday services attracted Natives from throughout Good's parish, the greatest number always came when Hills was in town. For days in advance they descended on St. Paul's and set up camp, each band flying the mission flag above its tents.[121] While he and his flock awaited the bishop, Good preached in the open air; his church was diminutive, and Hills generally arrived in the kind weather of spring or early summer. The spectacle of several hundred people congregated around Good's parsonage was dramatic, and he[122] and others[123] evoked it in rich prose.

The bishop's stay was usually brief and always frantic. Other than to check up on Good, the purpose of the trip was to examine candidates for the sacraments. In the mid-1870s, when Good's star was rising and so many of his flock were converting, the two men worked frenetically. Some days they held six separate services, each of which could last several hours; on Sunday 1 June 1873, Hills baptized over 100 Natives, receiving them from 7:30 am until past 10 at night.[124] During these services Good's charges had to face Hills and answer his questions. Most converts endured this rite of passage at some stage of their conversion, many more than once. The routine was always the same. In a formal ceremony, attended not only by Good but by many fellow Nlha7kápmx, candidates were required to recount the details of their conversion. This generally involved an admission of sin, an expression of remorse, and a testimony to new-found faith. Each individual was examined in turn, and Hills decided their fate. If they answered satisfactorily, the next sacrament was at hand; if not, it would likely be another year before the bishop returned. Hills recorded many of these Nlha7kápmx statements – their narratives of conversion to Christianity.

One cannot overstate the importance of these examinations. When we read of indigenous conversion, we are too often limited to bald statistics that privilege numbers and neglect process; here is evidence from Good, Hills, and others of the social context in which Natives attested to their faith. With this information, we can try to understand Native conversion *in situ*. Still, we must recognize the limits of reconstruction. The crucial distinction is between the text of conversion and the experience itself; between the narratives penned by Hills and the conversions they ostensibly signified. This distinction is central to Karl F. Morrison's incisive writing on understanding conversion. His main assumption, that it is impossible to recover the process of conversion and the emotions it entailed, is surely correct. And because 'the experience of conversion is lost,' it follows that 'all that exists for study is what texts call conversion.'[125] While we are unable to salvage Nlha7kápmx conversion itself, there is enough evidence to inspect the manner in which the experience of conversion became its narrative.

Consider a question derived from Good's report of the 1874 examinations: 'with the Bishop seated in the midst, the clergy at his side, the chiefs in a circle forming the Council, and the watchmen surrounding the whole, maintaining order' *is it surprising* that 'one by one these once pagan dwellers in darkness, turned by God's grace into other men, declare their allegiance to the Cross and Church of Christ'?[126] Or, to phrase the question another way, was it really God's grace that turned the Nlha7kápmx into other men (and women), or was their testimony in fact tied to the exercise of worldly power, manifested in this instance by a piercing, hierarchical gaze?

One could argue that this question is specious, for godly and human power do not belong to the same order of things. But even if we accept a theology of grace, should we ignore the ritual in which Native subjects, saved by the unmerited favour of God, professed their conversion to Christianity? Of course not. Ultimately there is no way to recover the impetus to conversion, be it worldly or divine or both, but it would be wrong to overlook social power, especially since Good, with Augustine, emphasized the role of the church in procuring converts. To read God into Nlha7kápmx conversion is to give the Anglicans the benefit of the doubt, but does not preclude situated analysis. Talal Asad makes this case better than most. He describes conversion as 'a process of divine enablement through which the intransitive work of becoming a Christian, of attaining true consciousness, can be completed. But that divine function has also been aided by human institutions that impose the conditions necessary for liberation from false consciousness. *The Church in this world has an essential task to secure the Truth through human power.'*[127] The purpose of this discussion is to show the power of ritual in determining the fact of conversion.

The vital feature of the examination is that it blended hierarchical observation and normalization in a single ritual of discipline. Hills was examiner and ultimate arbiter, but this was not a private affair. The candidate was examined before his or her peer group, and in the presence of clergy, chiefs, and watchmen. In Foucault's words, here was a 'normalizing gaze'[128] that inspected subjects and classified their faith. This gaze is apparent in accounts of examination for both catechumenship and baptism. Hills's first report is from his visit to Lytton in 1868, when he accepted four catechumens after public examination, and readmitted a penitent to the same rank. He described one of the men as formerly 'a notorious sorcerer, & steeped in crimes.' That this convert renounced his sins 'on his knees in the presence of the people' is clearly significant. As Hills emphasized, confidential confession this was not: 'A number of questions were asked him & the people were desired to say if they approved of his admission into the number of Catechumens.'[129] Good's account of the acceptance of catechumens more or less duplicates the bishop's: the examinee knelt, and examination occurred before a congregation.[130]

The first baptisms at St. Paul's Church took place in June 1872, when Spintlum and two dozen others were admitted after 'a most searching examination & investigation of character & repute.'[131] Good expanded on this account in a letter to his sponsors, again stressing that the candidates were examined in public, and that as such they were 'the cynosure of all eyes, the subject of an unsparing and searching investigation as to habit and practice,' for the duration of their interrogation.[132] Hills had the same take. 'Each case was watched silently,' he wrote of examinations in 1873; 'all eyes were gazing upon the person baptized.'[133]

The proof of conversion was established in the face of intense public scrutiny. Yet if the examination situated Natives in a field of surveillance, it also secured them in writing. The fact of being watched ensured the extraction of knowledge and the creation of a conversion story – recorded by the examiner. As the product of conversion but also its subject, the individual was constituted as both effect and object of knowledge. The conversion narrative captured this knowledge and made it the subject's truth. In what sense was this process normalizing? Certainly to the extent that Native conversion was to a common faith and identity. Furthermore, it was against a Christian norm that success and failure were gauged. Candidates were expected to demonstrate familiarity with the gospel, but it was not unknown for Hills to reject those whose knowledge or conviction withered under inspection.[134] The examination obliged, but did not guarantee, conformity; it measured faith, distributed rank, and either confirmed or refuted conversion.

Yet this ritual was normalizing in a more profound sense. To access this dimension, we need to question the form and function of conversion narratives. As Paula Fredriksen has shown, the fact that the convert articulates conversion a posteriori has significant implications. First, because the convert surveys the past from the present and composes an account of the past in light of that present, the story of conversion is always retrospective rather than contemporary. As a result, the conversion narrative describes not the past so much as the present it endorses. Second, the convert's present often involves membership of an institution that ratifies, and perhaps fostered, the conversion that has taken place. As such, there is generally a precedent for the new convert's conversion and a prevailing discourse for enunciating it. If the convert's own narrative does conform to an accepted paradigm of conversion, this personal account not only proves the authenticity of the convert but reinforces the theological tradition that he or she has joined.[135]

These comments bear directly on our reading of Nlha7kápmx conversion. When Natives stepped up to face Hills, the stories they told were not innocent tales of enlightenment. The conversion narrative necessarily muddied ingenuous sentiment with worldly discretion. The Anglican injunction was to pour forth one's pure religious spirit, but many Natives will have known the form and content of a judicious response – if only from observing the examination of peers. To tell of conversion was to define the past through the present, and the contemporary Nlha7kápmx predicament was that of a people encountering new faith; this was a religion with its own understanding of the conversion experience. When examinees stood as candidates for baptism or any other sacrament, they were expected not only to demonstrate steady belief but to describe conversion in terms acceptable to the church. Conversion was a personal experience, yet was only valid if it corresponded to an approved model of religious change. Thus, if Natives were judged by the evidence of their faith, they were also classified by the normality of their conversion. If their experience mirrored that of bona fide Christians, they were clearly real converts. If, however, their account was unfamiliar, they were either insincere or ignorant.[136]

Conformity entailed a normal conversion as well as a normal faith. We can gauge something of this typical conversion from Nlha7kápmx narratives. Its most conspicuous feature is the contrast between an enlightened present and a sinful past. 'Long ago I was very wicked,' Chil-lool-uk had said, 'now I repent & have my desire for baptism.' Other narratives offered the same stark distinction between then and now. These were the words of Isaac Vikilikapascut, baptized in 1872, as a candidate for confirmation the following year: 'From my birth (said Isaac) I grew up a liar & a thief, my whole soul was tainted & corrupt – but Mr. Good brought us God's grace & this has led me on.'[137] Although this form of testimony linked Natives to a state of original sin, contrition prepared the way for deliverance, and thus for the sanctification of an evil past. As Rafael argues in another context, this distinctive narrative structure 'splits the convert into a hierarchical opposition between a past, sinful self and a present interrogating conscience.'[138]

The roots of this understanding of conversion are with the Early Church, and in particular with the prototypical conversions of Paul and Augustine. Each man experienced a dramatic moment of conversion, Paul on the road to Damascus and Augustine in the garden at Milan. Both described conversion as a sudden but permanent change: the rebirth of a sinner. The essence of this classical narrative is that the old was wrong and the new is right; with conversion, bad habits are broken. This concept of a peripeteia has long served as the preeminent model of conversion to Christianity. Described in a celebrated book by A.D. Nock,[139] the notion of conversion as a radical break with the past normally assumes baptism as the moment of awakening to new life.

Yet recent scholarship has revamped this understanding of conversion, in large part by returning to Paul and Augustine and reconsidering their experiences. Fredriksen argues with the thesis that Paul's conversion is central to his theology, an assumption that, she suggests, has misled authors who, in consequence, overinterpret Paul's fleeting references to this event. She maintains, moreover, that the word conversion is itself deceptive, for Paul's was a lateral movement within Judaism (from the Pharisaic party to the Jesus party) rather than a conversion from one religion to another.[140] Morrison finds evidence that Paul's conversion was a gradual process, not a single, shattering revelation. The idea that his conversion entailed lasting moral reform sits uneasily with Paul's ongoing struggle with temptation.[141]

Morrison rethinks Augustine's experience along similar lines, and says that the mature Augustine doubted whether any conversion, including his own, was permanent and irreversible, and thus continued to struggle with uncertainty and fear during a gradual, erratic conversion that lasted, effectively, a lifetime.[142] Much the same point has been made by Peter Brown, who reads Augustine's debate with the Pelagians as a dispute over the meaning of conversion. Pelagius argued that conversion offered human perfection, in the sense that baptism signified divorce from the past, and thus from sin. The disciples of Pelagius were inclined 'to look at their own past from across the chasm of baptism' (a proclivity very much apparent in Nlha7kápmx conversion narratives). After W.H.C. Frend, Brown reads this Pelagian theology as a 'Christianity of discontinuity,' with baptism the disjuncture between sin and sanctity. This understanding of conversion, associated most closely with Gnosticism and common to Tertullian, Ambrose, and (maybe) Paul, was that of the younger Augustine, who interpreted his own conversion in this light. But against Pelagius, Augustine would ultimately deny that habit could be broken; he came to insist that humans could not achieve a truly virtuous life, and that since desire was never vanquished, baptism signified not a new start but a life of 'precarious convalescence.'[143]

Linked to this revisionism is the broader recognition that the meaning of conversion to Christianity is mutable. As scholars have reinterpreted Paul and Augustine, so it has emerged that the concept of a single moment of transformation is but one among many handles on the conversion experience. The idea of conversion has both a history and a geography.[144] Morrison examines understandings of conversion in twelfth-century western Europe, and concludes that at that time people thought of conversion as a continuous, testing process, not as a split between a sinful past and a blessed present.[145] Judith Pollmann makes an intriguing case for the fact that sixteenth-century Protestant models of conversion invoked evolutionary rather than revolutionary change. The Reformers were generally wary of a language of innovation. It was not Protestantism that was new, they argued, but Catholicism, for it was the Roman Church that corrupted ancient Christianity; since Protestantism was retailed as a religion of tradition rather than of change, the understanding of conversion as new life was inappropriate. Instead, Protestant conversion entailed 'learning old truths and ... unlearning bad habits.'[146]

The Nlha7kápmx came to the question of conversion through Good, and he approached it as a High Church Anglican but also, of course, as a missionary. The classical idea of conversion as a clean break with the past had an undeniable currency in Good's imperial world, which contrasted savagery with civility and rarely allowed for a murky middle ground. Theologies of conversion were refracted through discourses of empire, which traded in antipodes and thus could easily accommodate a dualistic model of religious change. If to convert the heathen was to make Christian, it was reasonable to assume that only dramatic enlightenment would purge the convert of savage residue. And indeed, it was more or less the traditional interpretation of Paul that Good, as an Anglican, advanced. In his *Laws of Ecclesiastical Polity*, Richard Hooker, the greatest systematic theologian of the Church of England, submitted that 'by Baptism we are made new creatures'; baptism 'both extinguisheth in [Christ] our former sin, and beginneth in us a new condition of life.'[147] Good's Tractarian sympathies will have reinforced his belief in baptism as peripeteia, which allowed for the rebirth of sinners and the colonization of their otherness.

This is not to suggest that empire allowed only one model of conversion.

As Sabine MacCormack demonstrates in her quite exceptional study of the Inca encounter with Christianity, some missionaries saw conversion as an extension and improvement of indigenous beliefs, not as a radical fracture. In early-seventeenth-century Peru, Garcilaso de la Vega identified continuity of both thought and ceremony between his Christianity and the religion of the Incas. To convert was not to replace falsity with truth but to attain spiritual maturity. Comparing Inca religion to his own childhood, De la Vega described conversion as a process of ageing rather than of rebirth.[148] While many discourses of empire likened Natives to children, some authors maintain that because this metaphor secured a powerful model of conversion as evolution, it was more essential to missionary discourse than to any other.[149]

Yet Good seldom referred to Natives as children; they were 'savages.' He saw no parallel between Nlha7kápmx religion and Christianity, and the conversion he promoted was not a process of elaboration on extant belief – he sought to tear his charges away from their custom.[150] Good himself associated this explicit cleavage with Paul and Augustine. The sharp contrast between old and new is the basis of many Nlha7kápmx narratives. Samuel Honhomslot, a chief of eight villages, recounted his awakening 'to newness of life.'[151] Another man, Huah-quelsh, spoke of a dark past and an enlightened present: 'I was black as night. The word came and made light (illumined) my heart.'[152]

It is important to note, however, that Good shared something of Augustine's doubt. He never imagined that his converts had achieved absolute virtue. Baptism *was* a significant divide, but although Nlha7kápmx Christians were no longer 'savages,' they would continue to fight temptation[153] and would not always prevail. Resigned to the fact that some would lapse, if not recant, Good impressed on converts the great weight of baptism and made it known that sin after this sacrament was not the same as sin before.[154] Conversion was ongoing in the sense that the struggle never ended, but it was in baptism that savagery effectively gave way to sanctity. In this sense Good's view of conversion, and the one he conveyed to his charges, was that of the Tractarian Pusey, who defined conversion as 'the first turning of the soul to God after it has been estranged from him,' but who also acknowledged that 'we all ... ever need conversion; we have ever some weaknesses.'[155]

But this sense of conversion as an uncertain, continuous process is not apparent in Nlha7kápmx conversion narratives; most of Hills's examinees claimed to have 'cast away' their sin, as one put it.[156] Their accounts invoke a new Truth incongruous with the error of old. But we should not be misled. The average Nlha7kápmx, according to Teit, saw 'no contradiction between the stories of his forefathers and those of the missionary,'[157] which suggests that the true Native perspective on conversion was *not* a sense of newness and enlightenment. How can we explain this disjuncture between the experience of conversion and its text? We must read beyond words to their context. The narrative of rebirth must be viewed against the backdrop of prolonged social discipline, and more especially in light of the examinations during which it took shape.

When candidates responded to the bishop's questions, their answers had to weather not only a public gaze but a regime of truth that included an orthodox account of conversion. It is clear that although some examinees gave poor testimony, there were means at hand to sanitize their narratives. Thus, when Archdeacon Wright accompanied Hills to Lytton in 1877, he was witness to an intriguing ritual. The examination service dragged on and on, for candidates were given several chances to describe their conversion properly. 'By allowing time for thought,' Wright wrote, 'we always secured a sensible answer.'[158] His comments point not only to the gap between experience and narrative but to the fact that the Anglicans had a particular conversion story in mind, and were prepared to wait to hear it. One wonders how many wrong answers were rejected first, and whether this method could weed out feigned conversions. Wright almost implies that conversion was assumed and that the examination was a foregone conclusion – not the way that Good had it.

Other evidence supports the view that conversion narratives were produced, not imparted. On 29 May 1868 the bishop heard a number of weak, inadmissible answers, at which point Spintlum intervened. 'The people had not answered well,' Hills wrote in his diary. 'They knew a good deal. [Spintlum] would speak for them. He would tell me what they knew.'[159] Again, this is a telling observation, for it draws back the veil of the conversion text. Behind this veil we find a strange ritual, during which Native fraternity, or Anglican patience, could turn tongue-tied confession into a lucid account of conversion – a narrative pleasing to the Anglicans. This does not prove a single Nlha7kápmx conversion to be less than genuine, but nor does it suggest devout, thirsty converts, convinced of their sin and content in a new faith. It is likely that some of those who faltered were earnest, and merely struggled to find their words. But maybe there were some who, subject to a normalizing power, conformed to the need to convert, with little understanding of what it meant and no familiarity with the god they ostensibly worshipped.

These caveats are critical to our understanding of Good's mission, if only because the Anglicans would have us believe that Nlha7kápmx conversion was a fait accompli. Their favourite word was 'reality.' Wright saw the examination answers as evidence of the 'reality' of Good's work,[160] and Woods, his predecessor as archdeacon and another eager visitor to St. Paul's, also spoke of the 'realness' of the mission's converts.[161] It was a powerful thesis, propagated by Hills too,[162] and when editors of the

Columbia Mission printed Nlha7kápmx testimonies in their fourteenth annual report, they marketed the text as a testament to the 'reality' of Native conversion.[163] We must read this discourse in the context of the exercise of power, for conversion was secured through discipline, and the truth of its reality was verified in ritual. Conversion narratives constitute proof only to the extent that the Nlha7kápmx summoned appropriate words – sometimes with prompting or assistance, and often in obedience rather than ardour. When Foucault says that power 'produces reality,'[164] this reality includes the 'reality' of conversion.

### Conversion to Christianity?

What then can we say of Nlha7kápmx conversion? Beyond the facts that many did convert, and that conversion was coursed through the exercise of worldly power, it is hard to reach any firm conclusions. As we have seen, conversion narratives probably say more about Anglican understandings of conversion than about Native experience of religious change. If we were to follow recent trends in scholarship on colonialism, we might think of these texts as examples of what Homi Bhabha calls anticolonial mimicry.[165] By this he means that indigenous affirmation of colonial Christian truth should be understood not as compliance but as covert resistance in the form of facetious parody. This interpretation would reduce conversion to Natives humouring the church to deflect its criticism – a case of tacit public acceptance, but private denial.

Does this perspective have any relevance to our understanding of Nlha7kápmx conversion? If Native interest in Good was purely spiritual, it does not. We must remember that for all Good's influence on his charges, they approached him at Yale rather than vice versa. His mission was not involuntary, and his was not a power that, by its very nature, obliged submission or resistance. The Nlha7kápmx were free to court other missionary churches, or indeed to ignore Christianity altogether – and some evidently did.[166] Teit did later maintain that many converts were only superficially Christian,[167] but to read this infraction as resistance is to suppose that conversion was an obligation. Within the immediate context of the Nlha7kápmx engagement with Christianity, it was not.

Yet mission work cannot be divorced from the more physical colonialism (such as seizure of land) that it often buttressed and masked. As we saw in Chapter 1, it is possible that some Nlha7kápmx embraced Good as an advocate in land disputes; Chapter 7 will offer further evidence for this motive. If it was indeed Good's worldly power that Natives coveted, their conversion has to be read as part of their broader response to a colonialism that *was* enforced. When the Nlha7kápmx were robbed of land and resources, they had to choose between surrender and insurgency, and to secure the aid of sympathetic colonizers was one way to resist.

Good's fear that Nlha7kápmx interest was disingenuous was certainly not ungrounded. There is no way of knowing how many Natives evaded Good's intent, but conversion was a means to indulge him and, through his agency, resist white power at large. This interpretation would appeal to Bhabha, who feels that where the colonized appropriate colonial knowledge, they put it to their own specific ends.[168] It seems likely that for some Nlha7kápmx, at least, conversion entailed an irreverent reading of Christianity and a politicization of its Truth.

This interpretation has its problems, however. Most significantly, it limits Native power and knowledge to the space of colonial discourse. This is the thrust of Benita Parry's criticism of Bhabha's thesis.[169] She argues that by locating indigenous people within the confines of colonial discourse – albeit in an inappropriate posture that disturbs the meaning and message of colonialism – Bhabha ignores alternative texts and other traditions of knowledge. His mimicry is purely an ironic imitation of dogma, and his resistance boils down to deconstruction of the textual footing of colonialism. In Parry's words, 'the scenario written by colonialism is given a performance by the native that estranges and undermines the colonialist script.'[170] Bhabha reduces Native agency to one dimension, namely perversion of colonial intent and displacement of its authority. Parry's concern is that this gesture overlooks knowledges that predate and survive colonialism.

These comments bear directly on the history of Nlha7kápmx belief during the era of Good's mission. If Bhabha's theory suggests an impious reading of Christianity, Parry inspires us to look beyond the scope of colonialist knowledge to different traditions of thought. In this respect Teit's ethnography is invaluable. He knew that Nlha7kápmx converts had not simply substituted one faith for another, yet he sensed that they had done more than infuse Christianity with Native content. Indeed, he describes Nlha7kápmx conversion much as MacCormack does Inca conversion – as a chapter in the history of *indigenous* religion, as well as a chapter in the history of Christianity.[171] It is clear, for instance, that a number of biblical tales, such as the great flood, and Adam and Eve in the Garden of Eden, infiltrated Nlha7kápmx mythology.[172] So did Christian spiritual beings, sometimes with ambiguous results; in one story recorded by Teit, the Nlha7kápmx 'Old-One' was confused with God.[173] This was not conversion as Good understood it. Native spirituality accommodated aspects of the faith he offered. Traditional Nlha7kápmx beliefs survived Good's mission, despite his efforts to extirpate them. Teit noted that even those converts who attended church regularly and consistently said their prayers would put the Bible aside at the end of the day and tell their children time-honoured Nlha7kápmx stories.[174] It may just be that the most enduring legacy of conversion was a Christian edge to these tales.

# 6
# Morals

Good was in British Columbia 'not only to evangelize but to civilize,'[1] for it was clear to him that the 'heathen' lacked Christian civility as well as Christian Truth. When he first lectured at Lytton in May 1867, he told his future charges that if he did establish a mission among them, moral reform would go hand in hand with religious teaching.[2] Like other Anglican missionaries, he was convinced that moral improvement required enlightenment. Thus, while the colonial government encouraged mission work as an important means to civilize Natives, the Anglicans saw it as the *only* means, for morality without religion was deemed morality without motive, and civilization without Christianity was therefore 'lame charity.'[3] A civilized Native population was by definition a Christian population. 'To preach Christ,' Good said of the Anglican burden in the mission field, 'must be our first purpose.'[4]

Moral reform was more than a handmaiden to evangelization. Mindful of feigned conversion, Good doubted the value of confession alone and required evidence of 'changed life' before he would baptize his charges. Although moral calibre became his principal barometer of Native faith, he did not belittle the examination ritual that verified conversion; he ruled, rather, that Natives should not get the chance to prove themselves to Hills 'upon their merely *saying* they believe.'[5] Assuming that daily conduct revealed the inner truth that words could obfuscate, Good established a set of ethical qualifications for baptism. He demanded 'effectual moral change of Heart & Feeling & an eradication of all superstitions and heathen fancies, with, of course, an outward abandonment of all old forms & ways that are positively antagonistical to moral & spiritual growth & development.'[6] More specifically, Natives were to forsake 'medicine-men' and traditional burial customs and to resist the temptations of gambling and alcohol.

The chief criterion of moral worth, however, was marital status. According to Michel Foucault, it is common for a single element of personal conduct to assume unusual importance in social constructions of morality.

He speaks of the 'determination of ethical substance' as the process by which this delimitation occurs. Individual men and women, he suggests, are encouraged to look upon one aspect of living as the 'prime material' of their moral being.[7] As subjects of St. Paul's, the Nlha7kápmx, many of whom were polygamous, were told that sexuality constituted ethical substance, and that monogamy was moral. As we shall see, Good was uneasy with this emphasis on sexuality and would have preferred to assess morality, and thus conversion, otherwise. But his mandate was nonnegotiable; the church decreed that polygamy was unchristian, so polygamists could not be baptized. This moral imperative dominated Good's mission despite his reservations, and must be tied to the politics of conversion, for a change of heart was gauged by works rather than by faith. Because the evidence for conversion was in morality, and because marital status determined ethical substance, the duality of polygamy and monogamy became the duality of heathen and Christian, and Good's appraisal of faith was reduced, *malgré lui*, to an arithmetics of sex.

Good's mission to civilize the Nlha7kápmx was of more lasting significance than his efforts to give them new faith. Natives could listen to the gospel and acknowledge its truth, and yet avoid its meaning; but either they were polygamists or they were not. Native conversion proves neither new beliefs nor the rejection of old ones, but because it entailed a particular way of life, conversion clearly *was* real for some Nlha7kápmx, especially for those for whom monogamy was foreign. Anglican moral codes were taken very seriously indeed and caused soul-searching and grief among both men and women. Indeed, Native resistance to monogamy may partly explain the collapse of Good's mission towards the end of the 1870s. James Teit, who argued that Nlha7kápmx Christianity was, in many cases, only skin deep, identified a decline in polygyny as one of the main products of conversion. Whereas in traditional Nlha7kápmx society most men had more than one wife, the majority were monogamous by the turn of the century.[8]

**Paralyzing Dogma**

The essential point is that sex was not only a matter of sensation and pleasure, of law and taboo, but also of truth and falsehood, that the truth of sex became something fundamental, useful, or dangerous, precious or formidable: in short, that sex was constituted as a problem of truth.
— Michel Foucault[9]

In his reminiscences Good tells the story of a Nlha7kápmx man named Peter Shako, an early convert to Christianity who married at St. Paul's before leaving his wife, Rebecca, for another (unnamed) woman.[10] Good had then told Shako that unless he relinquished his new partner and returned to his wife, he would be excluded from the church and treated as an outcast. Although for some time he rebuffed Good's authority, Shako had eventually crumbled, expressing remorse for his sins and begging forgiveness – which Good, delighted by this turn of events, gave. 'The restoration,' it says in Good's reminiscences, 'was complete.' All these years later, Good remembered Shako as the first of many converts to breach Anglican rules of sexual propriety, and, as he turned his mind back three decades, he wrote that 'the custom of concubinage and polygamy as practised by the Indian tribes had come to the front with us and caused us no small trouble and perplexity.'[11]

Good's struggle with Nlha7kápmx sexuality in general, and with polygyny in particular, was a persistent feature of his mission; it fractured otherwise strong bonds with many Native men and generated a grave dispute with Bishop Hills. The two men first discussed matters in 1868. Good, having encountered polygyny in Nanaimo,[12] had initially envisaged strict moral rules for Nlha7kápmx members of his mission: he would only baptize monogamists, and any convert who took up with additional spouses would be excommunicated. Yet when the bishop visited Lytton in 1868, Good confessed to serious doubts and suggested that they reconsider mission policy. He had one major change in mind: the church should welcome men who were already married to two or more women, while preventing monogamous male converts from taking a second wife. If Good were to have his way, the application of moral law would be prospective but not retrospective.[13]

It is important to stress that Good did not see this proposal as a capitulation to his charges. He was a sly man. Since instant assault on Nlha7kápmx ways would dull their enthusiasm for Christianity, long-term change was a safer objective than immediate moral reform. Good figured that if missionaries administered milk and then meat, Native beliefs would gradually pass away with the older generation, and a new crop would emerge 'speaking our language, adopting our habits, and possessing our faith.'[14] And to a degree he was right for, as Teit later observed, it was the younger Nlha7kápmx who adapted to colonial culture, and their elders who maintained tradition.[15] For the sake of real change in the long run, Good was willing to be less rigid in the short term. This much is evident in his perspective on polygyny. To accept polygamists was to tacitly accept Native custom and thus appease an inquisitive flock; but to insist that all others remain monogamous was to ensure that monogamy would ultimately prevail. Good's logic is hard to resist:

Had I for instance attacked Polygamy in the first instance and violently sought to rid individuals of what I might consider their superfluous household appendages, *before* they were full Catechumens even, much less baptized subjects of the New Kingdom of Light & Purity, I should, I feel sure, have killed the whole gravitating motion towards us and raised at once an insuperable barrier against our progress. But by laying down the rule to begin with, that all former contracts were to be respected and only subsequent matrimonial engagements were to be regulated by our own standard, I at once satisfied a sense of natural equity most keenly yet intensely regarded & upheld by this independent and clear sighted people, and at the same time prepared the way for the eventual extinction of the entire system.[16]

It is unclear whether this passage, written in the spring of 1870, refers to the twelve-month period prior to Good's discussion with Hills, or to the two years immediately after it. If Good's description was of his moral policy at the time of writing, he had studiously ignored his bishop, who in 1868 ruled that there would be no concession; monogamy would remain an absolute requirement for baptism. When Good recalled this judgment in his reminiscences, he gave every impression of having respected it, albeit with considerable misgiving.[17] One can only assume that the above passage pertains to Good's policy during his mission's first year, and that from 1868 he did not baptize polygamists. Hills was an imposing figure and Good, deep in debt and relying on the bishop to placate his concerned sponsors at the SPG, was in no position to question episcopal authority; he had to follow orders. As Alexander Pringle noted soon after arriving in British Columbia, Hills was a fine motivator but, one presumed, a formidable foe. 'His faith, zeal & determination are great incitements,' Pringle wrote, 'but any man who w[ould] *not* carry out his views, I take it w[ould] find his berth an uncomfortable one. – I am anxious to do my best to meet his wishes.'[18]

The bishop's judgment was final. Good had made a compelling case for relaxing Anglican ethics, but Hills remained true to his responsibility, as bishop, to enforce dogma. The Nlha7kápmx mission was in Good's hands but Hills would be held accountable for any irregularity; aware that this was the case, Good understood the bishop's ruling without agreeing with it. It did not strike him as a personal snub; the conscientious Hills was merely 'following the recommendation of the Church at large.'[19] The early years of the Columbia Mission revealed, in Hills, a bishop who was unprepared to rethink established principles. This caution sparked quarrels with other clergy as well as Good, and in each instance Hills was perfectly intransigent, largely, according to Joan Weir, due to fear of censure from the church in England.[20] Under Hills's episcopacy, any missionary unsure of Anglican policy consulted him before taking action, and he in turn deferred to definitive church standards. The 'cheerful pragmatists' at work among the Maisin of Papua in the early twentieth century are a striking contrast, for these Anglican missionaries, short on training and supervision, were unencumbered by dogma and could add a personal touch to the politics of conversion.[21] Agents of the Columbia Mission were allowed less latitude, and where they heeded their bishop it was often, as for Good, reluctantly.

One could argue that it was easier for Hills to remain dogmatic than it was for the likes of Good. Secure in his middle-class neighbourhood in Victoria, where he mixed with the upper crust of colonial society, the bishop only periodically interacted with Natives and could afford to remain aloof. His annual visits to St. Paul's and other missions were important to him, to be sure, but after touring his diocese he always returned to the familiar haven of white Victoria. This peculiar experience, at once missionary and administrator, may have shielded Hills from doubts that afflicted those more involved with Natives. If, as I argue below, Good's appreciation of Nlha7kápmx ways accounts for his willingness to compromise, perhaps the bishop's detachment explains his riposte. It is possible. My own feeling, though, is that Hills would not have bent however well he knew Good's charges. Conservatism was in his nature as well as in his office. Archdeacon Henry P. Wright, who probably knew Hills better than any other Anglican, said that he was a good man but liked to have his own way; he was not selfish so much as convinced that he was right. He was also oblivious to what other people believed, and why – 'ignorant of his fellow man,' in Wright's words.[22]

Hills, clearly, was lacking in empathy. Subsequent events at Lytton indicate that what little he knew of Nlha7kápmx culture did not impress him. From 1868 mission statutes ruled not only that monogamy was essential but that a man was only eligible for baptism if his partner was his first wife. Indeed, the bishop mocked one man who, in order to satisfy Good's moral criteria, had offered to leave his first three wives and retain the last.[23] This was unacceptable. In 1872, however, Hills changed his mind. In future, male candidates for baptism would be allowed to choose with which wife they remained. But it would be wrong to interpret the bishop's as a courteous gesture. Baffled by the Nlha7kápmx and their marriage customs, Hills saw little sense in retaining a law that Good could hardly be expected to enforce. Furthermore, he asked, why distinguish between true and untrue wives when the first spouse was probably married to several other men?[24] This claim was unsubstantiated but typical of the bishop; in Lytton only once a year, he did not know the Nlha7kápmx, and such observations as he offered were crudely pejorative.

After 1872 mission policy on polygyny remained constant. Hills was pleased to have mollified Good without violating the essence of the marriage contract (namely one man to one woman), but Good, for his part, was unimpressed with the bishop's ruling, which he regarded as mere embroidery – not the fundamental reassessment he continued to advocate. Still, many Nlha7kápmx couples did marry at St. Paul's – seventy in one batch in 1879[25] – and at least one critic, Oblate missionary A.G. Morice, was convinced that the Anglicans *had* capitulated. While his familiarity with Good's work is uncertain, Morice reckoned that the entire success of St. Paul's was rooted in concession to polygamy.[26] I am not sure about this; as Good himself emphasized, Hills had made only a very minor concession; monogamy was still compulsory. Yet we should not dismiss Morice out of hand, for the Anglicans had certainly surrendered some ground, and so often it was *they* who branded *Catholicism* the Christianity of compromise.[27]

If Hills was a stickler for tradition, what of Good's perspective on polygyny? Thus far I have presented Good as a fairly orthodox character, but his views on moral reform deviated from the party line. The longer he spent with the Nlha7kápmx, the more dogma concerned him. His growing conviction was that Anglican moral law was inappropriate in the mission field. But was not its truth his very reason for being there? Good had written in 1863 that conversion required the 'eradication of all superstitions and heathen fancies.' This destructive agenda assumed that any practice contradicting Christian morality was pernicious and had to be abolished. By 1868, when he and Hills first discussed marital law, Good was questioning this colonialist position, yet had not renounced it. Politics, not principles, explain his readiness to admit polygamists to baptism. Good still believed that monogamy was right and polygyny was wrong, but would humour the latter to allow the former time to take hold. He would recognize polygyny – where it predated his mission – but not its moral validity.

By the mid-1870s, however, Good had gone further still. Increasingly, he was forced to turn away Natives who were polygamous but well disposed towards Christianity in almost every other respect. This pained him. He felt that as a register of conversion, a simple arithmetics of sex was commonly misleading and in many cases entirely inaccurate. Among those excluded from the church for rejecting monogamy were some of his better pupils, ardent in prayer and steadfast in faith. To Good it seemed quite incongruous that a religion of ethics had no place for such 'good men.'[28] These were strong words. Good was in British Columbia on the assumption that morality required Christianity; lacking the gospel, Natives were ignorant and, therefore, sinful. On the face of it, to impute morality to polygamists was to oppugn mission theology, for the implication was that Christianity, which obliged monogamy, did not represent a universal code of ethics. There was virtue in sinners, Good appeared to be saying; otherness had moral credibility. If such was Good's thesis, he was questioning Christianity's most imperial conceits: that truth and morality are singular, and that difference of any kind must be reduced to sameness.

But Good's views on polygyny should not be taken for a disavowal of his mission, nor for a sudden change of heart. His central beliefs remained the same. For this mature Good, as for his younger self, a moral agenda was essential to mission Christianity. His identification of goodness in polygamists did not challenge the notion that morality resided in religion; it reconsidered, rather, the scope of Christian ethics, which is not to say that Good toppled the entire edifice of Anglican dogma; laws against drinking, gambling, and adultery remained sacrosanct. By the mid-1870s, however, Good no longer considered polygyny inherently unchristian. This proposition would have alarmed his colleagues, who would probably have accused Good of contesting the moral authority of Christianity. Yet they would have been wrong to do so. His concern was with Christianity's cultural specificity, and the possibility of a broader Christian ethics did not represent an abrupt sea change in his thought. Before rethinking polygyny, Good had accepted other Native customs that most missionaries banned. In 1869, for example, he delayed a church service in order that a potlatch could go ahead as planned.[29] The potlatch was not as important to the Nlha7kápmx as to Coast Salish peoples,[30] but was still common in Teit's day,[31] and while other missionaries required converts to forsake it,[32] Good reconciled its logic with Christian morality.

This elder Good was clearly something of a maverick, and we need to know why. In large part, his willingness to accommodate polygyny was tied to his appreciation of its role in Nlha7kápmx society and economy. He felt that his charges had excellent reason to refuse monogamy. Many men were anxious to convert, but unwilling to put aside women they had married 'in accordance with the custom of the tribe by exchange of gifts.'[33] In his ethnography of the Nlha7kápmx, Teit reported only that polygyny indicated wealth.[34] Elsewhere, he observed that men took up with other women if their first wife bore them no children; because the Nlha7kápmx saw polygyny as essential to their survival as a people, Teit wrote, they blamed Anglican marital law for depopulation.[35] Good may not have been aware of this, but he did read polygyny in its social context. Indeed, he would have had something to say about Ronald Hyam's claim that 'Victorian missionaries seldom stopped to enquire what structural function the practices they objected to so often performed in ensuring the cohesion of traditional societies.'[36] This was precisely Good's concern. He knew that polygyny had a social ingredient – even if he described it imprecisely – and that the social rationality of polygyny explained Nlha7kápmx resistance to monogamy. The greater his familiarity with Nlha7kápmx culture, the more Good respected the other-ness he was charged with reforming.

Other Anglicans also realized that Native sexual practices were embed-ded in well-established social relations. Alexander Garrett, for example, recorded a revealing Native response to a public address delivered by Arthur Kennedy, Governor of Vancouver Island. During his speech to Garrett's charges the governor spoke of the importance of observing Anglican moral laws, but when he specified monogamy one listener bris-tled. 'Had he but one wife,' Kennedy was told, 'one side would be cold all winter, and the great chief knows that would be bad for his health. Again had he but one wife, his potatoes would run short, his salmon remain uncured, his berries would not be gathered and for this reason he and his family would starve. With many wives, there was always warmth and plenty in the house.'[37] The difference between Good and peers such as Garrett was that *he* was swayed by the rationality of Native ways. If other missionaries identified reason in polygyny, this reason did not amount to civility, and thus did not diminish the urgency of moral reform.

Perhaps Good's greatest concern was that Anglican marital law limited his mission. If monogamy remained an absolute requirement for baptism, polygamous Nlha7kápmx would be denied conversion irrespective of faith, and St. Paul's would be considered only a partial success. This predicament was not unique to Good's mission. As Elizabeth Castelli has pointed out, missionary Christianity limits its purchase the more it assumes 'totalizing positions and unproblematized notions of identity.'[38] Good regarded his own commission as totalizing and, as such, prone to resistance. Indeed, he used the evocative phrase 'paralyzing dogma' to indicate that rigid moral law limited St. Paul's and threatened its very survival.[39] If the church was more open to cultural difference, Good main-tained, it could expand without restriction and truly become a religion for the world. Now Castelli's specific argument is that Christianity limits itself where its theology is Pauline, since Paul insisted on reducing all dif-ference to sameness. And yet although prepared to indulge certain Nlha7kápmx customs, Good refused to let go of Paul. Instead, he debated whether the Apostle really *had* withheld baptism from polygamists.[40] Rather than question Paul's indictment of difference and his imperative of mutual identity, Good chose to extend the compass of Christian sameness. In coming to this decision he had not renounced the task of colonizing his charges; but he knew that to colonize effectively and with minimal dissent, Christianity would have to be somewhat *less* colonizing.

The final explanation for Good's perspective on polygyny is compas-sion. As we shall see below, Good was concerned about the implications of monogamy for women whom men, if they converted, would be required to abandon. He also sensed that if dogma hampered his mission by deterring potential converts, it could be equally debilitating for the men who had to choose between spouses and faith. It would 'outrage every feeling and habit in which they have been nurtured' to make such a choice.[41] Consider, for example, Sashiatan, the man Good first received at Yale, whose early fealty to the Anglican mission was unmatched.[42] Good repeatedly hailed this 'earnest uncompromising thirsty reforming Christian.'[43] Sashiatan was renowned as the fearsome warrior who, some time before his meeting with Good, had attacked a Hudson's Bay Company train at Nicola Lake. In 1868, however, he impressed Bishop Hills with his 'fine, manly, intelligent countenance.'[44] His turn to Christianity, it seems, entailed remarkable moral reform; enlightenment banished a barbarian and unveiled Sashiatan the Christian gentleman.

Yet the change was not this categorical. At the bishop's bidding, Good had made monogamy an absolute requirement for baptism, and thus for conversion; but Sashiatan had three wives and was not prepared to relinquish two. Despite his zeal, he was never baptized. It is not easy to know how to interpret this story. Good never said a word against Sashiatan, who for many years frequented St. Paul's as a hearer; one suspects that Good was saddened by his friend's predicament. He would certainly not have agreed with Hills, who eventually condemned the man he had previously flattered – a Native who never quite acknowledged the error of his ways, and who in consequence died a 'miserable death' having 'gone back to enchantments.'[45]

It was Sashiatan's ill fortune that his quarrel with Christianity turned on its ethics of sex – for it was on this ethics that conversion depended. In the final reckoning, his devotion counted for naught, since faith was measured by morality, and morality meant monogamy. As Good was well aware, cultural differences separated Sashiatan from Hills and himself, and these differences made conversion a troubling option. To a people who structured marriage through wealth or barter or need, a religion that turned a particular sexuality into truth must have seemed strange. If we are to begin to understand the fate of men like Sashiatan, we need to ponder the implications of this oddity. Had Good required monogamy of Englishmen, for whom marriage *was* a moral concern and monogamy *was* the norm, his challenge would have been conventional. But to make this demand of Native men was to do much more than question their faith – for marriage was tacked to an entirely different order of things. Cultural difference ensured that Good's mission did not produce the converts it envisaged. Men who agreed to give up wives had not necessarily chosen truth, for polygyny, in their view of things, did not constitute error.

Because of cultural difference, qualification for baptism did not reduce to a choice between morality and immorality – as Hills presumed. It is to Good's credit that he knew otherwise. Perhaps the best way to characterize the bishop's ruling is to say that it generated uncertainty in the face of an unfamiliar dilemma. Some men, as we shall see, took the same course of action as Sashiatan, while others conformed to the church; but all hesitated. Homi Bhabha analyzes the production of doubt in the context of the evangelical mission to India:

> With the institution of what was termed 'the intellectual system' in 1829, in the mission schools of Bengal, there developed a mode of instruction which set up ... contradictory and independent textualities of Christian piety and heathen idolatry in order to elicit, between them, in an uncanny doubling, undecidability. It was *an uncertainty between truth and falsehood whose avowed aim was conversion, but whose discursive and political strategy was the production of doubt*; not simply a doubt in the content of beliefs, but a doubt, or an uncertainty in the native place of enunciation; at the point of the colonizer's demand for narrative, at the moment of the master's interrogation.[46]

Good's edicts had a similar effect on polygamous Nlha7kápmx men who were required to choose between church and custom, which the Anglicans described as antithetic moralities. Bhabha's thesis is that by making morality 'a space of contradictory and multiple belief,' mission instruction denied Natives an obvious option and thus ensured that any decision was at best equivocal. If Sashiatan chose Christ, he abandoned reason, but reason was itself now tempered by sin. Bhabha regards this quandary as 'a coercion of the native subject in which no truth can exist,'[47] and identifies doubt as its chief symptom.

Such doubt afflicted many of Good's male charges. He was especially grieved by the experience of a minor chief who, at his behest, both evangelized and supervised the people of his village. Good spoke proudly of this man's 'excessive zeal in defence & propagation of the cause we are here to espouse.' But with three wives, the chief was ineligible for baptism. Although 'persistently knocking at the Church's Door for admission into the Kingdom of God,' he would not abandon women with whom he had lived since long before Good arrived in the canyon, and with each of whom he had raised children. As Good described it, this man's decision to reject monogamy had not been easy: 'He could not however reconcile this voice of the Church with the voice of his inner consciousness, with his sense of right & obligation to his wives & children. He knew that those whom he publicly put away would be made conspicuous objects of shame & a prey to the vicious – and so tho' a believer, he barred himself from being admitted into the visible Household of Faith.' When the chief died of lung disease in 1874, Good's catharsis was a letter to his sponsors in which he denounced the policy imposed on him. He saw no logic in a morality that rebuffed a good man. Good maintained that paralyzing dogma had ultimately done for the chief, who died 'heathen' but with a copy of the New Testament in his hands.[48]

Another man plagued by doubt was Tosias Noe-kin-a-anaskut, who took up with a woman named Nicola who had been deserted by her husband. Tosias was no polygamist, but, as an adulterer, he had violated Anglican moral law. On learning of this affair, Good told Tosias and Nicola to separate and Tosias to 'go away on a long hunting expedition' until Hills arrived in Lytton to resolve the matter. The bishop's judgment was peremptory. 'My decision was that Nicola could not be his wife & he must give her up to her husband,' Hills wrote in his journal. When asked what he had to say for himself, Tosias, a baptized Christian, was uncertain. He wished to remain a Christian, but he also wanted to stay with Nicola. Yet he was forced to make a choice. Ultimately, he opted to conform, but the decision was equivocal, and it diminished him. He told Hills that leaving Nicola amounted to 'cutting off his right arm.'[49]

### Patriarchal Plurality?

Such stories were sharply gendered. Shako was obliged to select either his partner or his wife; Sashiatan and the other chief each had to decide between one spouse and three; and Tosias weighed his lover against his church. In each case *men* had to choose between sin and sanctity. 'It was,' as Foucault puts it, 'an ethics for men: an ethics thought, written, and taught by men, and addressed to men.'[50] Women were always treated as objects, never as subjects. Good announced that 'the restoration was complete' when Shako returned to his wife, but said nothing of the concubine cast aside – she vanishes. Yet Shako's wife is barely a subject either, for it *was* as wives, and not as women, that Good knew his married female charges. Female converts were not independent subjects, but 'wives and mothers' who approached Christ 'along with their husbands.'[51] Accounts of dramatic conversion and of relapse into savagery are almost invariably tales of men and a male God. In the sense that moral history is reduced to his-story, women are people *without* history.[52]

For this reason alone, it is difficult to ascertain the effect of Good's mission on Nlha7kápmx women, and even harder to distil their views on Christianity. As we saw in Chapter 3, Anglican missionaries installed a maternal femininity at the heart of their manifesto for social improvement. Yet Good, who certainly subscribed to an ideology of domesticity, called on Native *men* to ensure ethical conformity; he never asked Nlha7kápmx women to choose between lovers. Is there a contradiction here between the moral mechanics – driven by female sexuality – and the negotiation of sexual alliances – a strictly male affair? Not necessarily.

Most of Good's contact with Natives was with men, to whom he revealed the morals that women were expected to enforce. In his reminiscences Good recalls Nlha7kápmx men reacting strongly to lessons on precisely such matters. Indeed, one wonders at the content of the 'amusing illustrations' that startled them (the infamous missionary position?) But the more important point is this: while Good tutored men on sexual ethics, *women* were to act as 'burden bearers to the sterner sex' in these moral particulars.[53]

This theology of gender was a peculiar double bind. Women were to defend family and social morality, but were allowed no moral voice. In cases such as those recounted above, in which the outcome of mission discipline affected both sexes, responding to church directives was the man's prerogative. Of course, this does not mean that women played no role in making the decisions in question. In all likelihood they did. But as far as Good was concerned, men decided and women accepted. It is true that this bias was partly in the nature of the beast – it was polygyny, not polyandry, that the Anglicans battled, so naturally men were asked to make a choice. But there was an implicit assumption here that all wives *wanted* to stay with their polygamous husband. And, moreover, when Nicola left her husband for Tosias, it immediately became *his* moral dilemma; instead of telling Nicola to return to her spouse, Bishop Hills instructed Tosias to relinquish her.

Native women were seen as pawns, not players, in the exercise of moral discipline, and female welfare played second fiddle to the imposition of moral dogma. When he first discussed polygyny with his bishop in 1868, one of Good's main concerns was with the implications of monogamy for Nlha7kápmx women. He feared for the fate of those women whom men were obliged to give up. 'It was explained to me,' he wrote some years later, 'that for a man to put away a wife or concubine accepted under certain tribal stipulations of great moment and imposing obligations of the most binding nature, was tantamount to branding her as a harlot, and would most likely drive her either to follow an evil course or to end it by suicide.'[54] Opposed to dogma on various grounds, Good knew that improved morals would only come at great cost. He sensed the stigma of annulment and worried about the security of women thus shamed. Teit's Nlha7kápmx ethnography points to more material considerations. A man's 'effects' were distinct from his wife's (if he was given a gift, he kept it),[55] so she lost access to this property if she was abandoned.

In European colonies the world over, missionaries toiled to replace polygamy with monogamy, and many shared Good's anxiety regarding the consequences of dislocation.[56] But Bishop Hills refused to be moved when Good revealed his concerns in 1868. He was in Lytton as Good's supervisor, and as the man entrusted with hallowed dogma. Thus, although he agreed that to introduce monogamy might cause 'disappointment' to both men and women, Hills told Good that this was a worldly concern and, as such, was immaterial. Apparently Good protested, but for the bishop there was simply no question. In his journal he presented the issue as Truth against error, and emphasized that error was far more dangerous than grief. This was his logic: 'If however it is a fact that the first wife only is the true wife – & that the others are not wives – better that the poor creatures should be undeceived.' By 'poor creatures,' Hills meant Nlha7kápmx women who knew no better – women who might be deserted but, if they were, would be enlightened. Truth outweighed happiness, the bishop wrote, for the real crime to women was 'not in being put away, but in being kept in an unlawful state.'[57]

The bishop's argument needs to be carefully considered. Most obviously, this ruling privileged Anglican legality over social welfare. The Anglican mission constituted polygyny as a public problem, not the private affair that other colonists desired or disparaged but seldom sought to modify.[58] If Good considered Nlha7kápmx morality in the context of Nlha7kápmx social life, Hills effaced this backdrop and defined good Natives as worthy citizens of the British Empire. Thus, in the same moment that he removed Native ethics from one social register, the bishop bound them to another. The profit of a catholic moral law was to regulate the circulation of Native sexuality within its new circuit – the imperial public sphere.

With the marriage contract at hand, the Anglicans transformed ritual into crime and private into public, and thus linked the ethics of the body to the constitution of society at large. That this colonial bio-power[59] was cycled through a politics of gender is clear in the bishop's view of the changes he championed. In the sense that polygyny violated Anglican moral law, Hills maintained that Nlha7kápmx women were the victims of male deception. Men who retained unsanctioned wives betrayed not only mission rules but women who knew no better; it was Good's task to rescue these female victims of male sin. If Good was sceptical of this project, his bishop stressed that while monogamy might cause immediate distress, it would ultimately save Native women from their contemporary plight. This was a powerful thesis, central to the civilizing mission of British imperialism. Gayatri Spivak finds a similar assumption in British arguments against the Indian practice of widow-burning, or *sati*. Here, too, the Native woman was identified as an '*object* of protection from her own kind,' and her moral liberation stood as 'a signifier for the establishment of a *good* society.'[60] To impose monogamy was to shield Nlha7kápmx women from their men, and thus align Native sex with the morality of empire.

According to Hills, the disjuncture between Christian and Nlha7kápmx ethics was especially apparent in contrasting perspectives on relations of gender. Native heathenism was manifest in male dominance over mis-guided women, while the emancipation of female converts was a measure of Christian civility. Yet Good's mission scarcely encouraged sexual equal-ity or a spirit of female independence. The family life he vaunted was patriarchal, and his mission offered men and women entirely different possibilities. As the previous chapter demonstrated, Good trained men, often from as early as their boyhood, as his teaching assistants, and appointed men as watchmen in their respective villages. Women were singled out for marriage and motherhood.[61] As early as 1869, Good hatched plans to make 'superior wives & mothers' of Nlha7kápmx girls by teaching faith, domesticity and deference in a mission institution.[62] For a number of reasons, poor funding among them, Good shelved his plans, but E.L. Wright, one of his successors in the canyon, renewed the cause, arguing (like Reece) that unless Anglicans established schools for girls, they had little hope of converting the Native population.[63] In 1884 female missionaries arrived in Yale to staff the Ditchingham Sisterhood, which purported to offer Native girls 'womanly virtues.'[64]

All of this was after Good's day, however. The only children he schooled were boys, and to the extent that St. Paul's Mission impinged on women's lives, it was either as attendants at church services and participants in the sacraments, or as objects of the moral reformation that Good ven-tured. In some instances the introduction of Anglican ethics entailed nothing more than consecration of an existing relationship, but, where polygyny prevailed, women were at risk of rejection. Still, it would be wrong to represent Nlha7kápmx women as passive victims of mission rulings, which is more or less how Good imagined them. To insist on the power to colonize is not to deny the ability of the colonized to rework colonial intervention to their own ends. Recent scholarship suggests that indigenous women have in some instances used missionary religion to reenvision and reshape the skewed gender relations of their own soci-eties.[65] An excellent example is provided by Richard White, who shows that late-seventeenth-century Jesuit missions to the Great Lakes region attracted many Native women. White explains this interest in terms of the cult of the Virgin Mary, which invoked a female power based on chastity, and therefore appeared to offer women control over their bodies and lives.[66] Along similar lines, Birgitta Larsson argues that the Catholic mission to colonial Tanzania became a refuge for indigenous women, especially those forced into unwanted marriages under the conventions of their own society.[67]

Did St. Paul's Mission offer similar incentives to Nlha7kápmx women? It seems unlikely. Luther's understanding of female sexuality – namely that 'a woman is not created to be a virgin, but to conceive and bear children'[68] – was that of most Protestants, including the agents of the

Columbia Mission. Despite some claims to the contrary,[69] Hills was not an Anglo-Catholic, and as for many other Tractarians,[70] his opposition to cultic practices centred on the Virgin distinguished him from true Anglican Romanizers; he was firmly against such devotion.[71] For Good, too, Christian femininity reduced to the roles of (subordinate) wife and mother, and there is no evidence that Nlha7kápmx women identified a source of power in this European model of domesticity. If Anglican morality offered Native women an increased sense of control, it may have been in relationships with whites. Hills discovered that one reason why white men refused to marry Native partners was their impression that legal contract gave the women a leverage otherwise lacking. In 1863, for instance, the bishop met an Englishman who lived with but would not marry a Native woman, 'because if she knew he was legally bound to her she would probably fall back into her old habits & perhaps cohabit with Indian men & expect him to be home to keep her notwithstanding.' By way of justification, the man told Hills that 'this had happened in several cases when men had married.'[72]

If there is no proof that Christianity improved the lot of Nlha7kápmx women, can we advance the opposite case – that his mission worsened gender relations? Such has been the conclusion of several studies of the social impact of the Christian mission. Perhaps the most forceful proponent of this thesis is Carol Devens. In an effort to explain fraught gender relations within indigenous populations of the Great Lakes region, Devens holds that 'rather than being an "aboriginal" strain, fundamental to the social and ideological structures of Native American cultures, the friction between men and women is in fact the bitter fruit of colonization.'[73] She argues that Jesuit, Wesleyan, and Presbyterian missions have played a central role in introducing patriarchy to societies previously characterized by gender equality, and maintains that indigenous women received missionaries with less warmth than male counterparts because it was *female* power that Christianity threatened. While her reading of the female response to Jesuit teaching does not square with White's, and may be too monolithic, Devens makes a persuasive case. Numerous other scholars agree that the Christian mission has not benefited Native women.[74] Ron Bourgeault argues this case for British Columbia,[75] and other authors suggest that where missionary teaching *has* furthered women's rights, that contribution has been unwitting.[76]

My initial thinking, however, was that such claims do not hold for Good's Nlha7kápmx mission. One reason for my scepticism was our limited knowledge of the actual changes Good brought to social and family life; he clearly *intended* to limit women's work to caring for husbands and children, but his dream of a girls' school remained unfulfilled, and it is possible that Native women ignored the advice of his sermons. More important still, the evidence appeared to suggest that the precolonial Nlha7kápmx were not the egalitarian community that Jo-Anne Fiske associates with the precontact Carrier,[77] and that Bourgeault assumes for precontact British Columbia in general.[78] As Russell Smandych and Gloria Lee argue, 'An understanding of gender relations and the respective roles accorded to men and women in precontact Amerindian societies is an indispensable starting-point of any analysis of the later impact of colonialism.'[79] If indigenous Nlha7kápmx society was structured by unbalanced relations of gender, the introduction of Christianity would have to be cast in a different light.

This line of thought was based primarily on my reading of Teit. The ethnographer noted that even though Nlha7kápmx leaders were selected according to wealth and personal qualities rather than hereditary right, all chiefs were nonetheless men. At no stage, he observed, did women appear to have had any say in 'matters of importance,' and they were expected to show strict obedience to their husbands. There was also the matter of the traditional division of labour: men did the hunting, fishing, and other outdoor work, while women worked in the house and gathered and prepared food.[80]

These distinctions seemed to indicate some degree of Native patriarchy. I was alive to Wendy Wickwire's suspicion that Teit's images of inequality, sketched at the turn of the century, did not reflect precontact social relations so much as the effects of social and domestic reform under the Anglicans; nevertheless, I found her conclusion that Nlha7kápmx gender relations were characterized by 'a high degree of equity' at odds with the main thrust of Teit's writing.[81] Teit knew the Nlha7kápmx well, and his allusions to male dominance in public and private tally with what we can glean from Good – who not only lived among the Nlha7kápmx long before Teit but confessed to reinforcing existing Native power structures,[82] and never once mentioned a female figure of authority.

However, would Good have recognized such a woman? Indeed, would he have acknowledged female authority if he had been aware of its existence? Plenty of women were converted at St. Paul's and appear in the mission register,[83] but it is probably not insignificant that the conversion narratives discussed in Chapter 5 were *all* taken from men. It was important to educate and civilize Native women, to be sure, but the conversion of men, particularly chiefs, was Good's passion. Such turnings were the stuff of missionary lore and ignited public interest back in England. In general, it is fair to say that Good devoted far more attention to Nlha7kápmx men than women, and much detail associated with the latter undoubtedly eluded him. Furthermore, it is worth noting that European missionaries often encountered indigenous societies in which women *did* have authority, and that they were rarely impressed. Such power – in whatever form – did not square with orthodox Christian teaching on female subordination and deference.[84] It is possible that some Nlha7kápmx women were persons of considerable standing, and either Good failed to notice or, more likely, chose not to acknowledge those who transgressed the gender hierarchy of Christianity.

But there is a more fundamental issue at stake here. If we rely on Teit's or Good's analytical categories, we impose European concepts of power and identity on a culture to which they are foreign. Western thinking about social and familial authority accords great weight to particular roles and, significantly, to the spatial division of labour. But how relevant is it that Nlha7kápmx men did most of the outdoor work and women, apparently, were more domestic? Certainly Teit offers no evidence that Natives placed greater 'value' on activities in either domain. It is important not to be trapped by incongruous ideas of what constitutes power and prestige. Teit himself observed that many Nlha7kápmx shamans and prophets were women. Though Good was more interested in winning over chiefs (all men), his emphasis may reflect an ignorance, rather than an understanding, of Nlha7kápmx culture and the distribution of authority within it. Remember that Good *lost* his struggle to loosen the grip of the shamans on Native souls; here, clearly, was power, and women exercised it. Thus, I am increasingly convinced that Teit, and certainly Good, may be of little help in piecing together precolonial Nlha7kápmx gender relations.

As such, it is difficult to assess whether Christianity instituted or increased male dominance among the Nlha7kápmx. What we do know is that Bishop Hills was indifferent to the social dislocation threatened by his dictates, and that Good pursued a policy – monogamy – he seriously doubted. We also know that the Anglican Church treated men and women unequally – not only to the extent that different roles were allocated to each, or in the sense that women were excluded from the determination of Native ethics. Anglican moral law, quite simply, did not deal a fair hand. If a woman left her husband for another man because of his cruelty, she was obliged to return to her spouse; but if a man left his wife because she had committed adultery, he was allowed to remarry.[85] The Anglicans would have argued that adultery and cruelty were different sins altogether, and that only the former justified divorce. But there are no examples of men suffering at the hands of their wives, and Nicola was *not* allowed to wed Tosias, despite her husband's desertion.

Above all, we should dismiss the bishop's contention that his church saved Native women from male deception. When Good dubbed Nlha7kápmx polygyny a 'patriarchal plurality,'[86] his was *perhaps* an honest assessment of gendered relations of power. But when Hills identified polygyny as a male crime, his was less an observation on Native society and more a means to vindicate church law. To establish Nlha7kápmx women as objects requiring protection from Native men was to discount the iniquity of Anglican ethics. In denouncing Native social relations, Hills imputed morality to the Christian patriarchy on offer. To appreciate the effects of this mission, we would do better to listen not to the man who enforced dogma but to the man who questioned it, for although Good encouraged monogamy (and female domesticity with it), he knew that this fruit could be sour.

# 7
# Dissolution

At some time during 1878, St. Paul's Mission was disturbed by the arrival in the Fraser Canyon of a bizarre prophet. This man, a Flathead Indian referred to by the Anglicans as Qualis, had turned to Protestantism after recanting his Roman Catholic belief, but now found Anglicanism an impure faith. He announced himself to the Nlha7kápmx as the herald of 'a more advanced religious life.'[1] He claimed to possess supernatural power and, if this was the same troublesome prophet James Teit described two decades later, performed 'sleight-of-hand tricks.'[2] He urged the Nlha7kápmx to leave the Anglican Church and follow him instead. By year-end Qualis had disappeared (killed by shamans, according to Teit's informants), and Good looked back on the prophet's intervention as an 'evanescent movement.' But this dismissal belied the extent of Qualis's impact – the Reverend George Ditcham said that the man achieved a 'vast influence.'[3]

It is unlikely that Qualis would have swayed the Nlha7kápmx during the heyday of St. Paul's in the early 1870s, but by 1878 the mission was in decline and Good was vulnerable. Numerous factors conspired to weaken a mission that, as Bishop Hills noted when he visited Lytton in 1873 and 1874, had recently seemed in fine health. The bishop's own directives were partly to blame, for while Good was willing to relax church ethics to admit more converts, Hills was not, and his severity alienated many Natives. The great chief Spintlum, to whom Good initially devolved considerable power, would not change his habits and lost much of his authority as he drifted away from the church towards the end of the decade.[4] If Spintlum resented Anglican moral strictures, he was not alone. When Teit questioned the Nlha7kápmx on their view of the Anglicans, he found that despite a great variety of opinion, *all* were bitter about the church's marriage laws.[5] This anger undoubtedly contributed to the demise of St. Paul's.

By the late 1870s Good was also struggling against the pace of change in the canyon. As construction of the Canadian Pacific Railroad began in earnest, the social context of his mission shifted forever. He had anticipated this upheaval for some time – a party charged with surveying the railroad route had passed through Lytton in 1872 (the expedition secretary, a Presbyterian, had harsh words for Good's mission)[6] – but this did not soften the impact of thousands of construction workers, many Chinese, descending on the canyon. Good claimed that in one year some 3,000 men moved to Yale, and he worried about the 'steadfastness' of his flock.[7] When Bishop Sillitoe first visited the canyon in the summer of 1880, he found Good's mission seriously hampered by railroad construction.[8] Not only did the restless atmosphere militate against good morals but many Nlha7kápmx men were themselves taking railroad work, joining packers as the principal Native members of the local wage economy.[9] Good was cheered by this show of industry, but wage employment, combined with a prolific salmon season in 1881, kept his charges away from the reserves where he expected to find them.[10] As his grip on the Nlha7kápmx loosened, Good feared that as it stood St. Paul's was no longer an effective mission.[11]

Compounding these matters were escalating personal problems. Good had a long history of financial woe. During his tenure in Nanaimo, he had borrowed a significant sum from the Vancouver Coal Company. This debt accompanied him to the mainland and strained his first few years in Lytton, where the cost of living was higher than on the island.[12] Hills received word from London that the SPG had neither inclination nor means to bail Good out, and it is quite possible that Good would have resigned in 1869 had an anonymous benefactor in England not come to his aid.[13] Such relief was short-lived, however; into the next decade Good took on more debts. His sponsors again declined to help but, roused by his remarkable work with the Nlha7kápmx, eventually yielded.[14] They sent money tagged with a warning that further foul-ups would not be tolerated. 'His inconsiderate habits with money make it difficult for us in England to deal with him,' society secretary W.T. Bullock explained to Hills, 'however much we may honour his zeal and hard work.' The bishop was told to keep a closer eye on Good who, in turn, was asked to be more frugal.[15]

Yet Good continued to struggle to make ends meet[16] and relied on the diplomacy of friends and admirers to appease sponsors whose patience was wearing thin.[17] Unfortunately for Good, the stream of support soon ran dry. This was a watershed period for the Anglican Church in British Columbia. Henry Wright, who had gone back to England in 1865 after his stint as Archdeacon of Columbia, saw many changes when he returned a decade later as the new Archdeacon of Vancouver Island. The Edward Cridge schism had fractured church support in Victoria, and in the province at large Anglican progress was slow. Wright felt that it was time for Hills, a long-time friend, to retire, and firmly supported the division of the Columbia Diocese in 1879.[18] This division effectively scuppered Good; whereas previously he had in Hills a sympathetic supervisor, he now served Acton Sillitoe, who was unimpressed by his work and appalled by his blunders with money.

Sillitoe arrived in British Columbia to take charge of the newly formed Diocese of New Westminster, and, well-read in the literature of the Columbia Mission, he was eager to see Good's celebrated work. During his first summer in the province he travelled to Yale, which had been under Good's care since Ditcham departed in 1878 after a short period in charge. Although he did not make it up to Lytton, Sillitoe concluded that, judging by Good's work in the lower canyon, the flattering accounts of his mission had been 'unblushingly overstated.' In a candid letter to Good's sponsors, the bishop also denounced Hills, whose commission was now limited to Vancouver Island. According to Sillitoe, Good 'stood sadly in need of a controlling hand,' and 'for want of an overseer' had been 'his own master for too long'; Hills was not identified by name, but the criticism was thinly disguised. The new bishop of New Westminster, for his part, would not stand for any of Good's nonsense. Shocked to learn that Good pocketed the offertory and used it to pay for his laundry bills, Sillitoe at once stripped him of all financial responsibility.[19]

Under Sillitoe's administration, evidence of Good's faults mounted. In 1873 Hills had stifled rumours that Good had a penchant for the bottle,[20] but under the new scheme of things fellow Anglicans openly accused him of intemperance.[21] Good no longer had the protection of his peers, among whom he was now recognized as a prima donna. After 1880 there was a sense of inevitability about Good's fate. He was quite frank about his preference for Hills, and predicted that Sillitoe's ill will would be the death of his mission, for in such a dispute 'the weakest must go to the wall.'[22] This fear proved well founded. After two years of bickering with his new bishop, Good sensed in July 1882 that the end was nigh and resigned. In January 1883 he returned to Nanaimo.[23] 'At last the night has passed away,' wrote Sillitoe of the Nlha7kápmx mission that Good bequeathed, 'and the dawn of a new, and, we will hope, a more prosperous, day has broken.'[24]

If the reorganization of the Columbia Diocese marked the beginning of Good's demise, the context of this decline was a troubled domestic life. Paradoxically, the roots of this turmoil go back to the mid-1870s when, in terms of numbers of converts, St. Paul's experienced its greatest days. In 1875 Good again considered resigning his charge, this time because insolvency had forced him to sacrifice 'well nigh all home comforts' and his wife and children were suffering accordingly.[25] By the following spring the situation had deteriorated sufficiently for Good to ship his family off to Victoria, where he joined them each winter until they returned with him to Nanaimo.[26] During the winter, of course, the Nlha7kápmx, in riverine villages, were at their most accessible, so Good's winter absence from the canyon after 1876 probably cost him dearly. Perhaps he thought that improved productivity during the rest of the year would offset winter losses. He had always believed that 'volunteers from the ranks of celibacy' were the best missionary candidates – men free of domestic shackles could devote time and energy to their work[27] – and after his family departed, this was effectively Good's status. In the summer of 1876 he toured his parish extensively and seemed happy,[28] but with the fall came poor weather and, stranded in Lytton, he found secluded life little to his liking – his autonomy now a burden. Having once envied the freedom of single men, Good now wrote dimly of his 'loneliness of spirit and dreary isolation from kindred hearts in this moral wilderness.'[29]

Two years after his family left for Victoria, Good reconsidered his options. Back in 1873 Hills had amalgamated the Yale mission with St. Paul's (because Holmes had replaced Reece in the Cowichan Valley and there was no one to take his place),[30] and when Ditcham's brief incumbency ended in 1878, Good again took over Anglican operations throughout the canyon. At this juncture he decided to leave Lytton for Yale – in Stó:lō, not Nlha7kápmx, territory – in order to reunite his family. 'Here alone,' he said of Yale, 'we have a suitable Parsonage in which a family could comfortably reside.'[31] In moving to Yale in the spring of 1879, Good for the first time put his family before his mission. He finally acknowledged that his duty was to his wife and children as well as to his flock; sadly, it took personal inconvenience to open his eyes. Explaining his new perspective to his sponsors, Good admitted that 'it was my too great readiness in past years to undertake more than was prudent, that has cost me & mine more personal discomfort & trial than we should ever care to make known.'[32]

But things did not work out as planned. Good's family did not join him at Yale, largely, it seems, because Sarah decided against it.[33] She had never been especially happy in Lytton, possibly suffering from the depression that afflicted the wives of several other missionaries.[34] Living conditions were grim, and by the mid-1870s she had already lost three of her children. It is clear that when she took her remaining children to Victoria in 1876, the initiative was at least partly her own; medical and schooling facilities were vastly superior in the capital. Not surprisingly, Sarah was loath to return to the canyon in 1879. In any case the issue was soon taken out of her hands. Towards the end of the following year, Sillitoe relieved Good of his duties at Yale and sent him to Spence's Bridge – where he would remain until the bishop determined his long-term future.[35]

There is an important irony to this whole affair. Good knew that excessive zeal had previously obscured his judgment and compromised his domestic life; now, in moving to Yale on account of his family, Good undermined his mission. Working from Yale in 1879 and 1880, and dependent on Silas Nalee to keep St. Paul's in order, he waived his hold on the Nlha7kápmx. 'I was [in Lytton] two Sundays ago,' he wrote in September 1880, 'and I could see in a moment that things were going wrong.'[36] In the belief that family life infringed upon the Lord's work, Good had dispatched his family to Victoria, only to find that without Sarah he was unable to manage. In a belated effort to make amends, he took leave of his charge and saw his mission collapse. The irony was complete. Good regretted abandoning the Nlha7kápmx, but such was 'the inexorable force of circumstances, *private & domestic*,' that Yale appeared the only alternative.[37] Even Sillitoe acknowledged that family concerns, which Good had once set aside, now dictated the missionary's fate.[38]

It is possible, however, that Good knew his mission was doomed and saw nothing to lose in making a clean break. St. Paul's marital law had rankled the Nlha7kápmx (unnecessarily, as far as Good was concerned), and employment in the wage economy had exposed them to new, worldly forces. Moreover, Good had been shown to be powerless to halt the loss of Native land. He had petitioned both colonial and provincial governments on behalf of his converts, but these appeals were quashed by officials who privileged settlers over Natives and who, in this spirit, resented his intervention. As Good's impotence emerged, the Nlha7kápmx had begun to desert his mission.

**Colonial Land Policy, Missionary Mediation, and White Backlash**
'The very first operation is to obtain land,' wrote Edward Gibbon Wakefield of the art of colonialism; 'and land, with the essential addition of a good title to it, can only be obtained by the action of government in opening the waste to settlers by extensive and accurate surveys, and in converting it into private property according to law.'[39] These basic tenets steered colonial land policy both on Vancouver Island after 1849, and in the mainland colony after the gold rush.[40] In July 1858 Edward B. Lytton, secretary of state for the colonies, informed Governor Douglas that he was sending out a company of Royal Engineers to 'survey those parts of the country which may be considered most suitable for settlement.'[41] The Columbia Detachment of Sappers was on service in British Columbia for five years, during which time it laid out many town sites, including Yale, Hope, and Lytton, and constructed trails, roads, and bridges. Under the Pre-emption Act of January 1860, land surveyed by Colonel Moody's men was made available to settlers.[42]

The corollary of this policy was forthright boosterism. To encourage long-term agricultural settlement, the metropolitan press carried notices that, in retrospect, appear highly misleading. 'The face of the country in the interior,' reads one report in *The Times* (1861), 'bears in many respects a striking and grateful resemblance to the pastoral portions of England.'[43] Such words concealed British Columbia's true physical and human geographies – its rugged landscape and Native settlements – yet nonetheless failed to attract many settlers to the new colony. Miners dominated the immigrant population until the late 1860s, and while they often clashed with Natives, dispute over land ownership and use did not preoccupy colonial politicians until explicit claims to Aboriginal space were lodged. So long as the interior resisted European settlement, the government could elide the question of Native rights to own and work the land.[44] Douglas had determined that the Lands and Works Department, initially under Moody, would reserve to Natives their extant villages,[45] but the dearth of white settlement nourished neglect, and by 1865 few reserves had been set aside on the mainland.

As the 1870s approached, however, and non-Native settlement increased, demands on government land policy intensified. It was the misfortune of the First Nations that new administrators now formulated this strategy – men squarely associated with the values of a settler society. More than anyone else, Joseph Trutch, Moody's successor at Lands and Works, shaped the new colonial order and its politics of dispossession. In the summer of 1869 Anthony Musgrave, governor of British Columbia, visited Lytton with Trutch in tow, and there they received an anxious Nlha7kápmx deputation. With Good as mediator, the assembled Natives told Musgrave that colonial land policy concerned them; the handful of existing reserves covered only a small fraction of their territory, leaving the door wide open for settlers. To forestall future losses the Nlha7kápmx asked 'to have our villages & lands secured to us so that no one can make us afraid,' but the request fell on deaf ears. Trutch had no intention of granting new reserves, intending, rather, that Nlha7kápmx territory would be available for preemption. Good's angry reaction was to tell his sponsors that colonial land policy consisted of 'neglect and injustice.'[46]

Good knew that while European settlement remained sparse, his charges could continue, for the most part, to live and move where they wished. But as settlers arrived, Nlha7kápmx options dwindled, for while Douglas had allowed Natives to preempt land (at a time when they had no need), Trutch revoked this right in 1866, just as its value became clear.[47] Henceforth reserves, owned by the Crown, were the only *de jure* Native land, but in Good's parish they were paltry, and he realized that Trutch's refusal to add to them would mean friction. The Nlha7kápmx, Good observed, had been given few reserves, whereas their settlements 'dot the country in every direction.'[48]

His first taste of hostilities came in 1868. Several Nlha7kápmx bands lived at Nicola Lake in villages that Lands and Works had not converted into reserves. This oversight was immaterial in the early 1860s, but there was reason for alarm when settlers began to press their claims. The man on the spot was Peter O'Reilly, magistrate in Yale, who in June 1868 told Trutch that six preemption claims had been filed with his office, and that more were imminent. O'Reilly recommended that surveys be made and reserves set aside.[49] Trutch agreed. With a view to accompanying O'Reilly to Nicola Lake, and, en route, inspecting and reducing reserves along the Bonaparte River, he prepared for a trip to the mainland. But Governor Seymour challenged these plans. 'Would not this be very expensive?' he asked the land commissioner. 'Could not an officer of less importance than the Surveyor General do the work cheaper?' Trutch estimated his expenses at $700, and accepted that O'Reilly would have to do the work himself; reserves were low priority.[50]

With instructions to determine reserves as he saw fit and with ten acres per family as a general rule of thumb, O'Reilly travelled to Nicola Lake in August and allocated reserve land for two Nlha7kápmx bands. His main concern was to protect settler interests. Rather than assign land according to Native counsel, he tried to ensure that recent European claims were not violated,[51] and squeezed the reserves onto poorer land in between. Not surprisingly the Natives were enraged and sought redress, to which end Naweeshistan, a chief, approached Good, who understood their anger and wrote to Musgrave. Enclosing a petition from Naweeshistan, Good argued that O'Reilly had done a shoddy job, and that unless the reserves were extended and preemption was denied, white settlers would continue to take land and resources that belonged to Natives.[52] But Good's objection was to no avail. O'Reilly insisted that the reserves were adequate and that no changes were necessary, and his superiors accepted his defence. A restless Native voice, articulated by Good, had been silenced. The missionary then reeled off a second letter, this time a furious attack on the government in general, and on O'Reilly in particular.[53]

This would not be the last time that Good and O'Reilly clashed; their mutual dislike was common knowledge, and long remained fierce. In dismissing the criticism of his work at Nicola Lake, O'Reilly alleged that the Natives were happy with their reserves until Good stepped in. 'It is my opinion,' he said of the affair, 'that but for Mr. Good's interference from time to time the Indians would long since have ceased to consider they had a grievance.'[54] This was rubbish, of course, but O'Reilly's position represented a common view of missionary arbitration in colonial land policy.[55] Settlers of O'Reilly's ilk resented such intervention, and many claimed that the church manufactured Native dissent. When settlers at Nicola Lake faced ongoing Native protest after Naweeshistan's petition was ignored, they identified Good's meddling, not O'Reilly's parsimony, as the source of this trouble. In the spring of 1872 a Victoria paper published a stinging criticism of Good, written by seven residents of the land claimed by Naweeshistan. Good, they maintained, must be responsible for this Native protest, for 'The Indians are as well pleased with their reserves to-day, as the day when selected, and would not exchange them for any other part of the settlement.'[56] As O'Reilly had shown to good effect, blaming Good served to obscure Native ire and justify dispossession.

Good had encountered such attitudes before. In 1867 he petitioned the government on behalf of a Spence's Bridge Native in jail at New Westminster. Good learned from the magistrate at Lillooet, Mr Elliot, that the man had been convicted the previous year of stealing a horse, but Elliot was surprised that the sentence was still in effect. When Good contacted Seymour to seek release, the governor deferred to his attorney general, Edward Crease, who, after consulting Elliot, authorized the man's discharge.[57] But if Crease understood Good's concerns, he opposed his methods, which, Seymour was told, set an unhealthy precedent: 'I take occasion to recommend that the practice of Clergymen of any denomination being the medium of applications to government by Indians should be discouraged – and the Indians encouraged to revert to the old system of making their applications and procuring any favors from the Government thro' the local magistrate of their district. Many dangers ... will be thereby avoided.'[58] As the senior legal figure in the colony, Crease was a powerful man. Like O'Reilly, he preferred a colonialism with Europeans on one side and Natives on the other; missionaries seemed to upset this divide. Crease's were cautious words, but not far from the ugly rhetoric that reduced the mistreatment of Natives to a missionary myth.[59]

Unfazed, Good continued to act as spokesman for his charges. He would not sit idly by while the Nlha7kápmx were deprived of land and resources, and was optimistic that British Columbia's entry into Confederation in 1871 would be accompanied by a more generous land policy. Land questions in British Columbia were now couched in a broader political context, and Good felt that federal input would entail better treatment of Natives.[60] The province, however, resisted all overtures from the more liberal Dominion Government, and land policy remained as it had been. This impasse infuriated Good; to his mind, dispute between Ottawa and Victoria hurt everyone involved, not least Natives with no land rights and, from 1872, no voting rights either. In 1875 he wrote that 'the conflict between the Local Government & Canada in respect to native rights & titles, leaves those most affected by the dispute, in a state of chronic disaffection and doubt.'[61]

With the federal government exerting pressure on British Columbia to come into line with the rest of Canada, Lord Dufferin, the governor general, visited the province in 1876 to speak out against prevailing land policy. His stay in British Columbia was brief, but among his stops was St. Paul's Mission at Lytton; Good later pinpointed the governor general's visit as a turning point in the history of provincial land policy.[62] Partly in response to Dufferin's criticism, the province agreed to the establishment of a reserve commission along the lines of a proposal made by William Duncan. This commission would deal with disputed reserves and set aside new reserves where none yet existed. Three men were named to this committee, but by far and away its 'pivotal and most energetic member' was Gilbert Malcolm Sproat,[63] on whose shoulders the responsibility for laying out and enlarging reserves near Lytton now fell.

**The Land Question at Lytton**

In the neighbourhood of Lytton, as elsewhere in British Columbia, the history of the land is a history of Native dispossession. As a focal point of gold rush society, Lytton, unlike Nicola Lake, featured early in colonial land policy. Sproat noted that reserves were first set aside in 1862 by Captain Henry M. Ball,[64] but at least one reserve predated this work, and was probably established when the Royal Engineers surveyed the town site in 1860.[65] The Nlha7kápmx have never ratified the reserve system. According to Teit, they regarded the land as common property of the nation,[66] and because title to this land was never officially voided, they assumed it theirs through the colonial era and beyond. When Europeans divided Native territory into separate parcels of private property, they displaced Natives but not their claims to the land. 'I know no white man's boundaries or posts,' announced Spintlum against the intruders. 'If the whites have put up posts and divided my country I do not recognize them. They have not consulted me. They have broken my house without my consent.'[67]

When Sproat arrived in Lytton in the summer of 1878,[68] he discovered that the 590 people of the Lytton band had been allocated two reserves of just twelve and fourteen acres; a 185-acre reserve four kilometres to the north at the mouth of the Stein was not for the Lytton band.[69] Sproat's concerns, as reserve commissioner, were threefold. First, it was evident that many Nlha7kápmx villages were outside these reserves and that recent settlers, led to believe that anything but reserve was fair game, had claimed such land. Second, and plainly, the reserves were diminutive. Third, they had no water. As a case in point, Sproat described a newer reserve of thirty acres located across the Fraser from Lytton (see Figure 15), which the government had added in 1870, shoehorning it between preemptions. The Nohomeen Reserve was of terribly poor quality, and Sproat felt that perhaps only four or five acres could be cultivated. A creek ran through its midst, yet water rights to it were held by settlers – Messrs.

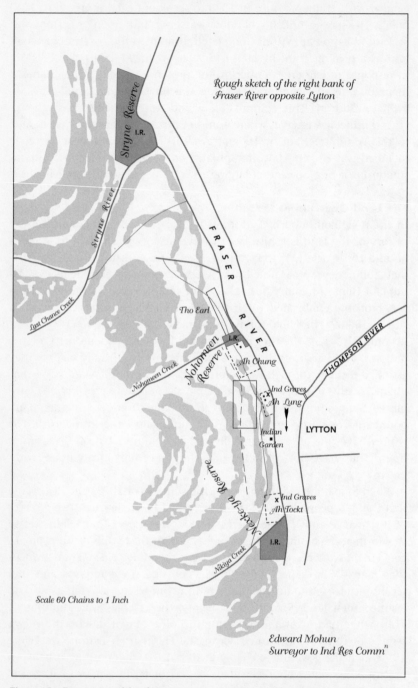

*Figure 15*  Reserves and land preemptions on the west bank of the Fraser River near Lytton, after E. Mohun, 1878

Earl and Chung – living on either side. Natives had long lived there but, according to Sproat, 'nearly all the good land has been "gouged out" of the "settlement" before it was made a "reserve."'[70]

Here as elsewhere Sproat distinguished between reserves and the Native settlements that preceded them. A settlement included not only land but what Sproat called its 'natural adjuncts,' by which he meant the resources that sustained those who lived there. The most obvious of these was water, but Sproat also considered access to fish and game as a basic ingredient of a liveable social space.[71] When he surveyed the reserves already set aside in the canyon, Sproat understood that Nlha7kápmx settlements had lost more than acreage, for land had been apportioned without the means to maintain it. Reserves were barren, even inhospitable, spaces. Government surveyors had abstracted patches of land from their environmental context to create what Henri Lefebvre would have called 'abstract space.'[72]

The manner in which reserves were delimited also contributed to their artificiality. Too often, Sproat maintained, surveyors had marked off reserve land with no appreciation for the local environment; either they pored over maps in the land office and added new lines to this colonial cartography, or they made a 'hasty visit' to the land in question before prescribing boundaries.[73] Either way, according to Sproat, reserves were conceived in abstraction. Before the joint reserve commission was formed in 1876, debate on reserves turned primarily on the question of how many acres should be allowed for each Native family.[74] Sproat considered this preoccupation misleading. To impose an abstract formula was to neglect local conditions, which varied greatly. No matter how many acres were set apart, the land was worthless if the terrain was rocky or if parched soil came without water to irrigate it. It was 'incredible' to Sproat that Victoria and Ottawa continued to argue over acreage, which he regarded as a 'bald question.'[75] Sproat's own inclination was to judge each case *in situ.*[76]

Sproat was a severe critic of prior land policy. As one example of how the reserve system compromised Natives, he identified its potential impact on Nlha7kápmx fisheries, particularly in the Fraser Canyon between Spuzzum and Lytton.[77] The canyon's few reserves had been set aside without rights to fish the river they abutted, and while Natives had not yet lost access to local fishing places, Sproat considered it important to include fishing rights with future reserves. If the Nlha7kápmx were restricted to lands already set aside, they would lose access not only to their main food source but, Sproat ventured, to an important pinion of the local trade economy. Fish constituted an exchange commodity as well as food. 'A hundred salmon for a horse,' Sproat learned, 'is an old Indian tariff.' It is clear from Sproat's comments that abstraction operated at a number of levels. Concern with reserve acreage privileged an abstract geometry over local context, allowing for space to be computed without respect for place; the fishery issue shows that reserves could also abstract place from space. Whereas Native settlements were embedded in a diffuse spatial economy, reserves were conceived as insular units of social and economic life. Not only Native trading systems spilled across this fragmented geography; Nlha7kápmx subsistence patterns assumed a mobility at odds with the fixity imposed by reserves.[78]

Water rights were also among Sproat's concerns. The Nlha7kápmx had been given reserve land and told to farm it, but were allowed no water. Henry Ball, in 1862 a gold commissioner and in 1878 a county court judge in the Cariboo, was forced to defend his early reserves against Sproat, who now accused him of having reneged on government promises to Natives. Ball maintained that when he set aside land for the Nlha7kápmx they had 'no wish or inclination ... to cultivate it,' and consequently 'no water in connection with the Land was received.' Sproat disagreed with Ball's assessment. A 'disposition to cultivate' was evident to him 'as early as 1860.'[79] The details of this quarrel are less interesting than the terms of its performance, which show that reserve endowments hinged on intent to farm. This in itself is telling; the Nlha7kápmx did not warrant land unless they were willing to cultivate it, for their own land use, like their culture, was invalid and thus wasteful. Such rhetoric of disuse is extremely important for it authorized dispossession, but my concern here is that where Natives *were* persuaded to farm, they were refused the necessary resources; twenty-seven water records were conferred in the Lytton area between 1861 and 1877, yet *none* went to the Nlha7kápmx.[80] As Sproat was well aware, this land policy was deceitful, for it denied the very life that it vaunted.

In effect, Sproat shared Good's objections to the Lytton reserves. The missionary had first protested to Ball in 1868, but Trutch, to whom Ball deferred the matter, barely registered the complaint and snuffed it out in an instant.[81] Like Sproat, Good was especially troubled by the lack of water. He argued that the government should exchange the small reserve hard by the town for 'some other piece of land capable of irrigation, where we should hope to see quite a civilized-looking native village soon being formed, with gardens and other accompaniments, by which the social as well as physical wellbeing of our converts might be materially changed and promoted.'[82]

Neither Sproat nor Good ever spoke out against the concept of reserve land, but rather against the manner in which it had been implemented in British Columbia, which they both regarded as clumsy and heartless. Sproat hoped to give the Lytton band new reserves with a tolerable water supply, but failed;[83] working alone after the joint commission disbanded in 1878, he faced determined resistance from the settler population and from the provincial government that represented it.[84] Since his mission policy encouraged agriculture, Good also wanted to increase Native access to water, but was no more successful than the reserve commissioner. Some authors now claim that missionaries made a real contribution to Native resistance to the state,[85] but we should not mistake humanist rhetoric and fruitless petitions for tangible aid. Good's solicitation of government bore no fruit. If we judge him by result rather than by intent – which in one sense was admirable – the picture is grim. To the extent that he pressed his flock to farm, Good was complicit with the land policy that both he and Sproat denounced, for he offered Natives a panacea that could not be achieved. In 1878 the Nlha7kápmx told a melancholy Sproat that 'the Queen had sent them seeds, but as they had no land nor water, they could not use them.'[86] If Good acknowledged this predicament, he did not admit that mission policy had aggravated it.

## Secularizing Resistance

Increasingly angered by their treatment, the Nlha7kápmx came together at Lytton in July 1879 to discuss the future. This meeting, a year in the planning, represented an attempt to formalize social organization within boundaries set by the federal government, in particular the Indian Act of 1876. The people elected a head chief and thirteen councillors, whose duty it was to establish rules and regulations across the whole gamut of social life – excluding church matters. As Douglas Harris has argued, this movement for local government within the Canadian state was an implicit affirmation of social contract. The Nlha7kápmx were telling white British Columbia that they would conform to white law, but were *also* asserting their right to equal treatment under that law.[87] Individual proposals covered schooling, medical care, and land ownership and use, and drunkenness, gambling, and the potlatch were banned.[88]

The content of these resolutions leads Cole Harris to suggest that they bear Good's hand,[89] and in one sense he is surely right. It is hard to imagine that the Nlha7kápmx agenda, loaded with moral resolve, was not influenced by a decade of Anglican instruction on precisely such matters. If the Nlha7kápmx wanted to demonstrate that they were law abiding (as Douglas Harris maintains), I would argue that they were also offering the government evidence of their civility. There can be no doubt that Good's teachings informed these moral resolutions. Yet on closer inspection the July meeting tells a more complex story about St. Paul's Mission. To punish individuals who violated their new rules, the Nlha7kápmx established a special committee of council that would take the administration of ethics *out* of Good's hands.[90] The Nlha7kápmx committee, not Good, would henceforth try Natives found drinking, gambling, or involved in a potlatch. In effect, sins against God had become crimes against society, with this secularization of morality rendering Good's weekly tribunals obsolete. As Teit later noted, many Nlha7kápmx elders felt that their people had been more moral before the missionaries arrived, so wresting moral authority from Good was in keeping with prevailing views of his mission.[91] And it is telling that the codes prescribed in 1879 did not include a marital law. The new resolutions drew selectively on Nlha7kápmx experience of Anglicanism but, if enforced, would clearly moderate Good's sway.

The July 1879 meeting was a secular affair, and Good, now living in Yale, was not present. Though he fully supported Nlha7kápmx claims for self-government[92] and was impressed by this particular initiative,[93] his direct influence on the meeting was minimal. Its secularity troubled some white settlers,[94] most of whom reacted to the gathering with a mixture of outrage and fear.[95] Gilbert Sproat, invited to the meeting by the Nlha7kápmx and identified by cynics as its principal architect,[96] was forced to explain why religion had had no place in the proceedings. In a letter to *The Daily Colonist*, he alluded to recurrent conflict among missionary churches in British Columbia and said that it would have been unfortunate for such rivalries to disrupt Nlha7kápmx plans. 'There is no more reason for introducing church matters into an official Indian Council,' maintained Sproat, 'than into the City Council of Victoria. The attempt would produce jealousies and confusion and do harm to mission-work.'[97] Good agreed. In a subsequent letter to the same newspaper, he defended Sproat against his critics; it was standard practice, Good claimed, for the church to 'stand aloof' from the reserve commissioner's work.[98]

The Nlha7kápmx, not Sproat, had proposed and organized the July gathering.[99] Was it their intention to exclude Good? It is possible. By now it was clear to them that Good, for all his support, was an impotent advocate. From as early as 1868, when Naweeshistan approached Good to forward his petition to Governor Musgrave, the missionary was the chief vehicle of Nlha7kápmx protest to the government – which, to date, had singularly failed. Every fruitless appeal diminished Good's standing. Long before the 1879 meeting, many Natives had already determined that he was worthless; disillusioned, they began to desert St. Paul's. Bishop Hills found that after 1875 his annual visits to Lytton attracted fewer Natives. Wondering why, he mused that 'There is certainly a strong feeling about the land.' The government's refusal to improve reserves was, he claimed, responsible for the Nicola Lake Nlha7kápmx abandoning St. Paul's in 1876.[100] Indeed, it was in that year that Good first acknowledged that provincial land policy was hurting him. He identified the 'neglect of Government to make a proper settlement with the Indians respecting their reserves' as a 'serious drawback to our work.'[101] Three years later Good had still failed to help the Nlha7kápmx cause. His absence from Lytton in July 1879 may be a measure of an increasingly disaffected flock.

Another indicator of Good's diminishing influence was the election of a man named Meshall as the new chief, for he was not one of Good's close allies, and the missionary was surprised by the appointment.[102] If the decision had been up to Good, Spintlum or Sashiatan, or maybe even Nalee, would probably have been picked. To my mind, Good was definitely aware that his charges now eluded him. In days gone by he had been a model of self-confidence, a man without the need or 'egotistical desire,' as he once put it, 'to sound my own trumpet.'[103] By contrast, his 1878 appeal for 'a controlling voice in all that is attempted [with the Nlha7kápmx] whether secular or civil' betrays a man alive to his own expendability.[104] When the press turned on Sproat for inciting the Nlha7kápmx to rebellion, Good found himself on the periphery of the storm. After the July meeting he tried to convince the public that 'If anybody is to blame for what was done at Lytton the other day I am that man,'[105] but by this stage few people were listening to him – least of all the Nlha7kápmx.

As he met and talked with Nlha7kápmx during the summer of 1878, Sproat began to understand their motives. They had relied on the church to defend their cause, but Good had not helped, and now they sought another channel of protest. They knew that British Columbia was part of a federation, and queried Sproat on the difference between 'church law' and the 'Queen's law.' When it emerged that the Queen was vested with the protection of her subjects through laws offering equal treatment to all, the Nlha7kápmx asked Sproat to tell Lord Dufferin, Her Majesty's representative in Canada, that while some were Roman Catholics and others were Anglicans, they were *'all as one for the Queen.'*[106] Church allegiance was now subordinate to fealty to the Crown for, according to the rhetoric of white law, the Queen enforced the justice that Good had failed to deliver. A transition in Nlha7kápmx politics was occurring; resistance was being secularized. The Nlha7kápmx were interested in Sproat as the Queen's arbiter of reserve land, for the church had been proven powerless. This shift from church to Queen suggests that obedience to Good was, in part, a political ruse; one old chief, for example, who had resisted mission ethics for many years, would set aside one of his three wives now that Sproat had come to solve the land question.[107]

All of this serves to explain the secularity of the 1879 meeting. The Nlha7kápmx had identified the Queen as their most likely benefactor and wanted *her* representative, not God's, at their side; Sproat was that man, for government officials would not attend. The meeting would show the Queen that the Nlha7kápmx accepted her laws; it also resolved to impose those laws on a provincial government that repeatedly ignored them –

especially insofar as it offered tiny reserves and refused to acknowledge Native land title.[108] When the Nlha7kápmx first mentioned the meeting to Sproat in the fall of 1878, they asked him to write to Ottawa and run the idea by the federal government. Sproat's response and the ensuing negotiations are revealing. Initially, Sproat resisted the request, telling the Natives to get 'a clergyman,' by whom he presumably meant Good, to approach Ottawa instead. But the Nlha7kápmx were having none of it and 'insisted' that Sproat help them. Only then did he accept.[109]

The 1879 meeting was a landmark event in the modern history of the Nlha7kápmx, for this was the first time since the early 1860s that they confronted white British Columbia without church aid; in 1867 they had replaced the Oblates with the Anglicans, but now they turned to a secular politics of arbitration. Treated poorly by a province that remained, effectively, a colony, they trusted that the federal government would intervene on their behalf. Unfortunately, Ottawa, swayed by the hostile reaction to the meeting in British Columbia, did not have the mettle to impose the rule of law and allowed the province to continue denying the Nlha7kápmx, as well as other First Nations, equal and fair access to land and resources. With their land claims unsettled and, after Sproat's resignation as reserve commissioner,[110] without a willing ally among whites, the Nlha7kápmx were left with no leg to stand on, and their plans for local government soon dissolved.

In its conception and content, the 1879 meeting represents the final chapter of Good's mission to the Nlha7kápmx. Convinced that Sproat could connect them, through the federal government, to a sympathetic Queen, the Nlha7kápmx abandoned Good. He remained in the Fraser Canyon until the early months of 1883, but after 1878 St. Paul's was never again the mission it had once been. The Nlha7kápmx had successfully solicited a new spokesman, while Good left his flock to reunite his family. The Nlha7kápmx struggle against colonialism went on, but Good made no further contribution – either to white power in the canyon, or to the resistance it generated. The missionary and his charges went their separate ways; he towards old age and retirement with his family,[111] and they towards an insecure future that saw further government initiatives fail to satisfy their land claims,[112] and that continues in this vein to the present day.

# Notes

**Introduction**

1 'Letter from the Rev. W.B. Crickmer, 1860-1,' BCA, E/B/C873.
2 Robin, 'Beyond the Bounds of the West,' is the only extant biography. But see also Peake, 'John Booth Good in British Columbia.'
3 See especially Fisher, *Contact and Conflict*, chapter 6.
4 Pagden, *Lords of All the World*, 12, 11.
5 Merivale, *Lectures on colonization and colonies*, 285.
6 Viswanathan, *Masks of Conquest*.
7 See especially Hanna and Henry, eds., *Our Tellings*.
8 Carey, 'The Church of England and the Colour Question,' 63.
9 See Christophers, 'Time, Space, and the People of God,' 10-25.

**Chapter 1: Beginnings**

1 Though Good arrived in Yale in mid-May, he was not appointed resident clergyman for the town until a month later. *British Columbia Tribune*, 21 May, 18 June 1866.
2 *Mission Life* 3, 1 (1872): 97.
3 *Columbia Mission Report* 9 (1867): 62.
4 Ibid., 76.
5 Good to the Secretary, SPG, RQE 31 December 1867, USPG, E Series, vol. 23, 1867-8. Many Anglicans invoked Paul thus. The CMS deemed Paul's summons to Macedonia 'the cry of Europe for the Gospel' and observed that the nineteenth century had reversed this geography – 'for now it is Europe that has the Gospel, and Asia that asks for it.' *Church Missionary Intelligencer* 1, 4 (1849): 75.
6 *Columbia Mission Report* 9 (1867): 67.
7 See, respectively, George Hills to W.T. Bullock, 18 October 1867, USPG, CLR Series, vol. 149, 1859-91; *Mission Life* 3, 1 (1872): 95-7.
8 Described by Carter, *The Road to Botany Bay*, 80, as 'a convenient device to gloss events that cause-and-effect explanations seemed unable to plumb.'
9 For an excellent example, see 'The voice of him that crieth in the wilderness,' 4-5.
10 *Columbia Mission Report* 9 (1867): 64.
11 Ibid., 74; 'who am I,' he wrote, 'that I should fight against God?'
12 John B. Good, 'The utmost bounds of the West. Pioneer jottings of forty years missionary reminiscences of the Out West Pacific Coast. A.D. 1861-A.D. 1900,' VST, PSA 52/9, 70. (Original copy in BCA; page references as per VST transcript.)
13 Rushdie, 'In God we trust,' in *Imaginary Homelands*, 378.
14 Some authors argue that Western historicism of any kind (whether its source is the Bible or Hegel) is colonialist, for 'others' are arrogated to a history with European parameters. For an excellent discussion of such matters, see Young, *White Mythologies*, especially chapter 1.

15 Stock, *One Hundred Years*, 2; original emphasis.
16 See, in particular, Pagden, *Lords of All the World*, 77-88, on how British imperialism mobilized the Roman Law argument of *res nullius*; also Bhabha, 'Conclusion' in his *The Location of Culture*, 246, who describes the colonial *terra nulla* as 'the empty or wasted land whose history has to be begun.' Louise Pratt, *Imperial Eyes*, explores these geographies of anticipation in the context of European travel writing in empire.
17 See, for instance, Good to the Secretary, SPG, RQE 31 December 1866, USPG, E Series, vol. 23, 1867-8; RQE 31 December 1876, USPG, E Series, vol. 31, 1876.
18 Good, 'The utmost bounds,' 66-7.
19 Ibid., 24.
20 Thompson, 'John West,' 44-57.
21 Good, 'The utmost bounds,' 4.
22 West, *The substance of a journal during a residence at the Red River colony, British North America*, 144-5.
23 John R. West to St. Augustine's, 16 August 1854, CCA, U88/A2/6/John Booth Good.
24 Good, 'The utmost bounds,' 9.
25 Neill, 'Christian Missions,' *Encyclopedia Britannica*, vol. 15, 576. Also, Pascoe, *Two Hundred Years*, ix. The SPG (1701) considerably predated the CMS (1799), and it was in part the SPG's emphasis on white settlers that inspired the evangelical society: 'there was room, and a call too, for the formation of a society whose distinct and proper work it should be to carry the Gospel to the heathen wherever they should be found.' *Church Missionary Gleaner* 1 (1874): 13.
26 Ernest Hawkins to Hills, 14 December 1860, USPG, CLS Series, vol. 107, 1859-1911; original emphasis. Also, *The Mission Field* 6 (1861): 145.
27 *Columbia Mission Report* 3 (1861): 50; original emphasis. This paragraph draws on several sources, primarily: Moir, *The Church in the British Era*, 8-25; Cnattingius, *Bishops and Societies*, 200-2.
28 Details provided in *Columbia Mission Report* 22 (1880-1): 16-23.
29 Simpson, 'Henry Press Wright,' 148.
30 Alexander Charles Garrett, 'Reminiscences,' VST, PSA 52/7, 32.
31 See the hostile words in Robson's Diary, BCA, H/D/R57/R57, especially 22 September 1861. When Robson left Nanaimo a couple of years later the Methodists replaced him with Cornelius Bryant and, briefly, Thomas Crosby.
32 Robin, 'Beyond the Bounds,' chapter 3, covers Good's Nanaimo years.
33 'Here miners going to the mines of the interior must stop at least one night, and on their return journey they are required to do the same.' *British Columbia Tribune*, 10 April 1866.
34 Good to the Warden, St. Augustine's, 6 November 1866, CCA, U88/A2/6/John Booth Good.
35 Alexander Pringle to David Pringle (father), 10 January and 7 April 1860, BCA, Add. MSS 369.
36 *Columbia Mission Report* 9 (1867): 71.
37 Weir, *Catalysts and Watchdogs*, 52.
38 Bishop George Hills, Diary, VST, 10 June 1860.
39 Pringle was uninterested in Native work: 'the white population is the charge I have undertaken.' Annual Return, 1860, USPG, E Series, vol. 8, 1860.
40 On Crickmer's conflict with Catholicism, 'Letter from the Rev. W.B. Crickmer, 1860-1'; on St. John the Divine, Downs, *Sacred Places*, 145-7. One visitor to colonial British Columbia claimed that Crickmer had been 'thoroughly unhinged by overwork in London.' D.B. Smith, ed., *Lady Franklin*, 54, entry for 8 March 1861.
41 As noted by Carey, 'The Church of England and the Colour Question,' 64. On Reeve's work in Yale, Simpson, 'Henry Press Wright,' 153. Hills, Diary, 20 June 1862, believed that the Chinese appreciated Reeve's attention.
42 *Columbia Mission Report* 9 (1867): 71.
43 Hills, Diary, 17 May 1867; 3 July 1860; 26 May 1868.
44 *Columbia Mission Report* 9 (1867): 63.
45 See, for example, *The Mission Field* 13 (1868): 137.

46 Frederick Seymour to Peter O'Reilly, 14 October 1867, BCA, A/E/Or3/Se91.
47 Seymour to O'Reilly, 21 June 1868, BCA, A/E/Or3/Se91.
48 See Cnattingius, *Bishops and Societies*, 30, 108.
49 Porter, 'Religion and Empire,' 380-2.
50 D.B. Smith, ed., *Lady Franklin*, 9, entry for 25 February 1861.
51 For this particular dispute and more general comments on church-state relations, Bagshaw, 'Church of England Land Policy,' 93-110.
52 McNally, 'Church-State Relations,' 107.
53 See, in particular, Townsend, 'Protestant Christian Morality.'
54 *The Churchman's Gazette and the New Westminster Diocesan Chronicle* 4, 1 (1884): 7. McNally, 'Church-State Relations,' 107, details Anglican and Catholic objections to secular schooling, as does Barman, 'The Emergence of Educational Structures,' 15, 19-22, 28-30. Viswanathan, *Masks of Conquest*, chapter 2, is a wonderful account of similar protest among evangelical missionaries in early-nineteenth-century India.
55 See particularly Bolt, *Thomas Crosby*, 54, 85.
56 Good, 'The utmost bounds,' 61.
57 Robson, Diary, 22 June 1862.
58 'Letter from the Rev. W.B. Crickmer, 1860-1.'
59 *Columbia Mission Report* 9 (1867): 74, 76.
60 Good to the Secretary, SPG, 5 August 1868, USPG, E Series, vol. 23, 1867-8.
61 Furniss, 'Resistance, Coercion, and Revitalization,' 240.
62 In discussing the Oblates I have had to rely on secondary sources in addition to Anglican and colonial office records; to the best of my knowledge, Good's arrival in Lytton is not mentioned in the records maintained by the Oblates.
63 O'Reilly to Sir Henry Pering Pellew Crease, 10 June 1867, BCA, A/E/C86/C86/Or3.
64 Bolt, *Thomas Crosby*, 54, identifies 'non-interference in the missions of another church' as 'one of the basic unwritten rules of Northwest Coast mission work.'
65 Morice, *History of the Catholic Church in Western Canada*, 353.
66 Seymour to O'Reilly, 14 October 1867.
67 O'Reilly, Diaries, BCA, Microfilm R12A, 31 October 1867.
68 'British Columbia, County Court Book, Lytton, 1859-1875,' BCA, GR 0594, 5 November 1867.
69 Hills, Diary, 28 May 1868; Good to the Secretary, SPG, RQE 30 September 1871, USPG, E Series, vol. 26, 1870-1.
70 O'Reilly to Seymour, 25 October 1867, BCA, A/E/Or3/Or3.18.
71 As noted by Robson, Diary, 5 July 1863.
72 O'Reilly to Seymour, 25 October 1867.
73 Hills, Diary, 28 May 1868.
74 O'Reilly to Seymour, 25 October 1867.
75 The Nlha7kápmx told ethnographer James Teit that the 'Black-Robes' were their first missionaries, 'but they left us after a time.' See his 'Mythology of the Thompson Indians,' 415.
76 Slater, 'New light on Herbert Beaver,' 16.
77 Smandych and Lee, 'Women, Colonization and Resistance,' 36.
78 Teit, 'The Thompson Indians of British Columbia,' 337-360.
79 Dickason, *Canada's First Nations*, 80.
80 The seminal statement of this theory is Horton, 'On the Rationality of Conversion,' 219-35, 373-99. For interesting reflections, see especially Geertz, '"Internal Conversion" in Contemporary Bali'; Comaroff and Comaroff, *Of Revelation and Revolution*, 248-51; Hefner, 'World Building and the Rationality of Conversion.'
81 Fisher, *Contact and Conflict*, 124.
82 Dickason, *Canada's First Nations*, 134, 242.
83 Teit, 'Mythology of the Thompson Indians,' 320-8.
84 I take 'pragmatic rationality' from Obeyesekere, *The Apotheosis of Captain Cook*, 18-21, who clings to the Weberian concept of rationality but denies its religious essentialism. Native uptake of Christianity can be seen as a rational choice even if its motive is worldly rather than spiritual.

85 Teit, 'Mythology of the Thompson Indians,' 410-2. R.C. Harris, 'The Fraser Canyon Encountered,' in his *The Resettlement of British Columbia*, unravels the Nlha7kápmx response to the miners.
86 Teit, 'The Thompson Indians of British Columbia,' 175-7.
87 *The Mission Field* 8 (1863): 11. See also Hills, Diary, 23 June 1862.
88 *Columbia Mission Report* 17 (1875): 25.
89 M. Williams, 'The Coming of the White Man,' 130-1.
90 Good to the Secretary, SPG, RQE March 1871, USPG, E Series, vol. 26, 1870-1.
91 *Columbia Mission Report* 9 (1867): 82.
92 See the excellent discussion in Bhabha, 'Signs Taken for Wonders,' in his *The Location of Culture*, especially 114.
93 Good to the Secretary, SPG, RQE 31 March 1870, USPG, E Series, vol. 25, 1869-70.
94 Bhabha, 'Signs Taken for Wonders.'
95 For a set of thoroughly contradictory comments, see Good to the Secretary, SPG, RQE 30 June 1876, USPG, E Series, vol. 31, 1876.

**Chapter 2: Redemption**
1 The phrase is from Said, *Culture and Imperialism*, 130.
2 Bhabha, 'The Other Question,' in his *The Location of Culture*, 70.
3 Young, *Colonial Desire*, 92, argues that from the 1880s 'permanent racial superiority' was 'the presiding, justifying idea of the [British] empire.'
4 Good to the Secretary, SPG, RQE 30 June 1876, USPG, E Series, vol. 31, 1876.
5 Good, 'The utmost bounds,' 29-30.
6 Good to the Secretary, SPG, RQE 30 June 1871, USPG, E Series, vol. 26, 1870-1. Neither discussion of this blunder was ever published. Good's June 1871 report *did* appear in an SPG publication (*The Mission Field* 16 [1871]: 293-7), but the section in which he criticized his editor was omitted. As for Good's protracted bid to publish 'The utmost bounds,' all his effort was in vain; see his early-twentieth-century letters to his alma mater, CCA, U88/A2/6/John Booth Good.
7 Bhabha, 'The Other Question,' 66.
8 Ibid.
9 Said, *Orientalism*, 38.
10 Good, 'The utmost bounds,' 74.
11 Thomas, 'Colonial Conversions,' 385.
12 West, *The substance of a journal*, 44, v.
13 *Columbia Mission Report* 9 (1867): 76.
14 Cf. Thomas, 'Colonial Conversions,' 387: 'Savagery was a contingent state of heathenism, illness, or adherence to false doctrine, not an immutable character of a distinct kind of human being.'
15 Brown, *Klatsassan*, 4.
16 *The Mission Field* 8 (1863): 8.
17 Ibid., 12 (1867): 46-7.
18 D. Scott, 'Colonial Governmentality,' 197.
19 See Kee, 'From the Jesus Movement,' 58-61.
20 Meeks, *The First Urban Christians*, 107.
21 *Columbia Mission Report* 13 (1871): 50. Elsewhere Good wrote of 'the common origins of all nations.' Good to the Secretary, SPG, RQE 30 September 1871, USPG, E Series, vol. 26, 1870-1.
22 Hills, Diary, 18 October 1871.
23 D.B. Smith, ed., *Lady Franklin*, 22, entry for 27 February 1861.
24 'Golden mediocrity' was how Matthew Parker, first Elizabethan archbishop of Canterbury, described the *via media* position of the Anglican Church; see Chadwick, *The Mind of the Oxford Movement*, 13. Bishop Hills denounced the Protestant tendency to lurch 'from one extreme to another' and appealed to fellow Anglicans to avoid extremes and ground themselves in 'broad truth.' Hills, Diary, 25 June 1863.
25 See most recently Bagshaw, 'The Hills Enigma,' in her *No Better Land*, 287-8.
26 Bagshaw, 'Jottings Made at the Time,' in ibid., 38.

27 Among those of influence in colonial British Columbia were William S. Reece, Archdeacon of Vancouver and advocate of ritualism, and Henry Wright, Archdeacon of Columbia and close friend of Hills.
28 Sohmer, 'Christianity without Civilization,' 174-97, especially 181-2.
29 Tomkins, 'The Anglican Communion,' 114. The Reverend E. Sambayya's essay on 'The Genius of the Anglican communion' talks about the corporatism of Anglicanism and its attendant missionary edge.
30 Young, *Colonial Desire*, 8, 11.
31 For one of Good's frequent, sketchy (and flawed) ruminations on the provenance of the Nlha7kápmx, see his 'The utmost bounds,' 79.
32 Pringle to the Secretary, SPG, 13 July 1860, USPG, E Series, vol. 8, 1860; Pringle to the Secretary, SPG, 15 December 1861, USPG, E Series, vol. 10, 1861; Pringle to the Secretary, SPG, 1 October 1860, USPG, E Series, vol. 8.
33 *A sermon preached in St. Stephen's*, 10.
34 Howay, 'The Negro Immigration,' 101-13, gives the main reasons for this black migration from California – which included both southern-born ex-slaves and freeborn northerners.
35 *The British Colonist*, 13 June 1859; original emphasis.
36 D.B. Smith, ed., *Lady Franklin*, 10, entry for 25 February 1861.
37 Kilian, *Go Do Some Great Thing*, 49-60.
38 The British were as bad as the Americans, according to the blacks, and contributed in equal measure to a racist rhetoric 'in which the words "niggers" and "slaves" dance in all the mazes of negro-hating parlance.' *The British Colonist*, 14 January 1860.
39 Hills, Diary, 15 March 1860. This woman was the wife of Joseph Trutch, a prominent figure in colonial British Columbia; see chapter 7.
40 *Columbia Mission. Occasional Paper*, 13; original emphasis. On Hills and Dundas, see Carey, 'The Church of England and the Colour Question'; on Cridge, Kilian, *Go Do Some Great Thing*, 36-7, 54-5.
41 *Columbia Mission Report* 9 (1867): 73.
42 On the worldliness and sociability of early Christian asceticism, see especially Chitty, *The Desert a City*; Rousseau, *Ascetics, Authority, and the Church*; and Robinson, 'Christian Asceticism.' On Donatism, Frend, *The Donatist Church*, is still the best general history.
43 See the excellent Babcock, 'Augustine and Tyconius,' 1209-15.
44 Meeks, *The First Urban Christians*, 8.
45 Ibid., 105.
46 Castelli, *Imitating Paul*, 117, 128.
47 Brown, *Augustine*, 224.
48 This brief overview comes primarily from Frend, *The Donatist Church*, 315-21, with caveats added from Eno, 'Some Nuances,' 417-21.
49 Brown, *Augustine*, 221, 214.
50 E. Barker, *The Ideas and Ideals*, 20. This paragraph also draws on several other sources, including Frend, *The Donatist Church*, 324-32; Morrison, 'Rome and the City of God'; and Pagden, *Lords of All the World*, 29.
51 *Church Missionary Intelligencer* 2, 1 (1851): 3.
52 Brown, *Augustine*, 223.
53 *Columbia Mission Report* 10 (1868): 38-9. This is a seminal statement as far as Good's mission is concerned. He often spoke of allowing the wheat and chaff to mingle. As Faul, 'Sinners in the Holy Church,' 404-15, points out, this was among Augustine's favourite metaphors. The church would contain good and bad, but the former would support and sway the latter through *charity*, the very substance of Christian life.
54 *Columbia Mission Report* (1860): 17. Good's prophecy was similar: he cherished the thought that his church might one day 'reach and embrace tribes and peoples most remote, till all the ends of this part of the earth shall have seen the salvation of our God.' *The Mission Field* 15 (1870): 294.
55 E.g., *Columbia Mission Report* 18 (1876): 28.
56 *The past and present extension of the Gospel*, 3.

57  Good to the sub-Warden, St. Augustine's College, 17 April 1905, CCA, U88/A2/6/John Booth Good.
58  *A sermon, preached at the farewell service*, 34.
59  I take 'moment within the Same' from Bernstein, 'Incommensurability,' 69.
60  As argued by Stoler, *Race and the Education of Desire*, 27.
61  Said, *Culture and Imperialism*, 130.
62  Said, *Orientalism*, 20.
63  The discourse of Orientalism posited a feminized Orient to be held in view by a male European observer; Said said little of this gendering, but other scholars have put right his omissions. Gregory, *Geographical Imaginations*, 175, introduces this subsequent literature; Lewis, *Gendering Orientalism*, is the latest monograph.
64  Said, *Culture and Imperialism*, 130. Other work has largely concurred. See, for example, Gregory, 'Between the Book and the Lamp,' 29-57.
65  Said, *Orientalism*, 55.
66  Fabian, *Time and the Other*, 16; original emphasis.
67  McClintock, *Imperial Leather*, 40-2. See also Low, *White Skins/Black Masks*, 75-84.
68  *Columbia Mission. Occasional Paper*, 6. See also extracts from speeches Hills made while in England in 1863, printed in *Columbia Mission Report* 5 (1863): 11-3.
69  Marx, *Grundrisse*, 524.
70  Hills, Diary, 12 December 1859.
71  See Fabian, *Time and the Other*, 26.
72  *Columbia Mission Report* 10 (1868): 99.
73  'Registrar's Register – Royal Letters Patent,' ADC, Text 168, 12 January 1859.
74  *A sermon, preached at the farewell service*, 31.
75  Clayton, *Islands of Truth*. See also A. Smith, 'The Writing of British Columbia History,' 73-102.
76  de Certeau, 'The Historiographical Operation,' 91; original emphasis.
77  Augustine, *Confessions*, I. xviii (28).
78  *A sermon, preached at the farewell service*, 10.
79  Bhabha's disquisition on 'the discourse of post-Enlightenment English colonialism' (in 'Of Mimicry and Man' in his *The Location of Culture*) comes to mind. At least one critic feels that in this respect, Bhabha offers the kind of totalizing account he would usually disparage. See Parry, 'Signs of Our Times,' 5.
80  Moir, *Church and State in Canada*, x. W.A. Scott, *Historical Protestantism*, 73, identifies the Church of England as the paradigmatic national church.
81  See, in particular, Dvornik, *National Churches and the Church Universal*.
82  Ibid., especially 34-48.
83  *Columbia Mission Report* 9 (1867): 66; Good to the Secretary, SPG, 26 July 1864, USPG, E Series, vol. 16, 1864.
84  *Columbia Mission Report* 5 (1863): 15.
85  *Church Missionary Intelligencer* 1, 3 (1849): 52.
86  Hills, Diary, 11 December 1859.
87  *Columbia Mission. Occasional Paper*, 13. See also Hills's response to the address he received upon arriving in Victoria: 'From the State we seek no exclusive privileges – we ask only for liberty, a fair field and no favor.' *The British Colonist*, 31 January 1860. The media continued to criticize the Anglicans, and Hills in particular. See *The Daily British Colonist*, 31 January and 11 September 1861.
88  Howay, *British Columbia*, 616; McNally, 'Church-State Relations,' sides with Howay; Bagshaw, 'The Hills Enigma' and 'Church of England Land Policy,' claims that Hills did not plan a state church.
89  Moir, *The Church in the British Era*, 206.
90  See, for example, comments made by John Downall, Archdeacon of Totnes, in *'The voice of him that crieth in the wilderness,'* 6, on allowing church and state to 'nurture and foster and bless each other' in the colonies.
91  Cited in *Columbia Mission Report* 5 (1863): 15.
92  *Church Missionary Intelligencer* 7 (1856): 5. See also ibid., 1 (1849): 3: 'To communicate the Gospel, as freely as we have ourselves received it, to the unevangelized tribes of

mankind, is a Christian duty of primary importance. It is one we cannot neglect without serious injury to ourselves and others, nor endeavour with fidelity to fulfil without receiving personal benefit.'

93 A note on terminology is necessary here. Since the Anglican Church is the national church of England, I discuss Anglican nationalist discourses as discourses of *Englishness*; I only refer to the *British* nation when I talk about political dominion, or when I use secondary materials that themselves prefer the broader ascription.

94 A copy of this hymn sheet can be found in the collected documents of Bishop Hills, VST, PSA 42/6.

95 *A sermon, preached at the farewell service*, 33-4.

96 The 'fatal impact' thesis was (and is) a colonialist narrative that Anglican missionaries found very convenient: mission work was readily justified by the thought that secular colonialism was deadly. As the Reverend John Sheepshanks, referring to British Columbia's First Nations, had it: 'Ought we not therefore to endeavour, that, since they have received evil from us, we may also impart to them some good?' *Columbia Mission Report* 6 (1864): 50.

97 Cited in Said, *Culture and Imperialism*, 123.

98 *Columbia Mission Report* 5 (1863): 18.

99 A Columbia Mission occasional paper of 1860 provides an evocative example of this therapeutic discourse. Empire was a means of national redemption: 'Reflecting then with grief upon the terrible history of the first family of America, it cannot fail to add a lively interest to the opening colony of Columbia to find within it a remnant of 75,000 natives. There, behind the Rocky Mountains, in their last refuge upon earth, they stand with painful wonder, while the smoke of the white man is rising up all around them; and Britain has before her another opportunity, on the same great Continent, while pursuing the path laid before her to further influence and prosperity, to give a different treatment to the Indian whose fair lands she is called upon to occupy and govern.' *Columbia Mission. Occasional Paper*, 29-30. See also part of a speech made by the bishop of London at the London Tavern in 1862: 'To the Indians we owe a deep debt for the mischief that has been inflicted upon them by the approach of European civilization, and the only way to wipe out that debt is by sending them, tardily though it may be, the blessings of European religion.' *Columbia Mission Report* 3 (1861): 57.

100 Colley, *Britons*, chapter 1; a rich account.

101 Collinson, 'The Protestant Nation,' 5; original emphasis.

102 Neill, *A History of Christian Missions*, 22-3. 'For there is no difference between the Jew and the Greek: for the same Lord over all is rich unto all that call upon him. For whosoever shall call upon the name of the Lord shall be saved' (Romans 10:12-3).

103 E.g., *Church Missionary Intelligencer* 3, 6 (1852): 137.

104 Ibid., 2 (1851): 2.

105 Ibid., 1 (1849): 52.

106 Ibid., 3 (1852): 138.

107 Ibid., 1 (1849): 76-7.

108 *A sermon, preached at the farewell service*, 23.

109 See, especially, B. Anderson, *Imagined Communities*, chapter 6; Bhabha, 'Of Mimicry and Man,' 86-8.

110 B. Anderson, *Imagined Communities*, 93.

111 Ibid., 11.

112 Suleri, *The Rhetoric of English India*, 7, maintains that Anderson is 'obsessed with the modernity of nationhood.'

113 B. Anderson, *Imagined Communities*, 7.

114 See, for example, Bhabha, 'Of Mimicry and Man'; Balibar, 'Paradoxes of Universality.' A more refined argument is offered by Stoler, *Race and the Education of Desire*, especially chapter 4.

115 B. Anderson, *Imagined Communities*, 17.

116 *Church Missionary Intelligencer*, 3 (1852): 138.

117 Bebbington, *Evangelicalism*, 41: 'it was increasingly held that human beings could be the appointed agents of bringing the gospel to unevangelised nations.' Also Dvornik, *National Churches and the Church Universal*, 50-2.

118  B. Anderson, *Imagined Communities*, 91-3.
119  Bhabha, 'Of Mimicry and Man,' 90. Bhabha's account is strongly influenced by Anderson's discussion of British nationalism and imperialism, and he cites approvingly the trope of 'the inner incompatibility of empire and nation' (87).
120  As encapsulated in the lecture *'Occupy till I come,'* especially 4.
121  This summary of Bhabha's ideas is derived from 'Of Mimicry and Man,' 85-90.
122  Good, 'The utmost bounds,' 90.

### Chapter 3: Reproduction

1  Hills, Diary, 8 August 1860.
2  *The Mission Field* 14 (1869): 194.
3  *Columbia Mission Report* (1860): 24. Lillooet missionary Brown, *British Columbia*, 55, offered perhaps the most eloquent critique: 'Mining, like life, is a lottery, (as in our ignorance we say,) whereof the blanks are many, and the prizes few.'
4  *The Mission Field* 6 (1861): 74.
5  Ibid., 7 (1862): 195.
6  See, for instance, the Reverend John Sheepshanks's comments in *Columbia Mission Report* 6 (1864): 49, or Good's in ibid., 10 (1868): 34.
7  This distinction is doubtless drawn too sharply. Bourgeault, 'Race, Class and Gender,' 95, maintains that many European fur traders regarded their Native concubines as sexual commodities. His claims certainly have some purchase for the colonial era, though how much is unclear.
8  *Columbia Mission Report* 9 (1867): 25, 72.
9  Loo, *Making Law*, chapter 7.
10  'Ungoverned passions' was Bishop Hills's sweeping summation of the colony's moral predicament; letter to James Douglas, 26 November 1860, CC, F340/4.
11  *The Churchman's Gazette*, March 1887, 392.
12  Weeks after arriving in British Columbia Hills disciplined an unnamed member of his clergy who had been accused of intemperance. The bishop's perspective on this impropriety is illuminating: 'How important is the utmost circumspection on our parts as clergy. What would be but an indiscretion in others is a crime in us. It must needs be that offences come but woe be to that man by whom the offence cometh. Ye are the light of the world – a city set on a hill cannot be hid. If the light that is in you be darkness – how great is that darkness.' Hills, Diary, 13 February 1860.
13  Stoler, 'Carnal Knowledge and Imperial Power,' 57. See also Jolly and Macintyre, introduction to *Family and Gender*, 3.
14  Brown, *British Columbia*, 53.
15  Ibid.: 'Often Religion itself does not seem permitted to effect the needed reformation without [women's] instrumentality.'
16  *A sermon, preached at the farewell service*, 29.
17  Ibid., 5. See also Hills on the need 'to plant broad and deep the foundations of that Church under which our mother-country has been blessed and prospered.' *Columbia Mission Report* 8 (1866): 63.
18  Hills, Diary, 5 March 1863.
19  See, for instance, Hall and Albion, *A History of England*, 662-6.
20  Mackie, 'The Colonization of Vancouver Island,' 38-9.
21  Wakefield, *A view of the art of colonization*, 53-4.
22  Ibid., 161.
23  *Columbia Mission Report* (1860): 24.
24  Some did, of course; on his trek through the interior in 1860, Hills met a nostalgic Englishman who felt that a greater Anglican presence would make British Columbia feel more like home. 'Tears filled his eyes,' the bishop recalled, 'when he talked of home.' Hills, Diary, 17 July 1860.
25  The Reverend J. Gammage described British Columbia's white population as an eclectic bunch, including 'a large proportion of heathen, and a larger proportion of rationalists and free-thinkers, with a still larger proportion of men caring "for none of these things."' *The Mission Field* 6 (1861): 16.

26 *Columbia Mission Report* 11 (1869): 62.
27 Good to the Secretary, SPG, 5 August 1868, USPG, E Series, vol. 23, 1867-8.
28 Wakefield, *A view of the art of colonization*, 155.
29 *The Times*, 18 July 1860, 12.
30 *The Mission Field* 6 (1861): 16.
31 *Columbia Mission. Occasional Paper*, 15; Hills, Diary, 4 April 1861.
32 Perry, '"Oh I'm just sick of the faces of men,"' 37.
33 Galois and Harris, 'Recalibrating Society,' 39.
34 Van Kirk, 'A Vital Presence.'
35 See, for example, Ormsby, ed., *A Pioneer Gentlewoman*, xxvii-xxx; Gresko, '"Roughing it in the bush,"' 41.
36 Hills, Diary, 14 June 1860.
37 See Perry, '"Oh I'm just sick of the faces of men,"' 41, who describes the 'lack of female solidarity' in British Columbia's white colonial society.
38 Hills, Diary, 13 June 1861.
39 Brown, *British Columbia*, 53.
40 On the homosocial world of colonial British Columbia, see Perry, '"How influential a few men and a few families become,"' 23-4; an excellent overview of relations between 'race,' gender, and sexuality in colonial British Columbia.
41 *Columbia Mission Report* 3 (1861): 51.
42 Pringle to the Secretary, SPG, 15 December 1861, USPG, E Series, vol. 10, 1861.
43 *Columbia Mission Report* 14 (1872): 29.
44 By 1871 Good felt that he had had some success in stopping concubinage between white men and Native women – 'very soon only the most reckless will openly dare so to defy the opinion of the day' – but he knew that he faced an uphill battle. Seven years later he observed that concubinage, while less common than before, was still prevalent. *The Mission Field* 16 (1871): 295; Good to the Secretary, SPG, RQE 31 December 1878, USPG, E Series, vol. 33, 1878.
45 Good to the Secretary, SPG, RQE September 1876, USPG, E Series, vol. 31, 1876.
46 *Columbia Mission Report* 10 (1868): 34.
47 Hills, Diary, 25 June 1862.
48 Stoler, *Race and the Education of Desire*, 123-36. See also Thorne, 'The conversion of Englishmen.'
49 Loo, *Making Law*, 146.
50 McClintock, *Imperial Leather*, 52. McClintock, like Stoler, identifies connections between 'race' and class in discourses of empire. 'The rhetoric of race,' she claims, 'was used to invent distinctions between what we would now call *classes*' (54; original emphasis). On the same theme, see Young, *Colonial Desire*, 95-6.
51 *Columbia Mission Report* 9 (1867): 72.
52 *Church Missionary Gleaner* 1 (1874): 61.
53 J.R. West to St. Augustine's, 16 August 1854, CCA, U88/A2/6/John Booth Good; original emphasis.
54 C.P. Williams, '"Not quite gentlemen,"' 302.
55 Hills, Diary, 8 August 1860.
56 As Loo, *Making Law*, 150-1, points out, it was not only Anglican missionaries who contrasted English civility with American barbarity; this tendency also characterized English settler discourses.
57 He claimed that the indigenous inhabitants of Vancouver Island had been 'fearfully vitiated through contact with those who disgrace the name of Christ & dishonour the country that gave them truth & sent them forth.' Good to the Secretary, SPG, 6 June 1863, USPG, E Series, vol. 14, 1863.
58 See, for example, *The 'Occasional Paper.'*
59 Two examples of this: on learning of a Langley white who prostituted Native women, the bishop's overriding concern was the man's nationality – 'we trust not an Englishman' (*Columbia Mission. Occasional Paper*, 19); similarly troubled when informed of a Lillooet man who paid $600 for a Native concubine, Hills was relieved to have his fears assuaged: 'I am glad to say this man is not an Englishman but a Southern American' (Diary, 10 June 1861).

60  Hills, Diary, 21 August 1865.
61  Brown, *British Columbia*, 60-1.
62  Low, *White Skins/Black Masks*, 19.
63  'The voice of him that crieth in the wilderness,' 7.
64  *Columbia Mission Report* 5 (1863): 17.
65  Loo, *Making Law*, chapter 4, assumes traditional stereotypes to be accurate.
66  Groeneveld-Meijer, 'Manning the Fraser Canyon Gold Rush,' chapter 3.
67  Robson, Diary, 4 October 1861.
68  Davidoff and Hall, *Family Fortunes*, 111.
69  'Some thoughts on the Service for the Admission of Students at Matriculation,' CCA, U88/A3/2/6.
70  Good to the Secretary, SPG, RQE 31 December 1870, USPG, E Series, vol. 26, 1870-1.
71  *Columbia Mission Report* 5 (1863): 10.
72  Ibid., 8 (1866): 55.
73  George, 'Homes in the Empire,' 98. See also McClintock, *Imperial Leather*, 47, who says that 'Controlling women's sexuality, exalting maternity and breeding a virile race of empire-builders were widely perceived as the paramount means for controlling the health and wealth of the male imperial body politic.'
74  'The whole question of Female agency in the Mission is most important, in order to prevent the sapping of the very lifeblood of the future population with unsound religion and infidelity.' *Columbia Mission. Occasional Paper*, 15.
75  *Columbia Mission Report* 8 (1866): 56, 57.
76  Davidoff and Hall, *Family Fortunes*, 124.
77  See, for example, *'Occupy till I come,'* 19.
78  Two recent articles address the work of female missionaries in late-nineteenth-century western Canada. On the involvement of Native women, see Whitehead, '"A useful Christian woman"'; on whites, Rutherdale, 'Revisiting Colonization.'
79  Rutherdale, 'Revisiting Colonization,' 21.
80  Grimshaw, 'New England Missionary Wives,' 26, argues that 'as the centre of a better-ordered family,' the missionary wife propagated a morality that 'would ripple outwards, redeeming not only wayward children and errant husbands, but the whole kingdom for godly living.'
81  *Columbia Mission Report* 11 (1869): 53. On Reynard's fate in the Cariboo, Weir, *Catalysts and Watchdogs*, 59-65. Reynard suffered hard times but, adding 'the Yorkshireman's pertinacity' to 'the Cariboo parson's *Ni espoir ni peur,'* persevered, until poor health and insufficient funds forced his hand – he left mining country in 1871. *Columbia Mission Report* 12 (1870): 66; ibid., 13 (1871): 53.
82  Robin, 'Beyond the Bounds of the West,' 115.
83  The shackles of home, according to Pringle, had precluded the establishment of a school for Native children at Hope; he told his sponsors that when such a school was eventually ready, 'my wife will give her aid when available & exempt from domestic duties. Had my own time been less occupied in domestic duties, the School for Indians w[oul]d have been commenced before.' Pringle, Annual Return, 1860, USPG, E Series, vol. 8, 1860.
84  Mary Louisa Pringle to Amy Pringle, 16 December 1860, BCA, Add. MSS 369.
85  D.B. Smith, ed., *Lady Franklin*, 16, entry for 26 February 1861.
86  Johnson, *Very far west*, 60.
87  *Columbia Mission Report* 3 (1861): 41, 42.
88  *The Times*, 30 January 1863, 7.
89  Macfie, *Vancouver Island and British Columbia*, 43.
90  *Columbia Mission Report* 3 (1861): 43.
91  Wakefield, *A view of the art of colonization*, 75.
92  He saw women's role in colonialism as 'so important that all depends on their participation' (ibid., 155).
93  *The Times*, 4 December 1861, 7. When John Garrett read from Brown's letter at the February 1862 meeting, he also read from a letter written by his brother, Victoria missionary Alexander, which emphasized the need for female domestics. See *Columbia Mission Report* 3 (1861): 40-1.

94 Davin, 'Imperialism and Motherhood,' 204.
95 *The Times*, 17 June 1861.
96 Pringle to the Secretary, SPG, 5 December 1859, USPG, E Series, vol. 6, 1859.
97 Bowen, *The Idea of the Victorian Church*, 29, notes Wilberforce's 'reputation as an orator.'
98 *Columbia Mission Report* 3 (1861): 53.
99 *The Times*, 7 April 1862, 6.
100 The best account of this emigration is Lay, 'To Columbia on the Tynemouth'; except where otherwise noted, I rely on this essay. Weir's version in *Catalysts and Watchdogs*, chapter 5, while dressed up as a new reading, is derivative and adds nothing to Lay.
101 Lay and Weir both plump for the figure sixty, but contemporary accounts disagreed about the number of women on board. *The Daily British Colonist* (19 September 1862, 3) put the original number at sixty-two, but noted that one had died en route. The Reverend Edward Cridge, dean of Victoria's Christ Church cathedral and chairman of the Immigration Committee established to cater for the women, said there were fifty-seven; Cridge to James Douglas, 14 July 1863, CC, F396/3.
102 *The Daily British Colonist*, 19 September 1862, 3.
103 Lugrin, *The Pioneer Women of Vancouver Island*, 156.
104 Hills, Diary, 4 October 1862.
105 Hills, Diary, 16 March 1863.
106 Macfie, *Vancouver Island and British Columbia*, 497.
107 Cridge to Douglas, 14 July 1863.
108 *The Daily British Colonist*, 29 September 1862, 3.
109 As Stoler, *Race and the Education of Desire*, 183, puts it, white women were trusted as 'guardians of European civility,' and when they flouted this role they were 'disavowed as good mothers and as true Europeans.'
110 Gresko, '"Roughing it in the bush,"' 46.
111 Hills, Diary, 16 January 1863.
112 *The Daily British Colonist*, 22 September 1862, 3.
113 Cridge to Douglas, 14 July 1863.
114 Pringle to David Pringle (father), 9 July 1862, BCA, Add. MSS 369; original emphasis.
115 *The Times*, 7 April 1862, 6.
116 Ibid., 19 March 1863, 7.
117 *Columbia Mission Report* 3 (1861): 40.
118 McClintock, *Imperial Leather*, 85, argues that in the nineteenth century, the middle class came to be defined by the use of domestic servants. Garrett had one who, he claimed, 'did better than any' (*Columbia Mission Report* 3 [1861]: 40), and another Anglican with a female servant was Sheepshanks (Pringle to the Secretary, SPG, 27 July 1860, USPG, E Series, vol. 8, 1860).
119 Cridge to Douglas, 14 July 1863.
120 *The Times*, 28 July 1862, 6. As Gresko, '"Roughing it in the bush,"' 42-5, shows, the scarcity of domestic servants in New Westminster left Mrs Moody 'plagued' by the problem of finding household help; she was, for the most part, her own servant. If Stoler, 'Carnal Knowledge and Imperial Power,' 71, is right, Colonel Moody's upbraiding of Rye was typical of the era. Stoler argues that male colonial officials often scorned the skilled female labour that arrived at the behest of metropolitan feminists.
121 Peterson, 'The Victorian Governess,' 7-26.
122 McClintock, *Imperial Leather*, 277, writes thus of the governess: 'Like a lady, yet not a lady, like a maid, yet not a maid.' See also Amies, 'The Victorian Governess,' 537-65.
123 Bush, '"The right sort of woman,"' 389.
124 Barman, *The West beyond the West*, 90.
125 Davidoff, 'Mastered for Life,' 409.
126 Stoler, 'Carnal Knowledge and Imperial Power,' 71.
127 On the secular tradition, see Pateman, *The Sexual Contract*, especially 50-4; on Christian patriarchy, Ruether, *Sexism and God-Talk*. 'Unto the woman he said, I will greatly multiply thy sorrow and thy conception; in sorrow thou shalt bring forth children; and thy desire shall be to thy husband, and he shall rule over thee' (Genesis 3:16). Eve's

transgression in the Garden of Eden explained the subordination of women to men, but the Anglicans (and others) insisted that social subordination did *not* preclude spiritual equality. On these discourses, see Davidoff and Hall, *Family Fortunes*, 114-8.

128   *Columbia Mission Report* 9 (1867): 79. Sheepshanks singled out obedience as a cardinal female virtue. See ibid., 6 (1864): 47.

129   On this see Jolly, 'Colonizing Women,' 113.

130   *Columbia Mission Report* 3 (1861): 52.

131   Ibid. 9 (1867): 24.

132   Lay, 'To Columbia on the Tynemouth,' 38.

133   See, for example, Chaudhuri and Strobel, eds., *Western Women and Imperialism*.

134   McClintock, *Imperial Leather*, 6.

135   See especially George, 'Homes in the Empire, Empires in the Home.'

136   Lugrin, *The Pioneer Women of Vancouver Island*, 1.

137   George, 'Homes in the Empire, Empires in the Home,' 97, makes a similar point.

138   See especially Stoler, 'Making Empire Respectable,' 634-60; also the interesting discussion in Young, *Colonial Desire*, chapter 6.

139   Brown, *British Columbia*, 53.

140   *Columbia Mission Report* 11 (1869): 66-7.

141   Good saw 'white men living in a state of open debauchery with Indian women' and complained that 'these men refuse to marry the women with whom they cohabit.' Good to the Secretary, SPG, 9 November 1861, USPG, E Series, vol. 10, 1861.

142   For details on Nanaimo, see Hills, Diary, 28 August 1865; on Lytton, Hills, Diary, 30 May 1873.

143   Perry, '"Oh I'm just sick of the faces of men,"' 41.

144   West, *The substance of a journal*, 26, 51, argued that marriage was an 'obligation' that Anglicans should 'enforce upon all' white men living with Native women.

145   See, for example, Hills, Diary, 7 April 1863 and 30 May 1873.

146   Stoler, 'Rethinking Colonial Categories,' 154.

147   Hills, Diary, 4 June 1860.

148   Crosby, *Among the An-ko-me-nums*, 66: through marriage 'we would to a large extent clear the country ... of this dreadful evil.'

149   See Perry, '"How influential a few men and a few families become,"' 6-7, 9-10; the quotation is from Macfie, *Vancouver Island and British Columbia*, 380, is on 7.

150   Crease to O'Reilly, [1868?], BCA, A/E/Or3/C86.

151   A trend well described in Himmelfarb, 'Marriage and Morals among the Victorians,' in her *Marriage and Morals among the Victorians and Other Essays*.

152   Slater, 'New light on Herbert Beaver,' 16, 20-1; as did West, *The substance of a journal*, 52-4.

153   Van Kirk, *'Many tender ties,'* 153-8. Van Kirk feels that these fur trade relationships were not the illicit and temporary affairs identified by missionaries (they were compassionate), but Bourgeault, 'Race, Class and Gender,' offers a less favourable assessment.

154   Good to the Secretary, SPG, 1 November 1858, USPG, E Series, vol. 3, 1858.

155   Hills to Crease, 2 May 1862, BCA, A/E/C86/C86/H55.

156   *Columbia Mission Report* 23 (1882-3): 12.

157   *The Churchman's Gazette and the New Westminster Diocesan Chronicle* 4, 1 (1884): 7.

158   Good to the Secretary, SPG, RQE September 1869, USPG, E Series, vol. 25, 1869-70.

159   Good to the Secretary, SPG, 9 April 1862, USPG, E Series, vol. 10, 1861.

160   Ruether, *Sexism and God-Talk*, 54.

161   See Gasparro, 'Asceticism and Anthropology,' 140-1.

162   Brown, *The Body and Society*, 153.

163   Davidoff and Hall, *Family Fortunes*, 110.

164   *Columbia Mission Report* 11 (1869): 64.

165   Ibid., 10 (1868): 78. Two years later Reece had a school for Native girls up and running, supervised by the wife of his catechist, W.H. Lomas, but attracting no more than a dozen pupils each day. See ibid., 12 (1870): 23. In such schools, Reece maintained, Native girls 'could be trained up to fulfill their future responsibilities as Christian mothers.' *The Mission Field* 14 (1869): 100. This emphasis on maternity parallels the approach favoured

in schools for white girls and also mirrors mission pedagogy in other parts of the British Empire; see, for example, Allman, 'Making Mothers,' 23-47.

166 Devens, "'If we get the girls, we get the race,"' 219-37. Baird worked for the Presbyterian Board of Foreign Missions in the late nineteenth century; see ibid., 225, for details.

167 I take 'theology of gender' from Roper, *The Holy Household*, 1.

168 *The Churchman's Gazette and New Westminster Diocesan Chronicle* 4, 1 (1884): 4.

## Chapter 4: Space

1 Lefebvre, *The Production of Space*, 111.

2 *Columbia Mission Report* 6 (1864): 46, 47.

3 Bagshaw, 'Jottings Made at the Time,' 26-7; see also her 'Settlement and the Church of England.'

4 Good to the Secretary, SPG, 30 June 1877, USPG, E Series, vol. 32, 1877.

5 *Columbia Mission Report* 6 (1864): 26-7.

6 In 1868 the Diocesan Church Society was established; in 1874, the Diocesan Synod. On the former, see *Columbia Mission Report* 10 (1868): 96; on the latter, *Synods, their constitution and objects*, and *Columbia Mission Report* 15 (1873): 40-4.

7 Hills, Diary, 13 January 1860: 'I learned how anxious the people are in that Colony [British Columbia] that I should come & live there. There is much rivalry between the two Colonies. I must endeavour to do what is right – both colonies are under my care.'

8 Also noted by Good in letter to the Secretary, SPG, 17 April 1861, USPG, E Series, vol. 10, 1861.

9 *Columbia Mission Report* 5 (1863): 5.

10 Ibid., 8 (1866): 11.

11 Ibid., 21 (1879): 29.

12 Ibid., 8 (1866): 63.

13 *Columbia Mission. Occasional Paper*, 5.

14 Loo, *Making Law*, chapter 1, describes the 'club law' of the Hudson's Bay Company; for a fuller discussion that gives more attention to company management of Natives, see R.C. Harris, 'Strategies of Power in the Cordilleran Fur trade' in his *The Resettlement of British Columbia*.

15 In addition to Loo, see especially Groeneveld-Meijer, 'Manning the Fraser Canyon Gold Rush,' chapters 4 and 5.

16 Loo, *Making Law*, chapter 3, especially 64-72.

17 *Columbia Mission Report* 3 (1861): 46.

18 Good to the Secretary, SPG, 1 January 1863, USPG, E Series, vol. 11, 1862.

19 Good to the Secretary, SPG, RQE 30 September 1872, USPG, E Series, vol. 27, 1871-2: 'in connection with my assigned District of Supervision embracing some 6000 sq. miles I can with truth affirm that not only is there not a settlement but not even perhaps a habitation whether of native or immigrant that I have not personally inspected and visited.'

20 Respectively: *Columbia Mission Report* 11 (1869): 23; Good to the Secretary, SPG, 1873 Annual Return, USPG, E Series, vol. 29, 1874.

21 See Best, 'The Evangelicals and the Established Church,' 75-6.

22 *A sermon, preached at the farewell service*, 24. Bagshaw, 'Jottings Made at the Time,' 27, notes Hills's urban emphasis.

23 I take this *suggested* chronology from Meinardus, *St. Paul in Ephesus*, vii.

24 See Meeks, *The First Urban Christians*, chapter 1. As Meeks (28) points out, our image of Paul's urban mission is influenced strongly by our sources. Acts gives the impression of a 'grand and public mission' with lots of public speaking to crowds; Paul's Epistles of a more nepotistic mission, where the 'families and houses of certain individuals seem to have been starting points' for his work in the city.

25 Neill, *A History of Christian Missions*, 29.

26 *Church Missionary Intelligencer* 8 (1857): 25.

27 *Columbia Mission Report* 16 (1874): 4.

28 *Church Missionary Intelligencer* 8 (1857): 25.

29 *Columbia Mission Report* 11 (1869): 36, 37.

30 See Morice, *History of the Catholic Church in Western Canada*, 307-27, on Oblate work in the lower Fraser Valley.

31 Hills to Douglas, 26 November 1860, CC F340/4. The bishop told the governor that the Columbia Mission would establish itself in the colony's 'central spots,' creating 'Christian villages' that would in turn exercise 'an important influence upon surrounding tribes.' Simpson, 'Henry Press Wright,' 151, says that Hills placed his missionaries at 'key points, so that all significant centres were served by the Church.'

32 Good to the Secretary, SPG, 1 November 1858, USPG, E Series, vol. 3, 1858.

33 Meeks, *The First Urban Christians*, 11.

34 See especially Foucault, 'Omnes et Singulatim'; and 'Governmentality,' 5-21.

35 Miller, *The Passion of Michel Foucault*, 301.

36 Foucault, 'Omnes et Singulatim,' 236.

37 Brown, *The Body and Society*, 306. On Chrysostom, Wilken, *John Chrysostom*.

38 McLynn, *Ambrose of Milan*, 248.

39 Brown, *The Body and Society*, 373.

40 Foucault, 'Omnes et Singulatim,' 240.

41 Ibid., 228: 'The shepherd wields power over a flock rather than over a land.' In 'Governmentality,' 10-2, Foucault fleshes out this image of a pastoral power that governs 'men and things' rather than 'territory.' It is a useful discussion, pivotal to Foucault's analysis of various arts of social governance, pastoral power prominent among them.

42 Meeks, *The First Urban Christians*, 29: 'Much of life was lived on the streets and sidewalks, squares and porticoes ... News or rumor would travel rapidly.'

43 Foucault, 'Omnes et Singulatim,' 229.

44 As Meeks, *The First Urban Christians*, chapter 1, intimates.

45 Neill, *A History of Christian Missions*, 29-30.

46 Of course, this observation pertains only to Foucault's discussions of pastoral power and governmentality. The spatial sense of much of his other work is now well-established. See, for instance, Philo, 'Foucault's Geography,' 137-61; also Marks, 'A New Image for Thought,' 66-76.

47 *Columbia Mission Report* 9 (1867): 29-30.

48 *Columbia Mission. Occasional Paper*, 12.

49 R.C. Harris, 'The Struggle with Distance,' in his *The Resettlement of British Columbia*.

50 *Columbia Mission Report* 12 (1870): 9.

51 As described by a correspondent for *The Times*, 8 August 1861, 7.

52 See especially Good to the Warden, St. Augustine's College, 6 November 1866, CCA, U88/A2/6/John Booth Good, for complaint that the missionary to Yale 'cannot depend upon any arrangement he may, after much trouble, have effected, holding good for any length of time.' According to Bagshaw, 'Jottings Made at the Time,' 28, there were similar concerns about Hope's suitability as a mission station.

53 Hills, Diary, 8 August 1860.

54 *The Times*, 17 November 1859, 10.

55 West, *The substance of a journal*, 144.

56 *The Mission Field* 7 (1862): 91.

57 *Columbia Mission Report* 12 (1870): 35. Missionaries of other denominations experienced similar problems in BC, among them the Methodist Thomas Crosby, whose work with the Port Simpson Tsimshian was inconvenienced by migrancy. See Bolt, *Thomas Crosby*, 49, 62.

58 *Columbia Mission Report* 8 (1866): 47.

59 Cited in Fisher, *Contact and Conflict*, 112.

60 Garrett to the Colonial Secretary, 24 November 1860, CC, F634/2.

61 Good made much the same case about Nanaimo: he argued that it too should be a focal point of Anglican work among Natives, for several migrations traversed the parish – 'Nanaimo, being situated just midway between Victoria and the Northern End of the Island, is the great stopping place for all Indians coming down and returning.' Good to the Secretary, SPG, 9 November 1861, USPG, E Series, vol. 10, 1861.

62 On Reynard's fate, see chapter 3, note 81.

63 See Garrett to the Secretary, SPG, 6 September 1863, USPG, E Series, vol. 14, 1863.

64 *The Mission Field* 14 (1869): 227.
65 Good claimed Lytton as 'the central home and rendezvous of the Thompson or Neklaka-pamuk tribe of Indians,' and maintained that the town 'owes its importance to its geographical and topographical position only.' See '"British Columbia," written by Mrs H. H. Bancroft to Mr Good's dictation at the Driard House, Victoria. May, 1878,' BL, Microfilm 107.18, 68; Good to the Secretary, SPG, RQE 30 June 1870, USPG, E Series, vol. 25, 1869-70.
66 Teit, 'The Thompson Indians of British Columbia,' 337: in Nlha7kápmx. mythology it was at Lytton that 'Coyote's son, when returning from the sky, reached the earth.'
67 The literature on Duncan is extensive; Usher, *William Duncan of Metlakatla*, remains the best overview; Clayton, 'Geographies of the Lower Skeena,' 41-5, discusses the moral geography of Duncan's mission.
68 See *The Mission Field* 8 (1863): 117.
69 Ibid., 14 (1869): 228.
70 Ibid.; 'twofold more the child of hell' is from Matthew 23:15.
71 *Columbia Mission Report* 19 (1877): 27.
72 Ibid., 11 (1869): 20, 21.
73 Good to Colonial Secretary W.A.G. Young, 28 November 1868, CC, F653/8.
74 *Columbia Mission Report* 11 (1869): 21.
75 O'Reilly to E. Graham Alston, 10 January 1870, CC, F13/17.
76 *Columbia Mission Report* 12 (1870): 39.
77 Good to the Secretary, SPG, RQE September 1870, USPG, E Series, vol. 26, 1870-1. Other missionaries expressed similar contempt for Lytton. The Methodist Ebenezer Robson said simply: 'Lytton is a small wicked place' (Diary, 29 June 1863). Bishop Hills was equally scornful; after his first visit to the town in 1860, he left 'without regret. It is a cold windy unsheltered flat & the people more alien than any place I have been in' (Diary, 3 July 1860).
78 Good to the Secretary, SPG, RQE 30 June 1870, USPG, E Series, vol. 25, 1869-70.
79 Teit, 'The Thompson Indians of British Columbia,' 192-4.
80 Boas, Introduction, 2.
81 Good to the Secretary, SPG, RQE 30 June 1870, USPG, E Series, vol. 25, 1869-70.
82 Ibid.
83 H.I. Smith, 'Archaeology of Lytton, British Columbia,' 129.
84 Teit, 'The Thompson Indians of British Columbia,' 169.
85 Ibid., 230-1.
86 Ibid., 249.
87 Hayden, 'Introduction,' in Hayden, ed., *A Complex Culture*, 26-9, muses possible explanations.
88 Teit, 'The Thompson Indians of British Columbia,' 169.
89 Ibid., 178-9.
90 Good to the Secretary, SPG, RQE March 1871, USPG, E Series, vol. 26, 1870-1.
91 *Columbia Mission Report* 12 (1870): 44.
92 Ibid., 37.
93 Trutch to Alston, 15 March 1870, CC, F13/18, puts the property at forty acres.
94 Good to the Secretary, SPG, RQE 31 March 1870, USPG, E Series, vol. 25, 1869-70.
95 On Good's division of the land, see *Columbia Mission Report* 12 (1870): 39; on Spintlum, see Teit, 'Mythology of the Thompson Indians,' 410-4.
96 *Columbia Mission Report* 20 (1878): 41.
97 Ibid., 12 (1870): 39.
98 Ibid., 20 (1878): 42.
99 See, for instance, Comaroff and Comaroff, *Of Revelation and Revolution*, 70-80.
100 Thus Bishop Hills celebrated that the 'forest has been driven back, and dwellings and gardens ... occupy its place.' *Columbia Mission Report* 6 (1864): 27-8.
101 Driver, 'Moral Geographies,' 275-87.
102 West, *The substance of a journal*, 25, 147. According to Moir, *The Church in the British Era*, 202, the Hudson's Bay Company criticized West's emphasis on Native settlement because 'every Indian who abandoned the nomadic life of a hunter was a loss to the fur trade.'

103  Devens, *Countering Colonization*, 20.
104  Moir, *The Church in the British Era*, 206.
105  *Mission Life* 7 (1876): 462.
106  *Columbia Mission Report* 13 (1871): 57.
107  Ibid., 11 (1869): 36.
108  Ibid., 12 (1870): 21-2.
109  Henderson, 'Missionary Influences,' 303-16.
110  Lovell, 'Mayans, Missionaries, Evidence and Truth,' 277-94, especially 280.
111  *Columbia Mission Report* 13 (1871): 57.
112  O'Reilly to Alston, 10 January 1870, CC, F13/17.
113  Good to the Secretary, SPG, RQE September 1876, USPG, E Series, vol. 31, 1876: the 'snares of death are everywhere around them.'
114  *Columbia Mission Report* 20 (1878): 42.
115  Hills, Diary, 10 September 1876.
116  Henderson, 'Missionary Influences,' argues that whereas the Methodist-led community at Skidegate prospered, the Anglican community at Masset floundered because it focused too narrowly on horticulture.
117  This idea that Good used St. Paul's Mission as the space in and through which to manage his dispersed charges is derived from de Certeau, *The Practice of Everyday Life*, 36, who talks of a power that assumes 'a *place* that can be delimited as its *own* and serve as the base from which relations with an *exteriority* composed of targets and threats (customers or competitors, enemies, the country surrounding the city, objectives and objects of research, etc.) can be managed' (original emphasis).
118  Good, 'The utmost bounds,' chapter 11.
119  Good to the Secretary, SPG, RQE 30 June 1877, USPG, E Series, vol. 32, 1877.

**Chapter 5: Conversion**
1  Hills, Diary, 2 May 1874.
2  Good to the Secretary, SPG, RQE 30 September 1877, USPG, E Series, vol. 32, 1877.
3  Galois and Harris, 'Recalibrating Society,' 46; Good to the Secretary, SPG, RQE 30 June 1881, USPG, E Series, vol. 36, 1881.
4  *Columbia Mission Report* 10 (1868): 37. Chadwick, *The Mind of the Oxford Movement*, 36, writes that the Tractarians called on Christian teachers to 'follow the apostolic example and begin with milk in order that the hearers may grow up and later receive meat.' The source was 1 Corinthians 3:1-2: 'And I, brethren, could not speak unto you as unto spiritual, but as unto carnal, even as unto babes in Christ. I have fed you with milk, and not with meat: for hitherto ye were not able to bear it, neither yet now are ye able.'
5  Chadwick, *The Mind of the Oxford Movement*, 36.
6  *Columbia Mission Report* 11 (1869): 21.
7  Pickering, *Anglo-Catholicism*, 69.
8  Good to the Secretary, SPG, RQE 30 June 1870, USPG, E Series, vol. 25, 1869-70.
9  See Fisher, *Contact and Conflict*, 122.
10  Good to the Secretary, SPG, 28 December 1863, USPG, E Series, vol. 14, 1863.
11  Hills, Diary, 30 June 1860.
12  *Columbia Mission Report* 19 (1877): 28.
13  Hills, Diary, 10 June 1872: 'He said why don't you trust us? I explained we were anxious for their admission but we knew that repentance was not easy & their belief should be intelligent or they would resist the Blessing & we wished them to come so well prefaced that they might find the blessing & be strengthened without a doubt.'
14  *The Mission Field* 13 (1868): 344-5.
15  Luria, 'The Politics of Protestant Conversion,' is an intriguing account of how both Protestant and Roman Catholic churches sought to prevent false conversions, for these insincere turns 'mix worldliness with sanctity and demean the gravity of a spiritual change' (23).
16  Good to the Secretary, SPG, RQE 31 March 1870, USPG, vol. 25, 1869-70.
17  See Bebbington, 'Evangelicalism,' 184; also Bebbington, *Evangelicalism in Modern Britain*, 64. The evangelical perspective was not unlike Paul's: 'For sin shall not have dominion

over you: for ye are not under the law, but under grace. What then? shall we sin, because we are not under the law, but under grace? God forbid' (Romans 6:14-5).

18 Chadwick, *The Mind of the Oxford Movement*, 49-50.

19 Good to the Secretary, SPG, RQE 31 March 1870, USPG, vol. 25, 1869-70; original emphasis.

20 The general message of this training was that medical inquiry and mission preaching should be thought of as mutually reinforcing practices. Students were 'not expected to become learned physicians, or expert surgeons,' but their medical instruction should enable them to 'occupy some middle point between the deeply learned and the entirely ignorant.' See 'The Calendar of the Missionary College of St. Augustine, Canterbury, for the year of our Lord, 1855,' Appendix C, CCA, U88/A2/1/6.

21 *Columbia Mission Report* 10 (1868): 38. Reverend William Edward Hyman, a member of the Royal College of Surgeons based at New Westminster, wrote that 'there is nothing so likely to get [Natives] to listen to religious instruction as being enabled to assist in alleviating or curing their bodily ailments ... A stepping-stone is of the greatest moment to introduce to the poor Indian the glad tidings of salvation.' Ibid., 9 (1867): 95-6. For a much fuller examination of mission medicine, see Vaughan, *Curing Their Ills*, chapter 3.

22 Teit, 'Attitude of Indians towards missionaries (Spence's Bridge Band),' unpublished ms, n.d., American Philosophical Society: Manuscripts relating to the American Indian, MSS 30(61), Microfilm 372, roll 4, 2.

23 Teit, 'Mythology of the Thompson Indians,' 404, notes that according to the Nlha7kápmx, Jesus took a *new* trail to be seated at God's right-hand side, not the single trail to the afterworld imagined in their own traditional mythology. 'Since then, good people when they die are said to go over the new trail; but before that, only the one trail was known, over which all Indians went to the world of the dead.' Teit, 'Attitude of Indians towards missionaries,' 1, notes that this was the single most important difference between the two belief systems.

24 Teit, 'The Thompson Indians of British Columbia,' 178.

25 Good argued that 'while civilization without Christianity is the precursor of the extermination of the red man, Christianity rightly exhibited and wisely disseminated, is found to be the only sort capable of preserving the generally ill-fated people from corruption and death.' See 'British Columbia,' 69.

26 Foucault, 'Omnes et Singulatim,' 234.

27 Augustine, *City of God*, XIX (14, 15).

28 Bernauer and Mahon, 'The Ethics of Michel Foucault,' 145.

29 The pastor 'watches over' his charges by night and day 'to constantly ensure, sustain, and improve the lives of each and every one.' Foucault, 'Omnes et Singulatim,' 230, 235.

30 *Columbia Mission Report* 11 (1869): 26.

31 See, for one of his many appeals, Good to the Secretary, SPG, RQE 31 December 1870, USPG, E Series, vol. 26, 1870-1. In 1874 Good *did* receive an assistant in the person of Mr G. Ditcham, a fellow graduate of St. Augustine's trained as a catechist – but Ditcham soon left Lytton to take charge of Hope and Yale, and by 1878 had moved out of the area altogether.

32 Foucault, 'Omnes et Singulatim,' 227: 'let us call pastorship the individualising power.' Foucault wrote often and forcefully about this individualizing tendency; see also 'The Subject and Power,' especially 214.

33 Good gives details of this progression in *Columbia Mission Report* 18 (1876): 26-7.

34 Good, 'The utmost bounds,' 70.

35 Ibid., 101.

36 Quoted in Chadwick, *The Mind of the Oxford Movement*, 139. This paragraph is a gloss on Chadwick's summary.

37 Pickering, *Anglo-Catholicism*, 34.

38 See, for instance, Grant, in *The past and present extension of the Gospel*, 70.

39 Augustine, *Confessions*, X. iii (4). See Brown, *Augustine*, 168-81.

40 Foucault, 'Omnes et Singulatim,' 238: 'As for self-examination, its aim was not to close self-awareness in upon itself, but to enable it to open up entirely to its director – to unveil to him the depths of the soul.'

41 According to Teit, Spintlum's interest in the church was minimal, despite his chiefly role and notwithstanding his nominal conversion to Christianity. Teit, 'Mythology of the Thompson Indians,' 413.

42 *Mission Life* 8 (1877): 533, as noted by H. Wright, Archdeacon of Vancouver.

43 Good to the Secretary, SPG, RQE 30 June 1870, vol. 25, 1869-70. Cf. Psalms 26:1-2: 'Judge me, O LORD; for I have walked in mine integrity: I have trusted also in the LORD; therefore I shall not slide. Examine me, O LORD, and prove me; try my reins and my heart.' Good's sponsors reported that he modelled his order of worship on the orthodox Anglican liturgy, but that he had made minor adjustments to suit 'the capacities and character of the people amongst whom he is labouring.' *The Mission Field* 15 (1870): 293.

44 Foucault, 'Omnes et Singulatim,' 240 (my emphasis).

45 Of Anglican conflict with Catholicism, Reece noted that Natives had difficulty in understanding 'how it is that two parties, both professing to be teachers of the same religion, and both having their improvement and good at heart, should yet be widely separated themselves.' *Columbia Mission Report* 9 (1867): 33.

46 Good accepted that the Bible contained all knowledge necessary for salvation, but, with the Tractarians, denied that the heathen could independently access that Truth and realize its full implications. As a result, the church had to act as guide to the Gospel. Newman wrote of the need 'for the Church to teach the truth, and then appeal to Scripture in vindication of its own teaching.' This High Church maxim that 'the Church is to teach, the Bible to prove,' was at odds with the views of evangelicals. Chadwick, *The Mind of the Oxford Movement*, 146, 37.

47 See chapter 1, especially 14-8.

48 Viswanathan, 'Coping with (Civil) Death,' 188.

49 Teit, 'Attitude of Indians towards missionaries,' 2-3.

50 Foucault, 'Omnes et Singulatim,' 237: 'His will is done, not because it is consistent with the law, and not just as far as it is consistent with it, but, principally, because it is his *will*' (original emphasis). Obedience was itself a virtue, and disobedience a sin.

51 Hills, Diary, 11 June 1872.

52 Teit, 'The Thompson Indians of British Columbia,' 175.

53 *Columbia Mission Report* 12 (1870): 38.

54 Good to the Secretary, SPG, RQE 31 December 1870, USPG, E Series, vol. 26, 1870-1.

55 *Columbia Mission Report* 9 (1867): 84-5.

56 Clifford, *Person and Myth*, 56, 77.

57 *Columbia Mission Report* 9 (1867): 85.

58 On Venn's theory that mission churches should accept indigenous leaders, see Fisher, *Contact and Conflict*, 134-5.

59 *Church Missionary Intelligencer* 1, 7 (1849): 149.

60 In church affairs Spintlum played second fiddle only to Sashiatan. See *Columbia Mission Report* 12 (1870): 43. As already noted, Spintlum was not a steadfast Christian (at note 41 above); and as we shall see in chapter 6, Sashiatan had his own problems with the Anglicans.

61 *Columbia Mission Report* 9 (1867): 80.

62 Hills, Diary, 27 May 1868.

63 Good to the Secretary, SPG, RQE 30 June 1882, USPG, E Series, vol. 37, 1882.

64 A 'long-pending charge against the late catechist' was 'fully proved' in Sillitoe's court of inquiry. *New Westminster Quarterly Paper*, 2, October 1884, 16, 17; also Gowen, *Church work in British Columbia*, 133. On Good's problems with Sillitoe, see chapter 7, 139-41.

65 Good to the Secretary, SPG, RQE 30 June 1873, USPG, E Series, vol. 28, 1873. See also *The Mission Field* 15 (1870): 291: Good praised the assistance of 'an earnest and growing body of native auxiliary exhorters, who have done much to stir and kindle up religious feeling and enthusiasm in the breasts of their countrymen and countrywomen.'

66 *Columbia Mission Report* 10 (1868): 35.

67 Good often spoke of Garrett's competence, and claimed that it was for his ability to 'open out communication with Indians along the route' that Hills had taken him to the Fraser Canyon in 1862: 'Mr. Garrett is the most accomplished Chinook scholar the

island possesses.' *The Mission Field* 7 (1862): 193. On Garrett's skills, see also D.B. Smith, ed., *Lady Franklin*, 14, entry for 26 February 1861; Simpson, 'Henry Press Wright,' 148.

68 *Columbia Mission Report* 18 (1876): 28: 'To preach Christ then, as revealed in his Word, as worshipped by the one Catholic and Apostolic Church of all ages, this must be our first purpose.'

69 Good, 'The utmost bounds,' 69.

70 Bhabha, 'The Commitment to Theory,' in his *The Location of Culture*, 33-4.

71 Rafael, *Contracting Colonialism*, 21, 117.

72 *Columbia Mission Report* 10 (1868): 35.

73 Good, 'The utmost bounds,' 76: 'our crude efforts must have sounded extremely childish and superfluous and a standing proof of our own ignorance at the time.'

74 Teit, 'The Thompson Indians of British Columbia,' 171.

75 See, for example, *The office for the Holy Communion translated into the Neklakapamuk tongue*. Good also furnished translations of the liturgy and of the offices for baptism and confirmation. He worked on these translations while wintering in Victoria, where the rest of his family moved in the mid-1870s. See Good to the Secretary, SPG, RQE 30 September 1877, USPG, E Series, vol. 32, 1877.

76 Good, 'The utmost bounds,' 80.

77 *Columbia Mission Report* 9 (1867): 64.

78 *The Mission Field* 15 (1870): 292.

79 Teit, 'The Thompson Indians of British Columbia,' 296, maintains that missionaries and Indian agents had a significant impact on Native leadership structures, generally promoting those who cooperated. Fisher, *Contact and Conflict*, 173, makes much the same point.

80 *Columbia Mission Report* 19 (1877): 28.

81 Hills, Diary, 2 June 1873.

82 *Columbia Mission Report* 12 (1870): 38.

83 Brown applauded Good on his 'bright idea.' *Mission Life* 3, 1 (1872): 106.

84 Furniss, 'Resistance, Coercion, and Revitalization,' 241. Loo, 'Tonto's Due,' 73-4, identifies similarities between the Durieu system of policing and surveillance strategies employed by Duncan at Metlakatla. And apparently the Methodist Crosby also used watchmen. See Bolt, *Thomas Crosby*, 67.

85 Southey, *History of Brazil*, 334, argues that in their mission to the Guáira region of what was then the Spanish territory of Paraguay, the Jesuits sought not to advance the Guaraní in civilization but 'to tame them to the utmost docility.' Many authors have since reproduced Southey's critique: among others, Merivale, *Lectures on colonization and colonies*, 283; Neill, *A History of Christian Missions*, 203; and, I suspect, Foucault, who certainly studied these missions and who elsewhere writes famously of 'docile bodies.' See, respectively, his 'Of Other Spaces,' 27, and his *Discipline and Punish*, 135-69. Note also that the Durieu system implemented by the Oblates in British Columbia was *itself* modelled in part on the Paraguay reductions, which the Oblates learned of through contact with Jesuit missionaries in Oregon. See Grant, *Moon of Wintertime*, 126.

86 *Columbia Mission Report* 18 (1876): 29; original emphasis. Exodus 18:18 tells Moses to unburden himself: 'Thou wilt surely wear away, both thou, and this people that is with thee: for this thing is too heavy for thee; thou art not able to perform it thyself alone.'

87 Good to the Secretary, SPG, RQE September 1869, USPG, E Series, vol. 25, 1869-70. See also *The Mission Field* 15 (1870): 291, where Good speaks of his 800 'closely guarded probationary disciples.'

88 See especially Brown, *Augustine*, chapter 21.

89 Good to the Secretary, SPG, RQE December 1868, USPG, E Series, vol. 25, 1869-70.

90 Cited in Brown, 'St. Augustine's Attitude to Religious Coercion,' in his *Religion and Society*, 263.

91 Ibid., 269.

92 Hills, Diary, 2 June 1873.

93 Good, 'The utmost bounds,' 76.

94 Foucault, 'Two Lectures,' in his *Power/Knowledge*, 107.

95 Good to the Secretary, SPG, RQE September 1870, USPG, E Series, vol. 26, 1870-1.

96 *Columbia Mission Report* 18 (1876) 25-6.
97 Hills, Diary, 3 May 1874.
98 Hills, Diary, 18 October 1871.
99 *The Mission Field* 14 (1869): 225.
100 Hills, Diary, 2 June 1873.
101 On *exomologesis* and the historical shift to private confession, see especially Foucault, 'Du gouvernement des vivants,' in his *Résumé des cours*; also, Asad, *Genealogies of Religion*, 97-105; Milbank, *Theology and Social Theory*, 291-3; Delumeau, *Le péché et la peur*, 219.
102 See Pickering, *Anglo-Catholicism*, 35, 78. Chadwick, *The Mind of the Oxford Movement*, 22, notes that the Tractarians made confession available to those who desired it.
103 Hills, Diary, 10 June 1872.
104 Foucault, *Discipline and Punish*, 181.
105 Whereas penance in the Early Church often did. See Asad, *Genealogies of Religion*, chapter 3.
106 *Columbia Mission Report* 19 (1877): 28.
107 Good to the Secretary, SPG, RQE 30 June 1874, USPG, E Series, vol. 29, 1874.
108 See especially Pasquino, 'Michel Foucault,' 100.
109 *Columbia Mission Report* 9 (1867): 63.
110 Good to the Secretary, SPG, RQE September 1870, USPG, E Series, vol. 26, 1870-1.
111 *Columbia Mission Report* 11 (1869): 26; my emphasis.
112 Both attempted to isolate potential Native converts from Natives who dismissed Christianity – from 'the temptations and influences of their non-Christian friends and relatives,' in the words of Bolt, *Thomas Crosby*, 23.
113 Foucault, *Discipline and Punish*, 184.
114 See especially 'St. Augustine's Missionary College, Canterbury,' *People's Magazine*, 1 April 1870, 243-8; also 'Some thoughts on the Service for the Admission of Students at Matriculation.'
115 Milbank, *Theology and Social Theory*, 291-4, has a sophisticated take on this aspect of Foucault's thought, and points to the gap between an individualizing pastoral power based on obedience and a more impersonal power based on self-discipline. Thus, while Foucault might be right that in twelfth-century confessional practice we have the first form of a disciplinary society, Milbank holds that this outcome was *not* latent in Christianity from the start.
116 Foucault, *An Introduction*, 144.
117 Foucault, 'Governmentality,' 19.
118 Foucault, *Discipline and Punish*, 170-84.
119 Ibid., 184-94. Much of the discussion in the pages that follow is derived from this account.
120 *Columbia Mission Report* 16 (1874): 1.
121 Hills, Diary, 1 May 1874.
122 *Columbia Mission Report* 16 (1874): 2.
123 E.g., Archdeacon Wright in ibid., 19 (1877): 27.
124 Hills, Diary, 1 June 1873.
125 Morrison, *Understanding Conversion*, xiv.
126 *Columbia Mission Report* 16 (1874): 2.
127 Asad, 'Comments on Conversion,' 266; my emphasis.
128 Foucault, *Discipline and Punish*, 184.
129 Hills, Diary, 27 May 1868.
130 Good to the Secretary, SPG, RQE 31 March 1870, USPG, E Series, vol. 25, 1869-70.
131 Good to the Secretary, SPG, RQE 30 June 1872, USPG, E Series, vol. 27, 1871-2.
132 Good to the Secretary, SPG, RQE 31 March 1873, USPG, E Series, vol. 28, 1873.
133 Hills, Diary, 1 June 1873.
134 E.g., Hills, Diary, 2 May 1874.
135 See Fredriksen, 'Paul and Augustine,' 3-34, especially 33-4.
136 Morrison, *Understanding Conversion*, xxii, argues that 'ways of understanding what was called conversion in a given society were defined by the particular environment in which

the experience and the understanding took place, by the mythic context that defined "templates" of credibility in that environment, and by the informal and formal institutions that enforced those definitions.'

137 Hills, Diary, 31 May 1873.
138 Rafael, *Contracting Colonialism*, 100.
139 Nock, *Conversion*.
140 Fredriksen, 'Paul and Augustine,' 15-6.
141 Morrison, *Understanding Conversion*, xii, 24.
142 Morrison, *Conversion and Text*, 1-38.
143 Brown, 'Pelagius and His Supporters,' in his *Religion and Society*, 200, 203. See also Fredriksen, 'Paul and Augustine,' 20-33, who notes that Augustine's early perspective on his own conversion was itself indebted to Paul, and that Augustine's eventual rejection of the idea of a radical break was based on his reconsideration of Paul's conversion – and in this respect Augustine's developing views on grace and predestination were critical.
144 See, for example, Luria, 'The Politics of Protestant Conversion,' 24.
145 Morrison, *Understanding Conversion*.
146 Pollmann, 'A Different Road to God,' 54.
147 Hooker, *Laws of Ecclesiastical Polity*, 264. The *Laws* were first published in eight volumes over several decades at the end of the sixteenth and beginning of the seventeenth century.
148 MacCormack, *Religion in the Andes*, especially 366-75.
149 See, for instance, Thomas, *Colonialism's Culture*, chapter 4, especially 135-6.
150 *Columbia Mission Report* 11 (1869): 21. Empire animated a myriad of different models of conversion, not all of which can be characterized as revolutionary (a clear fracture) or evolutionary (the unbroken transition to a more mature faith); as one other example, Clifford, *Person and Myth*, 78-90, describes Maurice Leenhardt's concept of conversion as a new amalgam of indigenous and Christian beliefs, with the emphasis on a more worldly understanding of God.
151 Hills, Diary, 31 May 1873.
152 Hills, Diary, 2 May 1874.
153 Good to the Secretary, SPG, RQE 30 September 1873, USPG, E Series, vol. 28, 1873: 'their course lies along the great world's Highway – exposed to all the ordinary daily temptations of the evil world around them.'
154 Good to the Secretary, SPG, RQE 31 March 1870, USPG, vol. 25, 1869-70: he insisted that 'a heathen's responsibilities are indefinitely increased after his reception into the ark of Christ's Church and that *sin after Baptism is not the same as sin before* tho' it be not necessarily in itself either deadly or unpardonable' (original emphasis).
155 Cited in Chadwick, *The Mind of the Oxford Movement*, 107.
156 Shakalok, in Hills, Diary, 2 May 1874.
157 Teit, 'Attitude of Indians towards missionaries,' 1.
158 *Columbia Mission Report* 19 (1877): 30.
159 Hills, Diary, 29 May 1868.
160 *Columbia Mission Report* 19 (1877): 35.
161 Ibid., 11 (1869): 33.
162 Hills, Diary, 11 June 1872: 'the clear & earnest statements of truth were strong proof of the realness of the good work.'
163 *Columbia Mission Report* 14 (1872): 7.
164 Foucault, *Discipline and Punish*, 194.
165 See especially Bhabha, 'Signs Taken for Wonders.'
166 Teit, 'Attitude of Indians towards missionaries,' 4, notes that of 211 Nlha7kápmx belonging to 2 bands near Spence's Bridge in the early twentieth century, 130 were Anglican, 4 were Catholic, and fully 77 were pagan.
167 Ibid., 3.
168 Bhabha, 'Signs Taken for Wonders,' 119-22.
169 Parry, 'Problems in Current Theories,' especially 39-43.
170 Ibid., 42.
171 MacCormack, *Religion in the Andes*, 11.

172 Teit, 'Mythology of the Thompson Indians,' 399-404.
173 Ibid., 400, footnote 2.
174 Teit, 'Attitude of Indians towards missionaries,' 1.

**Chapter 6: Morals**
1 Good to the Secretary, SPG, 6 June 1863, USPG, E Series, vol. 14, 1863.
2 *Columbia Mission Report* 9 (1867): 67.
3 *Church Missionary Intelligencer* 3 (1852): 138.
4 *Columbia Mission Report* 18 (1876): 28.
5 Good to the Secretary, SPG, RQE 30 September 1871, USPG, E Series, vol. 26, 1870-1; original emphasis.
6 Good to the Secretary, SPG, 28 December 1863, USPG, E Series, vol. 14, 1863.
7 Foucault, *The Use of Pleasure*, 26.
·8 Teit, 'The Thompson Indians of British Columbia,' 326.
9 Foucault, *An Introduction*, 56.
10 See Good, 'The utmost bounds,' 88-9; Lytton Mission Register, 164.
11 Good, 'The utmost bounds,' 89.
12 For details, see Good to the Secretary, SPG, 3 May 1864, USPG, E Series, vol. 16, 1864.
13 Hills, Diary, 1 June 1868.
14 *Columbia Mission Report* 6 (1864): 30.
15 Teit, 'The Thompson Indians of British Columbia,' 181.
16 Good to the Secretary, SPG, RQE 31 March 1870, USPG, E Series, vol. 25, 1869-70; original emphasis.
17 Good, 'The utmost bounds,' 89-90.
18 Pringle to Mary Louisa Pringle, 4 June 1860, BCA, Add. MSS 369; original emphasis.
19 Good, 'The utmost bounds,' 89.
20 Weir, *Catalysts and Watchdogs*, 43.
21 J. Barker, 'Cheerful Pragmatists,' 66-81.
22 Simpson, 'Henry Press Wright,' 171.
23 Hills, Diary, 1 June 1868.
24 Hills, Diary, 10 June 1872.
25 *Columbia Mission Report* 20 (1878): 40.
26 Morice, *History of the Catholic Church in Western Canada*, 353, has Good 'catering to the passions' of the Nlha7kápmx.
27 *Church Missionary Intelligencer* 4, 1 (1853): 5: 'It is not so much that the heathen surrender their heathenism to unite with Rome, as that Rome accepts of their heathenism to win the heathen; and Romanism in its Mission-fields is so diluted with new ingredients infused from heathenism, as to lose the tenacity and antagonistic vigor of action which distinguishes it in its European state.'
28 Good to the Secretary, SPG, RQE 30 June 1874, USPG, E Series, vol. 29, 1874.
29 *The Mission Field* 14 (1869): 226.
30 As noted by Boas, Introduction, 3.
31 Teit, 'The Thompson Indians of British Columbia,' 297.
32 Loo, 'Dan Cranmer's Potlatch,' 129, describes the potlatch as 'a lightning rod for the efforts of Christian missionaries bent on civilizing the province's native peoples.' For one example of the missionary assault on the potlatch, see Gough, 'A Priest versus the Potlatch,' 75-89. More generally, see Cole and Chaikin, *An Iron Hand upon the People*, 56-9, 144-6.
33 Good, 'The utmost bounds,' 90.
34 Teit, 'The Thompson Indians of British Columbia,' 326.
35 Teit, 'Attitude of Indians towards missionaries,' 2.
36 Hyam, *Empire and Sexuality*, 182.
37 Garrett, 'Reminiscences,' 25.
38 Castelli, *Imitating Paul*, 134.
39 Good to the Secretary, SPG, RQE 31 March 1870, USPG, E Series, vol. 25, 1869-70.
40 Good to the Secretary, SPG, RQE 30 June 1874, USPG, E Series, vol. 29, 1874. Good's doubts should not unduly surprise us; scholars still debate Paul's thinking on sexuality as it emerges in chapter 7 of the first book of Corinthians. See, for instance, Brown, *The*

*Body and Society*, 33-64, and Boyarin's critique of Brown's reading in his 'Body Politic among the Brides of Christ.'

41 Good to the Secretary, SPG, RQE 30 June 1874, USPG, E Series, vol. 29, 1874.

42 Good to the Secretary, SPG, RQE 31 December 1867, USPG, E Series, vol. 23, 1867-8: 'his attachment to us increases daily.'

43 Good to the Secretary, SPG, RQE 31 March 1870, USPG, E Series, vol. 25, 1869-70.

44 Hills, Diary, 1 June 1868.

45 Hills, Diary, 10 September 1877.

46 Bhabha, 'Articulating the Archaic,' in his *The Location of Culture*, 133 (my emphasis).

47 Ibid., 134, 135.

48 Good to the Secretary, SPG, RQE 30 June 1874, USPG, E Series, vol. 29, 1874.

49 Hills, Diary, 4 May 1874.

50 Foucault, *The Use of Pleasure*, 22. If this mission ethics was conceived by and directed to men, so too is the colonial interrogation discussed by Bhabha (at note 46 above), yet he says nothing of this bent – the colonialism he describes is very much a male encounter from which women are excluded.

51 *The Mission Field* 14 (1869): 225.

52 This phrase is pinched from Wolf, *Europe and the People without History*.

53 Good, 'The utmost bounds,' 91.

54 Ibid., 90.

55 Teit, 'The Thompson Indians of British Columbia,' 293.

56 As one example, Langmore, 'The Object Lesson,' 91-2, reports similar concerns among missionaries of various denominations to pre-war Papua.

57 Hills, Diary, 1 June 1868.

58 Nussbaum, 'The Other Woman,' 143, claims that in Africa it was only really missionaries who worried about polygamy to the extent of intervention; the same is true of colonial British Columbia.

59 As Foucault describes it, bio-power links the regulation of individual bodies to the government of the population at large; sexuality, as for the Anglicans, is central to this articulation. With Stoler, *Race and the Education of Desire*, 40-1, we can represent this colonial management of sexuality 'not as a coherent and comprehensive regime of biopower, but with many of its incipient elements.'

60 Spivak, 'Can the Subaltern Speak,' 299, 298; original emphasis.

61 Jolly, 'Sacred Spaces,' 231-3, reports that the same distinction held for the High Church Anglican mission to Melanesian men and women.

62 Good to the Secretary, SPG, RQE September 1869, USPG, E Series, vol. 25, 1869-70.

63 Wright claimed that 'unless we have large boarding and industrial schools, carried on with the help either of sisters or other ladies, the Indians must still remain ignorant.' *New Westminster Quarterly Paper* 1 (June 1884): 18.

64 Ibid., 2 (October 1884): 15. On All Hallows School, which included the sisterhood but also had European and Native boys as pupils, see Lyons, *Milestones on the Mighty Fraser*, 40-1; Nicolai C. Schou, 'Report on the examination of the All Hallows Mission School, Yale, British Columbia, Mid-Summer 1890,' University of British Columbia Library, Vancouver, BC, Microfilm Collection, CIHM 16095; 'All Hallows School, Yale: "Our Indians in British Columbia,"' BCA, Add. MSS 273.

65 This general point is made by Few, 'Women, Religion, and Power,' 627-37, especially 633-4.

66 White, *The Middle Ground*, 67-72.

67 Larsson, *Conversion to Greater Freedom?* Larsson makes an important caveat: Catholic insistence on monogamy was one reason for the increase in prostitution under colonial rule, for where men put aside women in order to qualify for baptism, some of those who were rejected supported themselves by selling sex. See 116-20 in particular.

68 Cited in Ozment, *Protestants*, 155.

69 Sage, 'The Early Days of the Church of England,' 9, has Hills with 'Anglo-Catholic tendencies'; cited in Bagshaw, *No Better Land*, 287.

70 Pickering, *Anglo-Catholicism*, 38, identifies devotion to the Virgin Mary as the most obvious distinction between Tractarians and Anglo-Catholics.

71  Hills, Diary, 8 July 1860.
72  Hills, Diary, 7 April 1863.
73  Devens, *Countering Colonization*, 5. K. Anderson, *Chain Her by One Foot*, makes a similar argument.
74  See, for instance, Ralston, 'Changes in the Lives of Ordinary Women.'
75  Bourgeault, 'Race, Class and Gender,' especially 89.
76  See in particular the excellent Fiske, 'And Then We Prayed Again'; also her 'Carrier Women and the Politics of Mothering,' especially 200-4.
77  Fiske, 'And Then We Prayed Again,' 64-74.
78  Bourgeault, 'Race, Class and Gender,' 91-4.
79  Smandych and Lee, 'Women, Colonization and Resistance,' 30.
80  Teit, 'The Thompson Indians of British Columbia,' 289-96.
81  Wickwire, 'Women in Ethnography,' 555-6.
82  Good to the Secretary, SPG, RQE 31 March 1870, USPG, E Series, vol. 25, 1869-70.
83  Hills baptized 122 Natives here on 1 June 1873, of whom sixty-eight were women (Hills, Diary, 2 June 1873). Analysis of the mission register suggests that over the lifespan of the mission, men and women were baptized in roughly equal numbers.
84  See, for example, Ralston, 'Changes in the Lives of Ordinary Women,' 60.
85  Hills, Diary, 4 May 1874, discusses two such cases: first, he consented to the remarriage of Percy Quos-a-tas-kut, who left his wife on account of her adultery (verified by village watchmen); second, he ordered an unnamed woman to return to her husband despite his alleged cruelty.
86  Good to the Secretary, SPG, RQE 30 June 1874, USPG, E Series, vol. 29, 1874.

### Chapter 7: Dissolution

1  *Columbia Mission Report* 20 (1878): 37.
2  Teit, 'The Thompson Indians of British Columbia,' 366.
3  *Columbia Mission Report* 20 (1878): 37-8. The emergence of prophets was very common among First Nations cultures; see Abel, *Drum Songs*, 128-31.
4  Teit, 'Mythology of the Thompson Indians,' 413. Gowen, *Church work in British Columbia*, 133, notes that when Bishop Sillitoe visited Lytton in the summer of 1884 to introduce the Nlha7kápmx to their new missionary, the Reverend Richard Small, he investigated a charge of drinking and gambling that had been brought against 'the recognized chief of all the Thompson River tribes' – presumably Spintlum.
5  Teit, 'Attitude of Indians towards missionaries.'
6  Grant, *Ocean to ocean*, 307, reported 'No sign of progress' at Lytton, where the expedition stopped for the night of 2 October: 'Its population of perhaps an hundred souls is made up of Canadians, British Yankees, French, Chinamen, Siwashes, half-breeds; all religions and no religion.'
7  Good to the Secretary, SPG, RQE 30 June and 30 September 1880, USPG, E Series, vol. 35, 1880.
8  Gowen, *Church work in British Columbia*, 17.
9  Boas, Introduction, 2; Galois and Harris, 'Recalibrating Society,' 46.
10 Acton W. Sillitoe to Henry W. Tucker, 4 January 1882, USPG, CLR Series, vol. 149, 1859-91.
11 Good to the Secretary, SPG, RQE 30 June 1881, USPG, E Series, vol. 36, 1881, maintained that 'this new condition of things' obliged a 'new distribution of our pastoral and teaching power.'
12 Good to W.T. Bullock, 30 October 1868, USPG, CLR Series, vol. 149, 1859-91.
13 Bullock to Hills, 31 July and 17 September 1869, USPG, CLS Series, vol. 107, 1859-1911, detail SPG objections to relieving Good of his debt; Hills to Bullock, 16 September 1869, USPG, CLR Series, vol. 149, 1859-91, reports Good thinking about tendering his resignation; Bullock to Good, 3 January 1870, USPG, CLS Series, vol. 107, 1859-1911, relays the good news.
14 Bullock to Good, 22 July 1874, USPG, CLS Series, vol. 107, 1859-1911, lays down the law: missionary funding comes from within the diocese, not from the SPG coffers in London; Bullock to Good, 9 January 1875, USPG, CLS Series, vol. 107, 1859-1911,

confirms SPG loan of £150, which makes Good's case 'an exception to [the Society's] rule.'

15 Bullock to Hills, 22 July 1874; Bullock to Good, 26 October 1876; both in USPG, CLS Series, vol. 107, 1859-1911.

16 Good to Tucker, 8 August 1879, USPG, CLR Series, vol. 149, 1859-91, details his difficulty 'not only to provide for daily wants but also to get even with the past.'

17 Hills supported Good throughout; Wright, who learned of Good's problems from Mrs Good on visiting St. Paul's in 1877, urged the SPG to treat Good considerately. See Simpson, 'Henry Press Wright,' 166-7.

18 Simpson, 'Henry Press Wright,' 168-72.

19 Sillitoe to Tucker, 16 August 1880, USPG, CLR Series, vol. 149, 1859-91. Note that when Sillitoe *did* eventually visit Lytton and inspect Good's progress at St. Paul's, he was far more impressed. 'There has certainly been work done here in the past,' he reported. See Sillitoe to Tucker, 28 January 1881, USPG, CLR Series, vol. 149, 1859-91.

20 Hills, Diary, 9 November 1873.

21 Reverend Horlock, stationed at Yale from January 1882, was highly critical of Good. Horlock to Tucker, Christmas 1882, USPG, CLR Series, vol. 149, 1859-91, states that Good was 'known to celebrate the Holy Communion after having been seen emerging from a saloon in a state of semi-intoxication.'

22 Good to Tucker, 24 January 1881 and 16 November 1882, USPG, CLR Series, vol. 149, 1859-91.

23 Good to Tucker, 4 July 1882 and 23 January 1883; Sillitoe to Tucker, 11 and 14 July 1882; all in CLR Series, vol. 149, 1859-91.

24 *New Westminster Quarterly Paper* 2 (October 1884): 11. Good did not have an immediate successor in Lytton; the Reverend Robert C. Whiteway performed occasional services in the town until Small arrived in May 1884 to take up a full-time position. On Whiteway, Sillitoe to Tucker, 4 January 1882, CLR Series, vol. 149, 1859-91. On Small, Williams and McGeachie, *Archdeacon on Horseback*.

25 Good to the Secretary, SPG, RQE 31 December 1875, USPG, E Series, vol. 30, 1875.

26 Good to the Warden, St. Augustine's, 20 April 1876, CCA, U88/A2/6/John Booth Good, cites 'economical & family reasons' for the relocation of his family. This was not the first time that they had been forced to live apart. Back in 1869, when Good first considered resignation, Sarah and the children spent a number of months in New Westminster. See Good to the Secretary, SPG, RQE June 1869, USPG, E Series, vol. 25, 1869-70.

27 Good to the Secretary, SPG, RQE 31 December 1870, USPG, E Series, vol. 26, 1870-1.

28 Good to the Secretary, SPG, RQE September 1876, USPG, E Series, vol. 31, 1876.

29 Good to the Secretary, SPG, 22 November 1876, USPG, E Series, vol. 31, 1876.

30 Good to the Secretary, SPG, RQE 31 December 1873, USPG, E Series, vol. 29, 1874.

31 Good to the Secretary, SPG, RQE 31 October 1878, USPG, E Series, vol. 33, 1878.

32 Good to the Secretary, SPG, RQE 30 June 1879, USPG, E Series, vol. 34, 1879.

33 See Robin, 'Beyond the Bounds of the West,' 129.

34 One example is Emma Crosby; see Bolt, *Thomas Crosby*, 98-9.

35 It was this decision that cemented Good's opposition to Sillitoe. See Good to Tucker, 24 January 1881, USPG, CLR Series, vol. 149, 1859-91.

36 Good to the Secretary, SPG, RQE 30 September 1880, USPG, E Series, vol. 35, 1880.

37 Good to Tucker, 24 January 1881, USPG, CLR Series, vol. 149, 1859-91; my emphasis.

38 Sillitoe to Tucker, 16 August 1880, USPG, CLR Series, vol. 149, 1859-91, puts Good's failure down to 'his isolation and independence, added, perhaps, to the burden of domestic embarrassments.'

39 Wakefield, *A view of the art of colonization*, 211.

40 Cail, *Land, Man, and the Law*, chapter 1, is a useful introduction to this history.

41 Lytton to Douglas, 31 July 1858, cited in Woodward, 'The Influence of the Royal Engineers,' 14.

42 Woodward, 'The Influence of the Royal Engineers,' 18-9.

43 *The Times*, 21 September 1861.

44 The same was not true on southern Vancouver Island, where early colonial settlement had obliged Douglas to confront the issue of aboriginal title. He did so according to the

terms of the Royal Proclamation of 1763; to cede land to the Crown Douglas first had to acknowledge Native title, and then extinguish it in a formal treaty with the peoples concerned. For discussion of the fourteen treaties that Douglas signed on Vancouver Island, see Fisher, *Contact and Conflict*, 66-8; and Tennant, *Aboriginal Peoples and Politics*, chapter 2.

45  Notably, aboriginal title was never recognized in the mainland colony. Why Douglas now discounted the Royal Proclamation (having observed it before 1854) is not entirely clear. The conventional wisdom has been that insolvency forced his hand, but Tennant offers a more plausible case – that by the early 1860s Douglas no longer deemed aboriginal title relevant, for Natives were expected to assimilate, and a society of equals had no place for rights based on ethnicity. 'Douglas ignored treaty-making on the Mainland,' concludes Tennant, *Aboriginal Peoples and Politics*, 36, 'because his system anticipated assimilated Indians who, having abandoned traditional communities for their homesteads, would maintain neither Indian identity nor Indian land claims.'

46  Good to the Secretary, RQE September 1869, USPG, E Series, vol. 25, 1869-70. This was a favourite theme; elsewhere Good condemned government policy towards the 'natural owners of the country we now call our own,' and said that Native reserves were generally 'quite unsuitable and useless.' Good to the Secretary, SPG, RQE September 1870, USPG, E Series, vol. 26, 1870-1. Bishop Hills also spoke out against the appropriation of Native lands; see Bagshaw, *No Better Land*, 33.

47  See Fisher, 'Joseph Trutch and Indian Land Policy,' 3-33; also his *Contact and Conflict*, 162-5.

48  Good to the Secretary, RQE March 1871, USPG, E Series, vol. 26, 1870-1. This report articulates Good's main concerns.

49  O'Reilly to Trutch, 19 June 1868, *Papers connected with the Indian land question*.

50  Trutch to the Colonial Secretary, 30 June 1868; Seymour to the Colonial Secretary, 3 July; Trutch to the Colonial Secretary, 6 July; CC F1289. This correspondence is not included in the *Papers connected with the Indian land question* collection, which otherwise provides a thorough treatment of the Nicola Lake controversy. Tennant, *Aboriginal Peoples and Politics*, x, maintains that *Papers* contains a 'complete record of the beginnings and early history of the [Native land question],' but some important records clearly are omitted.

51  Trutch to O'Reilly, 5 August 1868; O'Reilly to Trutch, August 29th; *Papers connected with the Indian land question*, 50-1. See also O'Reilly, Diaries, 21-3 August 1868.

52  Good to Musgrave, with enclosed petition from Naweeshistan, 19 December 1870, ibid., 86-7.

53  Colonial Secretary to Good, 18 January 1871, with O'Reilly report of 12 January enclosed; Good to the Colonial Secretary, 3 February; ibid., 88-90.

54  O'Reilly report, 12 January. Good denied that this was the case: 'Lastly, I am charged with inciting the chief to consider himself aggrieved, who would otherwise have remained quiescent. In answer to this, I have to say that the Chief, as soon as he realized his condition, hastened to me, so long ago as the fall of 1868, and with bitter tears and lamentation besought my interference.' Good to the Colonial Secretary, 3 February.

55  Another missionary accused of stirring up Natives over the land question was the Methodist Crosby. Bolt, *Thomas Crosby*, chapter 5, provides a careful commentary on Crosby's role (or otherwise) in Tsimshian disputes with the provincial government in general, and O'Reilly in particular; see especially 73-8.

56  *The Victoria Weekly Standard*, 29 May 1872.

57  Good to Seymour, 3 July 1867; Crease to Elliot, 16 July; Elliot to Crease, 3 August; CC F653/5.

58  Crease, [comments for attention of Seymour?], scrawled on Crease to Elliot, 16 July.

59  Today, certain whites are still accused of stirring up dissent; Tennant, *Aboriginal Peoples and Politics*, 229, identifies an obvious parallel between the 1860s and the 1980s: 'In the early period white politicians blamed white agitators, especially missionaries, for giving the Indians new ideas and false hopes. [In the 1980s] Social Credit spokesmen blamed the federal government.' More recently, the Reform Party accused the New Democrats of similar meddling.

60 Good to the Secretary, SPG, RQE March 1871, USPG, E Series, vol. 26, 1870-1, is decidedly upbeat.
61 Good to the Secretary, SPG, RQE 31 December 1875, USPG, E Series, vol. 30, 1875. On the strained relationship between British Columbia and the Dominion Government in regard to Native land rights in the early 1870s, see Tennant, *Aboriginal Peoples and Politics*, 42-8.
62 Good to the Secretary, SPG, RQE September 1876, USPG, E Series, vol. 31, 1876, has details of Dufferin's visit. For Good's later reflections on Dufferin, see 'The utmost bounds,' 114-5: 'It was through his strenuous interposition the native land grievances were righted.' This statement gives a false impression of the development of provincial land policy; Good's perspective seems to have changed more than the policy itself.
63 The assessment is Fisher's, in his *Contact and Conflict*, 189.
64 Sproat, 'Field minute on the Lytton Subgroup of the Lytton group of Nekla. kap. a. muk. Indians,' 24 July 1878, RG10, vol. 3666, file 10, 176 (2).
65 See Groeneveld-Meijer, 'Manning the Fraser Canyon Gold Rush,' 109-12.
66 Teit, 'The Thompson Indians of British Columbia,' 293.
67 Teit, 'Addenda to publication. Historical-Geographical,' Unpublished ms, n.d., American Philosophical Society: Manuscripts relating to the American Indian, MSS 30(61), Microfilm 372, roll 4.
68 R.C. Harris, 'The Fraser Canyon Encountered,' 118-29, offers a fine account of Sproat's work in the canyon that summer.
69 Sproat, 'Field minute on the Lytton Subgroup.'
70 Ibid. The other Lytton reserves were no better. Sproat wrote to Ball in July 1878 and accused him of having neglected his remit, which, as defined by Douglas (and advocated by Sproat), stipulated that evidence of Native residence should discount all European claims, and that Natives themselves should determine the location and size of reserves. What really got Sproat's goat was the fact that at the larger reserve upstream of Lytton, Ball irrigated *his own adjacent land* (staked in 1864) with water that *should* have gone to the reserve. Sproat to Ball, 15 July 1878, RG10, vol. 3666, file 10, 176 (2).
71 Sproat, 'Field minute on the Lytton Subgroup.'
72 Lefebvre, *The Production of Space*, 285-91.
73 Sproat to the Superintendent General of Indian Affairs, 9 January 1878, RG10, vol. 3657, file 9193.
74 See Tennant, *Aboriginal Peoples and Politics*, 44, 46-7, 49.
75 Sproat to Captain de Winton, 16 November 1882, RG10, vol. 3617, file 4563.
76 This was also the basis of Duncan's initial proposal. See Fisher, *Contact and Conflict*, 188.
77 Sproat also commented on loss of fishing privileges on the Thompson; see Sproat, 'Fishing places,' 4 February 1878, RG10, vol. 3657, file 9361.
78 Sproat, 'Field minute on the Lytton Subgroup'; Sproat to the Superintendent General of Indian Affairs, 15 November 1878, RG10, vol. 3611, file 3755; Fisher, *Contact and Conflict*, 194.
79 Sproat to Ball, 15 July 1878, RG10, vol. 3666, file 10, 176 (2); Ball to Sproat, 29 July 1878, RG10, vol. 3666, file 10, 176 (1); Sproat to the Superintendent General of Indian Affairs, 15 August 1878, RG10, vol. 3666, file 10, 176 (2).
80 R.C. Harris, 'The Fraser Canyon Encountered,' 125.
81 Ball to Trutch, 30 October 1868; Trutch to Ball, 20 November 1868; *Papers connected with the Indian land question*, 53. Good's letter is missing.
82 *Columbia Mission Report* 10 (1868): 32-3.
83 Sproat, 'Field minute on the Lytton Subgroup.'
84 See Fisher, *Contact and Conflict*, 195-8.
85 Grant, *Moon of Wintertime*, 142, concludes that 'missionaries contributed significantly to the native cause'; Weir, *Catalysts and Watchdogs*, 107, maintains the 'efficacy of the mediation provided by ... individual clergy.'
86 Sproat to the Superintendent General of Indian Affairs, 17 August 1878, RG10, vol. 3611, file 3755.

87  D. Harris, 'The Nlha7kápamx Meeting at Lytton,' 5-25. R.C. Harris, 'The Fraser Canyon Encountered,' 128-9, also discusses this meeting, as does Fisher, *Contact and Conflict*, 178-80.
88  Details included in Sproat's 'Rules and regulations formed by the Nekla-kap-a-muk Council, sitting at Lytton, British Columbia, the 17th July 1879, for their own people,' RG10, vol. 3696, file 15, 316. See also Sproat's letter to *The Daily Colonist*, 21 August 1879.
89  R.C. Harris, 'The Fraser Canyon Encountered,' 128.
90  See D. Harris, 'The Nlha7kápamx Meeting at Lytton,' 8-9, 12.
91  Teit, 'Attitude of Indians towards missionaries,' 1.
92  See especially Good to the Secretary, SPG, January 1876, USPG, E Series, vol. 31, 1876.
93  Good to the Secretary, SPG, RQE 30 June 1879, USPG, E Series, vol. 34, 1879, gives details of the meeting.
94  A group of 'Concerned Citizens' tabled several objections to the meeting, including a concern that Natives intended a system of government 'which ignores religious teaching.' See A.C. Anderson, William Duncan, Roderick Finlayson, William J. Macdonald, J.W. Mackay, Archibald McKinlay, W.F. Tolmie, Charles Vernon, Captain James Prevost to George A. Walkem (premier of British Columbia), 25 September 1879, RG10, vol. 3669, file 10, 691.
95  Outrage that Natives should articulate displeasure with their treatment by the province, and fear that confederated Natives might threaten white safety and property (rumours that Natives in the interior were planning to attack white settlers had been circulating for many years now). R.C. Harris, 'The Fraser Canyon Encountered,' 129, describes the 'howls of white indignation' that the 1879 meeting provoked; D. Harris, 'The Nlha7kápamx Meeting at Lytton,' 12-7, provides a full treatment of this response. Sproat was highly critical of the manner in which settlers reacted. He labelled their preferred Indian policy 'terrorism' and condemned their 'race-prejudice.' Sproat to the Superintendent General of Indian Affairs, 5 September 1879, RG10, vol. 3669, file 10, 691.
96  In particular newspaper editor Amor de Cosmos, who, upon learning of the proposed meeting the previous fall, declared immediately that the notion 'originated with the Commissioner.' *The Daily Standard*, 26 November 1878.
97  *The Daily Colonist*, 9 September 1879.
98  Ibid., 12 October 1879.
99  Although he admitted that the Nlha7kápmx wanted him 'on the spot, when the meeting was held, to advise them what to discuss, and to tell them what was within the law, and afterwards to communicate with Ottawa,' Sproat insisted on their 'independence' in resolving to gather. Sproat to the Superintendent General of Indian Affairs, 6 November 1878, RG10, vol. 3669, file 10, 691. Noting that Good supported this version of events, D. Harris, 'The Nlha7kápamx meeting at Lytton,' 9, sides with Sproat against de Cosmos.
100 Hills, Diary, 10 September 1876. According to Hills, Naweeshistan had refused a $500 gift from Dr. Israel Powell, the province's superintendent of Indian Affairs (who criticized Sproat's role in the 1879 meeting), 'lest the land question might be compromised thereby.'
101 *Mission Life* 7, 2 (1876): 458-9. Good was not the only missionary to suffer from land disputes; Furniss, 'Resistance, Coercion, and Revitalization,' 246-8, shows that relations between the Shuswap and their Oblate priests soured in the late 1870s as it became clear that the Oblates could not help the Shuswap to improve their reserves.
102 *The Daily Colonist*, 12 October 1879.
103 Good to the Warden, St. Augustine's, 6 February 1867, CCA, U88/A2/6/John Booth Good.
104 Good to the Secretary, SPG, RQE 31 December 1878, USPG, E Series, vol. 33, 1878.
105 *The Daily Colonist*, 12 October 1879.
106 Sproat to the Superintendent General of Indian Affairs, 17 July 1878, RG10, vol. 3666, file 10, 176 (2); my emphasis.
107 Sproat to the Superintendent General of Indian Affairs, 6 November 1878, RG10, vol. 3669, file 10, 691.
108 As argued by D. Harris, 'The Nlha7kápamx Meeting at Lytton.'

109 Sproat to the Superintendent General of Indian Affairs, 6 November 1878, RG10, vol. 3669, file 10, 691, is the resulting communication.
110 See Fisher, *Contact and Conflict*, 198.
111 Robin, 'Beyond the Bounds of the West,' chapters 6 and 7.
112 In particular the McKenna-McBride Commission of 1913 to 1916, as discussed by Schurmann, 'Reinscribing Colonialism.'

# Bibliography

**Primary**

**Manuscript collections**
American Philosophical Society Library. Philadelphia, PA
Archives of the Diocese of Columbia. Victoria, BC
Archives of the Ecclesiastical Province of British Columbia. Vancouver School of Theology, Vancouver, BC
Archives of the United Society for the Propagation of the Gospel. Rhodes House Library, Oxford, UK
Bancroft Library. Berkeley, CA
British Columbia Archives. Victoria, BC
Canterbury Cathedral Archives. Canterbury, UK
University of British Columbia Library. Vancouver, BC

**Published**
*A sermon, preached at the farewell service celebrated in St. James's Church, Piccadilly, on Wednesday, Nov. 16, 1859, the day previous to his departure for his diocese, by George Hills, D.D. Bishop of Columbia. With an account of the meeting held on the same day at the Mansion House of the City of London, in aid of the Columbia Mission*. London: Rivingtons 1859
*A sermon preached in St. Stephen's, Westminster, on the Sunday before Advent, 1860. By John Garrett, M.A. Vicar of St. Paul, near Penzance, and Commissary to the Bishop of Columbia*, London: Rivingtons 1861
Augustine. *City of God*. Trans. Henry Bettenson. London: Pelican Press 1972
–. *Confessions*. Trans. Henry Chadwick. Oxford: Oxford University Press 1991
Boas, Franz. Introduction to *Traditions of the Thompson River Indians of British Columbia*, by James Teit. American Folk-Lore Society 1898
Brown, Robert C.L. *British Columbia: An essay*. New Westminster, BC: Royal Engineer Press 1863
–. *Klatsassan, and other reminiscences of missionary life in British Columbia*. London: Gilbert and Rivington 1873
*Columbia Mission. Occasional Paper*. London: Rivingtons 1860
*Columbia Mission. Occasional Paper*. London: Rivingtons 1861
Crosby, Thomas. *Among the An-ko-me-nums, or Flathead tribes of Indians of the Pacific Coast*. Toronto: William Briggs 1907
Gowen, Herbert H. *Church work in British Columbia: being a memoir of the episcopate of Acton Windeyer Sillitoe, D.D., D.C.L., First Bishop of New Westminster*. London: Longmans, Green and Co. 1899
Grant, George M. *Ocean to ocean: Sandford Fleming's expedition through Canada in 1872*. Toronto: Belford Brothers 1877

Hooker, Richard. *Laws of Ecclesiastical Polity. Vol. II.* Oxford: Clarendon Press 1820
Lugrin, Nancy de Bertrand. *The Pioneer Women of Vancouver Island, 1843-1866*, edited by
  John Hosie. Victoria: The Women's Canadian Club of Victoria 1928
Macfie, Matthew. *Vancouver Island and British Columbia: their history, resources, and
  prospects.* London: Longman Green 1865
Merivale, Herman. *Lectures on colonization and colonies. Delivered before the University of
  Oxford in 1839, 1840, and 1841. Vol. I.* London: Longman 1841
Morice, A.G. *History of the Catholic Church in Western Canada: From Lake Superior to the
  Pacific (1659-1895), Vol. II.* Toronto: Musson Book Company 1910
*The 'Occasional Paper.' Two letters from the Bishop of Columbia to the Rev. E. Cridge and
  Bishop Demers.* Victoria: British Colonist Office 1860
*'Occupy till I come.' A sermon, preached at the first annual service of the Columbia Mission,
  in the church of St. Martin's-in-the-Fields, on Wednesday, June 6, 1860. By the Rev. Henry
  Mackenzie, M.A. Prebendary of Lincoln; Chaplain to the Bishop of that diocese; proctor in
  convocation for the clergy of the same, andc. andc.* London: Rivingtons 1860
*The office for the Holy Communion translated into the Neklakapamuk tongue, for the use of
  the Indians of the St. Paul's Mission, Lytton, British Columbia.* Victoria: St. Paul's Mission
  Press 1878
Ormsby, Margaret, ed. *A Pioneer Gentlewoman in British Columbia: The Recollections of
  Susan Allison.* Vancouver: UBC Press 1976
*Papers connected with the Indian land question.* Victoria: Richard Wolfenden 1875
*The past and present extension of the Gospel by missions to the heathen: considered in eight
  lectures, delivered before the University of Oxford, in the year MDCCCXLIII. At the lecture
  founded by John Bampton, M.A. canon of Salisbury. By Anthony Grant, D.C.L. Vicar of Rom-
  ford, Essex, and late Fellow of New College.* London: Rivingtons 1845
*Report of the Second Session of the First Synod of the Diocese of British Columbia.* Victoria:
  Alex Rose 1876
Smith, Dorothy Blakey, ed. *Lady Franklin visits the Pacific Northwest: being extracts from
  the letters of Miss Sophia Cracoft, Sir John Franklin's niece, February to April 1861 and April
  to July 1870.* Provincial Archives of British Columbia Memoir No. XI. Victoria 1974
Smith, Harlan I. 'Archaeology of Lytton, British Columbia.' In *The Jesup North Pacific
  Expedition, Memoirs of the American Museum of Natural History. Vol. 2.* New York 1899
*Synods, their constitution and objects. A sermon, preached in Christ Church and St. John's,
  Victoria, January 1874, by the Right Rev. George Hills, D.D., Lord Bishop of British Colum-
  bia.* Victoria Standard Office 1874
Teit, James. 'Mythology of the Thompson Indians.' In *The Jesup North Pacific Expedition,
  Memoirs of the American Museum of Natural History. Vol.8.* New York 1912
—. 'The Thompson Indians of British Columbia.' In *The Jesup North Pacific Expedition,
  Memoirs of the American Museum of Natural History. Vol. 1.* New York 1900
*'The voice of him that crieth in the wilderness.' A sermon, preached in St. James' Church, Pic-
  cadilly, at the annual service of the Columbia Mission, on the festival of St. Barnabas, 1861.
  By John Downall, M.A., Archdeacon of Totnes.* London: Rivingtons 1861
Wakefield, Edward Gibbon. *A view of the art of colonization, with present reference to the
  British Empire; in letters between a statesman and a colonist.* London: John W. Parker 1849
West, John. *The substance of a journal during a residence at the Red River colony, British
  North America; and frequent excursions among the North-West American Indians, in the
  years 1820, 1821, 1822, 1823.* London: L.B. Seeley and Son 1824

**Newspapers and periodicals**
*British Columbia Tribune*
*Church Missionary Gleaner*
*Church Missionary Intelligencer*
*The Churchman's Gazette and New Westminster Diocesan Chronicle*
*Columbia Mission Report*
*The Daily British Colonist*
*The Gospel Missionary*
*The Mission Field*

Mission Life
New Westminster Quarterly Paper
People's Magazine
The Times
The Victoria Daily Standard
The Victoria Weekly Gazette
The Victoria Weekly Standard

**Secondary**

**Published**

Abel, Kerry. *Drum Songs: Glimpses of Dene History*. Montreal and Kingston: McGill-Queen's University Press 1993

Allman, Jean. 'Making Mothers: Missionaries, Medical Officers and Women's Work in Colonial Asante, 1924-1945.' *History Workshop Journal* 38 (1994): 23-47

Amies, Marion. 'The Victorian Governess and Colonial Ideals of Womanhood.' *Victorian Studies* 31, 4 (1988): 537-65

Anderson, Benedict. *Imagined Communities: Reflections on the Origin and Spread of Nationalism*. London: Verso 1991

Anderson, Karen. *Chain Her by One Foot: The Subjugation of Native Women in Seventeenth-Century New France*. New York: Routledge 1991

Asad, Talal. 'Comments on Conversion.' In *Conversion to Modernities: The Globalization of Christianity*, edited by Peter Van der Veer. New York: Routledge 1996

–. *Genealogies of Religion: Discipline and Reasons of Power in Christianity and Islam*. Baltimore: Johns Hopkins University Press 1993

Babcock, W. 'Augustine and Tyconius: A Study in the Latin Appropriation of Paul.' *Studia Patristica* 17, 3 (1982): 1209-15

Bagshaw, Roberta L. 'Church of England Land Policy in Colonial British Columbia.' In *British Columbia: Geographical Essays*, edited by Paul M. Koroscil. Burnaby: SFU Department of Geography 1991

–, ed. *No Better Land: The 1860 Diaries of Anglican Colonial Bishop George Hills*. Victoria: Sono Nis 1996

Balibar, Etienne. 'Paradoxes of Universality.' In *Anatomy of Racism*, edited by David Theo Goldberg. Minneapolis: University of Minnesota Press 1990

Barker, Ernest. *The Ideas and Ideals of the British Empire*. Cambridge: Cambridge University Press 1946

Barker, John. 'Cheerful Pragmatists: Anglican Missionaries among the Maisin of Collingwood Bay, Northeastern Papua, 1898-1920.' *Journal of Pacific History* 22, 2 (1987): 66-81

Barman, Jean. 'The Emergence of Educational Structures in Nineteenth-Century British Columbia.' In *Children, Teachers and Schools in the History of British Columbia*, edited by Jean Barman, Neil Sutherland, and J. Donald Wilson. Calgary: Detselig Enterprises 1995

–. *The West beyond the West: A History of British Columbia*. Toronto: University of Toronto Press 1991

Bebbington, David W. 'Evangelicalism.' In *The Blackwell Encyclopedia of Modern Christian Thought*, edited by Alister E. McGrath. Oxford: Blackwell 1993

–. *Evangelicalism in Modern Britain: A History from the 1730s to the 1980s*. London: Unwin Hyman 1990

Bernauer, James W., and Michael Mahon. 'The Ethics of Michel Foucault.' In *The Cambridge Companion to Foucault*, edited by Gary Gutting. Cambridge: Cambridge University Press 1994

Bernstein, Richard J. 'Incommensurability and Otherness revisited.' In *The New Constellation: The Ethical/Political Horizons of Modernity/Postmodernity*. Cambridge, MA: MIT Press 1992

Best, G.F.A. 'The Evangelicals and the Established Church in the Early Nineteenth Century.' *Journal of Theological Studies* 10, 1 (1959): 63-78

Bhabha, Homi K. *The Location of Culture*. London: Routledge 1994

Bolt, Clarence. *Thomas Crosby and the Tsimshian: Small Shoes for Feet Too Large*. Vancouver: UBC Press 1992

Bourgeault, Ron. 'Race, Class and Gender: Colonial Domination of Indian Women.' In *Race, Class, Gender: Bonds and Barriers*, edited by Jesse Vorst et al. Winnipeg: Society for Socialist Studies 1989

Bowen, Desmond. *The Idea of the Victorian Church: A Study of the Church of England, 1833-1899*. Montreal: McGill University Press 1968

Boyarin, Daniel. 'Body Politic among the Brides of Christ: Paul and the Origins of Christian Sexual Renunciation.' In *Asceticism*, edited by Vincent L. Wimbush and Richard Valantasis. New York: Oxford University Press 1995

Brown, Peter. *Augustine of Hippo*. Berkeley: University of California Press 1967

–. *The Body and Society: Men, Women and Sexual Renunciation in Early Christianity*. London: Faber and Faber 1990

–. *Religion and Society in the Age of Saint Augustine*. London: Faber and Faber 1990

Bush, Julia. '"The right sort of woman": Female Emigrators and Emigration to the British Empire, 1890-1910.' *Women's History Review* 3, 3 (1994): 385-409

Cail, Robert E. *Land, Man, and the Law: The Disposal of Crown Lands in British Columbia, 1871-1913*. Vancouver: UBC Press 1974.

Carey, Simon H.D. 'The Church of England and the Colour Question in Victoria, 1860.' *Journal of the Canadian Church Historical Society* 24, 2 (1982): 63-74

Carter, Paul. *The Road to Botany Bay*. London: Faber and Faber 1987

Castelli, Elizabeth A. *Imitating Paul: A Discourse of Power*. Louisville: Westminster/John Knox Press 1991

Chadwick, Owen. *The Mind of the Oxford Movement*. Stanford: Stanford University Press 1960

Chaudhuri, Nadur, and Margaret Strobel, eds. *Western Women and Imperialism: Complicity and Resistance*. Bloomington: Indiana University Press 1992

Chitty, Derwas J. *The Desert a City: An Introduction to the Study of Egyptian and Palestinian Monasticism under the Christian Empire*. Oxford: Blackwell 1966

Clayton, Daniel. 'Geographies of the Lower Skeena.' *BC Studies* 94 (1992): 29-58

–. *Islands of Truth: Vancouver Island from Captain Cook to the Beginnings of Colonialism*. Berkeley: University of California Press, forthcoming

Clifford, James. *Person and Myth: Maurice Leenhardt in the Melanesian World*. Berkeley: University of California Press 1982

Cnattingius, Hans. *Bishops and Societies: A Study of Anglican Colonial and Missionary Expansion 1698-1850*. London: S.P.C.K. 1952

Cole, Douglas, and Ira Chaikin. *An Iron Hand upon the People: The Law Against the Potlatch on the Northwest Coast*. Vancouver: Douglas and McIntyre 1990

Colley, Linda. *Britons: Forging the Nation 1707-1837*. London: Pimlico 1994

Collinson, Patrick. 'The Protestant Nation.' In *The Birthpangs of Protestant England: Religious and Cultural Change in the Sixteenth and Seventeenth Centuries*. New York: St. Martin's Press 1988

Comaroff, Jean, and John Comaroff. *Of Revelation and Revolution: Christianity, Colonialism, and Consciousness in South Africa. Volume 1*. Chicago: University of Chicago Press 1991

Cooper, Frederick, and Ann Laura Stoler, eds. *Tensions of Empire: Colonial Cultures in a Bourgeois World*. Berkeley: University of California Press 1997

Creese, Gillian, and Veronica Strong-Boag, eds. *British Columbia Reconsidered: Essays on Women*. Vancouver: Press Gang Publishers 1992

Davidoff, Leonore. 'Mastered for Life: Servant and Wife in Victorian and Edwardian England.' *Journal of Social History* 7, 4 (1974): 406-28

Davidoff, Leonore, and Catherine Hall. *Family Fortunes: Men and Women of the English Middle Class, 1780-1850*. Chicago: University of Chicago Press 1987

Davin, Anna. 'Imperialism and Motherhood.' In *Patriotism: The Making and Unmaking of British National Identity. Vol. 1*, edited by Raphael Samuel. London: Routledge 1989

De Certeau, Michel. 'The Historiographical Operation.' In *The Writing of History*, trans. Tom Conley. New York: Columbia University Press 1988

–. *The Practice of Everyday Life*. Berkeley: University of California Press 1984

Delumeau, Jean. *Le péché et la peur: la culpabilisation en Occident (XIIIe – XVIIIe siècles)*. Paris: Fayard 1983

Devens, Carol. *Countering Colonization: Native American Women and Great Lakes Missions, 1630-1900*. Berkeley: University of California Press 1992

—. '"If we get the girls, we get the race": Missionary Education of Native American Girls.' *Journal of World History* 3, 2 (1992): 219-37

Dickason, Olive P. *Canada's First Nations: A History of Founding Peoples from Earliest Times*. Toronto: McClelland and Stewart 1992

Downs, Barry. *Sacred Places: British Columbia's Early Churches*. Vancouver: Douglas and McIntyre 1980

Driver, Felix. 'Moral Geographies: Social Science and the Urban Environment in Mid-nineteenth Century England.' *Transactions: Institute of British Geographers* 13 (1988): 275-87

Dvornik, F. *National Churches and the Church Universal*. Westminster: Dacre Press 1945

Eno, R.B. 'Some Nuances in the Ecclesiology of the Donatists.' *Studia Patristica* 14, 3 (1976): 417-21

Fabian, Johannes. *Time and the Other: How Anthropology Makes Its Object*. New York: Columbia University Press 1983

Faul, D. 'Sinners in the Holy Church: A Problem in the Ecclesiology of St. Augustine.' *Studia Patristica* 9, 3 (1966): 404-15

Few, Martha. 'Women, Religion, and Power: Gender and Resistance in Daily Life in Late-Seventeenth Century Santiago de Guatemala.' *Ethnohistory* 42, 4 (1995): 627-37

Fisher, Robin. *Contact and Conflict: Indian-European Relations in British Columbia, 1774-1890*. Vancouver: UBC Press 1992

–. 'Joseph Trutch and Indian Land Policy.' *BC Studies* 12 (1971-2): 3-33

Fiske, Jo-Anne. 'Carrier Women and the Politics of Mothering.' In *British Columbia Reconsidered: Essays on Women*, edited by Gillian Creese and Veronica Strong-Boag. Vancouver: Press Gang Publishers 1992

Foucault, Michel. *Discipline and Punish: The Birth of the Prison*. London: Penguin 1977

–. 'Governmentality.' *Ideology and Consciousness* 6 (1979): 5-21

–. *An Introduction*. Vol. 1 of *The History of Sexuality*. Trans. Robert Hurley. New York: Vintage Books 1990

–. 'Omnes et Singulatim: Towards a Criticism of "Political Reason."' In *The Tanner Lectures on Human Values*, vol. 2, edited by Sterling M. McMurrin. Salt Lake City: University of Utah Press 1981

–. 'Of Other Spaces.' *Diacritics* 16 (1986): 22-7

–. *Power/Knowledge: Selected Interviews and Other Writings, 1972-1977*, edited by Colin Gordon. Brighton: Harvester Press 1980

–. *Résumé des cours, 1970-1982*. Paris: Julliard 1989

–. 'The Subject and Power.' In *Michel Foucault: Beyond Structuralism and Hermeneutics*, edited by Hubert L. Dreyfus and Paul Rabinow. Brighton: Harvester Press 1982

–. *The Use of Pleasure*. Vol. 2 of *The History of Sexuality*. Trans. Robert Hurley. New York: Vintage Books 1990

Fredriksen, Paula. 'Paul and Augustine: Conversion Narratives, Orthodox Traditions, and the Retrospective Self.' *Journal of Theological Studies* 37, 1 (1986): 3-34

Frend, W.H.C. *The Donatist Church: A Movement of Protest in Roman North Africa*. Oxford: Clarendon Press 1952

Furniss, Elizabeth. 'Resistance, Coercion, and Revitalization: The Shuswap Encounter with Roman Catholic Missionaries, 1860-1900.' *Ethnohistory* 42, 2 (1995): 231-63

Galois, Robert, and R. Cole Harris. 'Recalibrating Society: The Population Geography of British Columbia in 1881.' *Canadian Geographer* 38, 1 (1994): 37-53

Gasparro, Giulia Sfameni. 'Asceticism and Anthropology: *Enkrateia* and "Double Creation" in Early Christianity.' In *Asceticism*, edited by Vincent L. Wimbush and Richard Valantasis. New York: Oxford University Press 1995

Geertz, Clifford. '"Internal Conversion" in Contemporary Bali.' In *The Interpretation of Cultures*. New York: Basic Books 1973

George, Rosemary Marangoly. 'Homes in the Empire, Empires in the Home.' *Cultural Critique* (winter 1993-4): 95-127

Gough, Barry M. 'A Priest versus the Potlatch: The Reverend Alfred James Hall and the Fort Rupert Kwakiutl, 1878-1880.' *Journal of the Canadian Church Historical Society* 24, 2 (1982): 75-89

Grant, John Webster. *Moon of Wintertime: Missionaries and the Indians of Canada in Encounter since 1534*. Toronto: University of Toronto Press 1984

Gregory, Derek. 'Between the Book and the Lamp: Imaginative Geographies of Egypt, 1849-50.' *Transactions: Institute of British geographers* 20 (1995): 29-57

–. *Geographical Imaginations*. Oxford: Blackwell 1994

Gresko, Jacqueline. '"Roughing it in the bush" in British Columbia: Mary Moody's Pioneer Life in New Westminster, 1859-1863.' In *British Columbia Reconsidered: Essays on Women*, edited by Gillian Creese and Veronica Strong-Boag. Vancouver: Press Gang Publishers 1992

Grimshaw, Patricia. 'New England Missionary Wives, Hawaiian Women and "the cult of true womanhood."' In *Family and Gender in the Pacific: Domestic Contradictions and the Colonial Impact*, edited by Margaret Jolly and Martha Macintyre. Cambridge: Cambridge University Press 1989

Gutting, Gary, ed. *The Cambridge Companion to Foucault*. Cambridge: Cambridge University Press 1994

Haig-Brown, Celia. *Resistance and Renewal: Surviving the Indian Residential School*. Vancouver: Tillacum Library 1988

Hall, Walter Phelps, and Robert Greenhalgh Albion. *A History of England and the British Empire*. 3rd ed. Boston: Ginn and Company 1953

Hanna, Darwin, and Mamie Henry, eds. *Our Tellings: Interior Salish Stories of the Nlha7kápmx People*. Vancouver: UBC Press 1995

Harris, Douglas. 'The Nlha7kápamx Meeting at Lytton, 1879, and the Rule of Law.' *BC Studies* 108 (1995-6): 5-25

Harris, R. Cole. *The Resettlement of British Columbia: Essays on Colonialism and Geographical Change*. Vancouver: UBC Press 1997

Hayden, Brian, ed. *A Complex Culture of the British Columbia Plateau: Traditional Stl'átl'imx Resource Use*. Vancouver: UBC Press 1992

Hefner, Robert W., ed. *Conversion to Christianity: Historical and Anthropological Perspectives on a Great Transformation*. Berkeley: University of California Press 1993

–. 'World Building and the Rationality of Conversion.' In *Conversion to Christianity: Historical and Anthropological Perspectives on a Great Transformation*. Berkeley: University of California Press 1993

Henderson, John R. 'Missionary Influences on the Haida Settlement and Subsistence Patterns, 1876-1920.' *Ethnohistory* 21, 4 (1974): 303-16

Himmelfarb, Gertrude. *Marriage and Morals among the Victorians and Other Essays*. London: I.B. Tauris 1989

Horton, Robin. 'On the Rationality of Conversion.' *Africa* 45 (1975): 219-35, 373-99

Howay, F.W. *British Columbia from the Earliest Times to the Present*. Vol. 2. Vancouver: S.J. Clarke Publishing 1914

–. 'The Negro Immigration into Vancouver Island in 1858.' *British Columbia Historical Quarterly* 3, 2 (1939): 101-13

Hyam, Ronald. *Empire and Sexuality: The British Experience*. Manchester: Manchester University Press 1990

Jolly, Margaret. 'Colonizing Women: The Maternal Body and Empire.' In *Feminism and the Politics of Difference*, edited by Sneja Gunew and Anna Yeatman. Halifax: Fernwood 1993

–. 'Sacred Spaces: Churches, Men's Houses and Households in South Pentecost, Vanuatu.' In *Family and Gender in the Pacific: Domestic Contradictions and the Colonial Impact*, edited by Margaret Jolly and Martha Macintyre. Cambridge: Cambridge University Press 1989

Jolly, Margaret, and Martha Macintyre, eds. *Family and Gender in the Pacific: Domestic Contradictions and the Colonial Impact*. Cambridge: Cambridge University Press 1989

Kee, Howard Clark. 'From the Jesus Movement toward Institutional Church.' In *Conversion to Christianity: Historical and Anthropological Perspectives on a Great Transformation*, edited by Robert W. Hefner. Berkeley: University of California Press 1993

Kilian, Crawford. *Go Do Some Great Thing: The Black Pioneers of British Columbia.* Vancouver: Douglas and McIntyre 1978

Langmore, Diane. 'The Object Lesson of a Civilized, Christian Home.' In *Family and Gender in the Pacific: Domestic Contradictions and the Colonial Impact*, edited by Margaret Jolly and Martha Macintyre. Cambridge: Cambridge University Press 1989

Larsson, Birgitta. *Conversion to Greater Freedom? Women, Church and Social Change in North-Western Tanzania under Colonial Rule.* Stockholm: Almquist and Wiksell International 1991

Lay, Jackie. 'To Columbia on the Tynemouth: The Emigration of Single Women and Girls in 1862.' In *In Her Own Right: Selected Essays on Women's History in BC*, edited by Barbara Latham and Cathy Kess. Victoria: Camosun College 1980

Lefebvre, Henri. *The Production of Space.* Oxford: Basil Blackwell 1991

Lewis, Reina. *Gendering Orientalism: Race, Femininity and Representation.* London: Routledge 1996

Loo, Tina. 'Dan Cranmer's Potlatch: Law as Coercion, Symbol, and Rhetoric in British Columbia, 1884-1951.' *Canadian Historical Review* 73, 2 (1992): 125-65

-. *Making Law, Order, and Authority in British Columbia, 1821-1871.* Toronto: University of Toronto Press 1994

-. 'Tonto's Due: Law, Culture, and Colonization in British Columbia.' In *Making Western Canada: Essays on European Colonization and Settlement*, edited by Catherine Cavanaugh and Jeremy Mouat. Toronto: Geramond Press 1996

Lovell, W. George. 'Mayans, Missionaries, Evidence and Truth: The Polemics of Native Resettlement in Sixteenth-Century Guatemala.' *Journal of Historical Geography* 16, 3 (1990): 277-94

Low, Gail Ching-Liang. *White Skins/Black Masks: Representation and Colonialism.* London: Routledge 1996

Luria, Keith P. 'The Politics of Protestant Conversion to Catholicism in the Seventeenth-Century France.' In *Conversion to Modernities: The Globalization of Christianity*, edited by Peter Van der Veer. New York: Routledge 1996

Lyons, C.P. *Milestones on the Mighty Fraser.* Vancouver: Evergreen Press 1950

McClintock, Anne. *Imperial Leather: Race, Gender and Sexuality in the Colonial Contest.* New York: Routledge 1995

MacCormack, Sabine. *Religion in the Andes: Vision and Imagination in Early Colonial Peru.* Princeton: Princeton University Press 1991

Mackie, Richard. 'The Colonization of Vancouver Island, 1849-1858.' *BC Studies* 96 (1992-3): 3-40

McLynn, Neil B. *Ambrose of Milan: Church and Court in a Christian Capital.* Berkeley: University of California Press 1994

McNally, Vincent J. 'Church-State Relations and American Influence in British Columbia before Confederation.' *Journal of Church and State* 34, 1 (1992): 93-110

Marks, John. 'A New Image for Thought.' *New Formations* 25 (1995): 66-76

Marx, Karl. *Grundrisse.* Harmondsworth: Penguin 1973

Meeks, Wayne A. *The First Urban Christians: The Social World of the Apostle Paul.* New Haven: Yale University Press 1983

Meinardus, Otto F.A. *St. Paul in Ephesus and the Cities of Galatia and Cyprus.* Athens: Lycabettus Press 1973

Milbank, John. *Theology and Social Theory: Beyond Secular Reason.* Oxford: Blackwell Publishers 1990

Miller, James. *The Passion of Michel Foucault.* London: Harper Collins 1993

Moir, John S. *Church and State in Canada, 1627-1867: Basic Documents.* Toronto: McClelland and Stewart 1967

-. *The Church in the British Era: From the British Conquest to Confederation.* Toronto: McGraw-Hill Ryerson 1972

Morgan, E.R., and Roger Lloyd, eds. *The Mission of the Anglican Communion.* London: S.P.C.K. and S.P.G. Books 1948

Morrison, Karl F. *Conversion and Text: The Cases of Augustine of Hippo, Herman-Judah, and Constantine Tsatsos*. Charlottesville: University Press of Virginia 1992
–. 'Rome and the City of God: An Essay on the Constitutional Relationships of Empire and Church in the Fourth Century.' *Transactions of the American Philosophical Society* 54, 1 (1964)
–. *Understanding Conversion*. Charlottesville: University Press of Virginia 1992
Neill, Stephen C. 'Christian Missions.' *Encyclopedia Britannica*. Vol. 15. 1973
–. *A History of Christian Missions*. Harmondsworth: Penguin 1964
Nock, Arthur D. *Conversion: The Old and the New in Religion from Alexander the Great to Augustine of Hippo*. New York: Oxford University Press 1933
Nussbaum, Felicity. 'The Other Woman: Polygamy, *Pamela*, and the Prerogative of Empire.' In *Women, 'Race,' and Writing in the Early Modern Period*, edited by Margo Hendricks and Patricia Parker. London: Routledge 1994
Obeyesekere, Gananath. *The Apotheosis of Captain Cook: European Mythmaking in the Pacific*. Princeton: Princeton University Press 1992
Ozment, Steven. *Protestants: The Birth of a Revolution*. New York: Doubleday 1992
Pagden, Anthony. *Lords of All the World: Ideologies of Empire in Spain, Britain and France c. 1500-1800*. New Haven: Yale University Press 1995
Palmer, R.R., ed. *Rand McNally Atlas of World History*. New York: Rand McNally 1965
Parry, Benita. 'Problems in Current Theories of Colonial Discourse.' *Oxford Literary Review* 9 (1987): 27-58
–. 'Signs of Our Times: Discussion of Homi Bhabha's *The Location of Culture*.' *Third Text* 28-9 (1994): 5-24
Pascoe, C.F. *Two Hundred Years of the S.P.G.* Vol. 1. London: S.P.G. 1901
Pasquino, Pasquale. 'Michel Foucault (1929-84): The Will to Knowledge.' *Economy and Society* 15, 1 (1986): 97-109
Pateman, Carole. *The Sexual Contract*. Stanford: Stanford University Press 1988
Peake, Frank A. 'John Booth Good in British Columbia: The Trials and Tribulations of the Church, 1861-1899.' *Pacific Northwest Quarterly* 75, 2 (1984): 70-8
Perry, Adele. '"Oh I'm just sick of the faces of men": Gender Imbalance, Race, Sexuality, and Sociability in Nineteenth-Century British Columbia.' *BC Studies* 105-6 (1995): 27-43
Peterson, M. Jeanne. 'The Victorian Governess: Status Incongruence in Family and Society.' *Victorian Studies* 14, 1 (1970): 7-26
Philo, Chris. 'Foucault's Geography.' *Environment and Planning D: Society and Space* 10 (1992): 137-61
Pickering, W.S.F. *Anglo-Catholicism: A Study in Religious Ambiguity*. New York: Routledge 1989
Pollmann, Judith. 'A Different Road to God: The Protestant Experience of Conversion in the Sixteenth Century.' In *Conversion to Modernities: The Globalization of Christianity*, edited by Peter Van der Veer. New York: Routledge 1996
Porter, Andrew. 'Religion and Empire: British Expansion in the Long Nineteenth Century, 1780-1914.' *Journal of Imperial and Commonwealth History* 20, 3 (1992): 370-90
Pratt, Mary Louise. *Imperial Eyes: Travel Writing and Transculturation*. London: Routledge 1992
Rafael, Vicente L. *Contracting Colonialism: Translation and Christian Conversion in Tagalog Society under Early Spanish Rule*. Manila: Ateneo de Manila University Press 1988
Ralston, Caroline. 'Changes in the Lives of Ordinary Women in Early Post-contact Hawaii.' In *Family and Gender in the Pacific: Domestic Contradictions and the Colonial Impact*, edited by Margaret Jolly and Martha Macintyre. Cambridge: Cambridge University Press 1989
Robinson, Samuel. 'Christian Asceticism and the Emergence of the Monastic Tradition.' In *Asceticism*, edited by Vincent L. Wimbush and Richard Valantasis. New York: Oxford University Press 1995
Roper, Lyndal. *The Holy Household: Women and Morals, in Reformation Augsburg*. Oxford: Clarendon Press 1989
Rousseau, Philip. *Ascetics, Authority, and the Church in the Age of Jerome and Cassian*. Oxford: Oxford University Press 1978

Ruether, Rosemary Radford. *Sexism and God-Talk: Toward a Feminist Theology.* Boston: Beacon Press 1983

Rushdie, Salman. *Imaginary Homelands: Essays and Criticism 1981-1991.* London: Granta Books 1991

Rutherdale, Myra. 'Revisiting Colonization through Gender: Anglican Missionary Women in the Pacific Northwest and the Arctic, 1860-1945.' *BC Studies* 104 (1994): 3-23

Sage, Walter N. 'The Early Days of the Church of England on the Pacific Slope, 1579-1879.' *Journal of the Canadian Church Historical Society* 2, 1 (1953): 1-17

Said, Edward W. *Culture and Imperialism.* London: Chatto and Windus 1993

–. *Orientalism.* Harmondsworth: Penguin 1985

Sambayya, E. 'The Genius of the Anglican Communion.' In *The Mission of the Anglican Communion,* edited by E.R. Morgan and Roger Lloyd. London: S.P.C.K. and S.P.G. Books 1948

Scott, David. 'Colonial Governmentality.' *Social Text* 43 (1995): 191-220

Scott, William A. *Historical Protestantism: An Historical Introduction to Protestant Theology.* Englewood Cliffs, NJ: Prentice-Hall 1971

Simpson, Donald H. 'Henry Press Wright: First Archdeacon of Columbia.' *BC Historical Quarterly* 19, 3-4 (1955): 123-86

Slater, G. Hollis. 'New Light on Herbert Beaver.' *BC Historical Quarterly* 6, 1 (1942): 13-29

Smandych, Russell, and Gloria Lee. 'Women, Colonization and Resistance: Elements of an Amerindian Autohistorical Approach to the Study of Law and Colonialism.' *Native Studies Review* 10, 1 (1995): 21-46

Smith, Allan. 'The Writing of British Columbia History.' *BC Studies* 45 (1980): 73-102

Sohmer, Sara H. 'Christianity without Civilization: Anglican Sources for an Alternative Nineteenth-Century Mission Methodology.' *Journal of Religious History* 18, 2 (1994): 174-97

Southey, Robert. *History of Brazil.* Vol. 2. London: Longman 1817

Spivak, Gayatri Chakravorty. 'Can the Subaltern Speak?' In *Marxism and the Interpretation of Culture,* edited by Cary Nelson and Lawrence Grossberg. Urbana: University of Illinois Press 1988

Stock, Eugene. *One Hundred Years: Being the Short History of the Church Missionary Society.* London: Church Missionary Society 1898

Stoler, Ann Laura. 'Carnal Knowledge and Imperial Power: Gender, Race, and Morality in Colonial Asia.' In *Gender at the Crossroads of Knowledge: Feminist Anthropology in the Postmodern Era,* edited by Micaela di Leonardo. Berkeley: University of California Press 1991

–. 'Making Empire Respectable: The Politics of Race and Sexual Morality in 20th-Century Colonial Cultures.' *American Ethnologist* 16, 4 (1989): 634-60

–. *Race and the Education of Desire: Foucault's History of Sexuality and the Colonial Order of Things.* Durham: Duke University Press 1995

–. 'Rethinking Colonial Categories: European Communities and the Boundaries of Rule.' *Comparative Studies in Society and History* 31, 1 (1989): 134-61

Suleri, Sara. *The Rhetoric of English India.* Chicago: University of Chicago Press 1992

Tennant, Paul. *Aboriginal Peoples and Politics: The Indian Land Question in British Columbia, 1849-1989.* Vancouver: UBC Press 1990

Thomas, Nicholas. 'Colonial Conversions: Difference, Hierarchy, and History in Early Twentieth-Century Evangelical Propaganda.' *Comparative Studies in Society and History* 34, 2 (1992): 366-89

–. *Colonialism's Culture: Anthropology, Travel and Government.* Princeton: Princeton University Press 1994

Thompson, Arthur N. 'John West: A Study of the Conflict between Civilization and the Fur Trade.' *Journal of the Canadian Church Historical Society* 12, 3 (1970): 44-57

Thorne, Susan. '"The conversion of Englishmen and the conversion of the World Inseparable": Missionary Imperialism and the Language of Class in Early Industrial Britain.' In *Tensions of Empire: Colonial Cultures in a Bourgeois World,* edited by Frederick Cooper and Ann Laura Stoler. Berkeley: University of California Press 1997

Tomkins, Oliver S. 'The Anglican Communion and the Œcumenical Movement.' In *The Mission of the Anglican Communion*, edited by E.R. Morgan and Roger Lloyd. London: S.P.C.K. and S.P.G. Books 1948

Usher, Jean. *William Duncan of Metlakatla: A Victorian Missionary in British Columbia*. Ottawa: National Museums of Canada 1974

Van der Veer, Peter, ed. *Conversion to Modernities: The Globalization of Christianity*. New York: Routledge 1996

Van Kirk, Sylvia. *'Many tender ties': Women in Fur-Trade Society in Western Canada, 1670-1870*. Winnipeg: Watson and Dwyer 1980

-. 'A Vital Presence: Women in the Cariboo Gold Rush, 1862-1875.' In *British Columbia Reconsidered: Essays on Women*, edited by Gillian Creese and Veronica Strong-Boag. Vancouver: Press Gang Publishers 1992

Vaughan, Megan. *Curing Their Ills: Colonial Power and African Illness*. Cambridge: Polity Press 1991

Viswanathan, Gauri. 'Coping with (Civil) Death: The Christian Convert's Rights of Passage in Colonial India.' In *After Colonialism: Imperial Histories and Postcolonial Displacements*, edited by Gyan Prakash. Princeton: Princeton University Press 1995

-. *Masks of Conquest: Literary Study and British Rule in India*. New York: Columbia University Press 1989

Weir, Joan. *Catalysts and Watchdogs: B.C.'s Men of God, 1836-1871*. Victoria: Sono Nis Press 1995

White, Richard. *The Middle Ground: Indians, Empires, and Republics in the Great Lakes Region, 1650-1815*. Cambridge: Cambridge University Press 1991

Whitehead, Margaret. '"A useful Christian woman": First Nations' Women and Protestant Missionary Work in British Columbia.' *Atlantis* 18, 1-2 (1992-3): 142-66

Wickwire, Wendy. 'Women in Ethnography: The Research of James A. Teit.' *Ethnohistory* 40, 4 (1993): 539-62

Wilken, R.L. *John Chrysostom and the Jews: Rhetoric and Reality in the Late Fourth Century*. Berkeley: University of California Press 1983

Williams, C.P. '"Not quite gentlemen": An Examination of "middling class" Protestant Missionaries from Britain, c. 1850-1900.' *Journal of Ecclesiastical History* 31, 3 (1980): 301-15

Williams, Cyril E.H., and Pixie McGeachie. *Archdeacon on Horseback: Richard Small, 1849-1909*. Merritt, BC: Sonotek 1991

Williams, Mary. 'The Coming of the White Man.' Trans. Mamie Henry. In *Our Tellings: Interior Salish Stories of the Nlha7kápmx People*, edited by Darwin Hanna and Mamie Henry. Vancouver: UBC Press 1995

Wimbush, Vincent L., and Richard Valantasis, eds. *Asceticism*. New York: Oxford University Press 1995

Wolf, Eric. *Europe and the People Without History*. Berkeley: University of California Press 1982

Woodward, Frances M. 'The Influence of the Royal Engineers on the Development of British Columbia.' *BC Studies* 24 (1974-5): 3-51

Young, Robert J.C. *Colonial Desire: Hybridity in Theory, Culture and Race*. London and New York: Routledge 1995

-. *White Mythologies: Writing History and the West*. New York: Routledge 1990

**Unpublished**

Bagshaw, Roberta L. 'Settlement and the Church of England in the Bishopric of British Columbia, 1859-1863.' Master's thesis, Simon Fraser University 1987

Christophers, Brett. 'Time, Space, and the People of God: Anglican Colonialism in Nineteenth Century British Columbia.' Master's thesis, University of British Columbia 1995

Fiske, Jo-Anne. 'And Then We Prayed Again: Carrier Women, Colonialism, and Mission Schools.' Master's thesis, University of British Columbia 1981

Groeneveld-Meijer, Averill. 'Manning the Fraser Canyon Gold Rush.' Master's thesis, University of British Columbia 1994

Perry, Adele. '"How influential a few men and a few families become": White Women,

Family, and Colonialism in Nineteenth-Century British Columbia.' Paper presented at the International Congress of Historical Sciences, Montreal 1995

Robin, Peter William. 'Beyond the Bounds of the West: The Life of John Booth Good, 1833-1916.' Master's thesis, University of Victoria 1991

Schurmann, Nadine C. 'Reinscribing Colonialism: The Royal Commission on Indian Affairs in Nlha'pamux and Stl'atl'imx Territory, 1914.' Master's thesis, University of British Columbia 1996

Townsend, Joan Helen. 'Protestant Christian Morality and the Nineteenth Century Secular and Non-sectarian British Columbia Public School System.' Master's thesis, University of British Columbia 1974

# Index